# CAMBRIDGE SERIES ON
# HUMAN–COMPUTER INTERACTION 9

Information Seeking in Electronic Environments

Cambridge Series on Human–Computer Interaction

*Managing Editor*
Professor John Long, Ergonomics Unit, University College, London

# Information Seeking in Electronic Environments

Gary Marchionini

*University of Maryland*

CAMBRIDGE
UNIVERSITY PRESS

PUBLISHED BY THE PRESS SYNDICATE OF THE UNIVERSITY OF CAMBRIDGE
The Pitt Building, Trumpington Street, Cambridge CB2 1RP, United Kingdom

CAMBRIDGE UNIVERSITY PRESS
The Edinburgh Building, Cambridge CB2 2RU, UK    http: //www.cup.cam.ac.uk
40 West 20th Street, New York, NY 10011-4211, USA    http: //www.cup.org
10 Stamford Road, Oakleigh, Melbourne 3166, Australia

First published 1995
Reprinted 1996
First paperback edition 1997
Reprinted  1998

Printed in the United States of America

Typeset in Times

*A catalogue record for this book is available from the British Library*

*Library of Congress Cataloguing-in-Publication Data is available*

ISBN 0-521-44372-5 hardback
ISBN 0-521-58674-7 paperback

# Contents

# Figures and tables

## Figures

## Tables

# Preface

For a quarter century we have been inundated by prognostications about the information society and changes in the world's economies and cultures. With apologies to Samuel Clemens, I believe that reports of the demise of society and culture have been greatly exaggerated. I do believe, however, that information technologies (computers and communication networks) are bringing about qualitative changes in how we learn and work. In particular, our abilities and capabilities to seek and use information are strongly influenced by these environments. This book aims to explicate some of these changes so that information workers can better prepare for the ongoing changes ahead and system designers can better understand the needs and perspectives of information seekers.

As a teacher, I have always been troubled by students' confusion about memory and learning. Memory is necessary but not sufficient for learning and understanding, and this confusion reflects larger distinctions among information, knowledge, and wisdom. It is this concern that has led me to consider information seeking as a broader process rather than the more limited notion of information retrieval. The book presents a framework for understanding information seeking and applies the framework to an analysis of search strategies and how they have been affected by electronic technology. Based on 10 years of user studies, this book describes how formal, analytical search strategies have been made more powerful by technology and argues for systems that also support intuitive browsing strategies.

Several themes undergird the discussion. First, there is a strong belief in user-centered design that proceeds from empirical evidence regarding how people define information problems, seek information related to those problems, and evaluate and use what they find. I argue that electronic systems should amplify our natural abilities and proclivities rather than create new methods and tools that themselves must be learned. This is essentially an argument for augmentation of the intellect through successive amplification (significant quantitative change leads to qualitative change) rather than augmentation through invention and optimization. Second, I present evidence and arguments to illustrate how electronic environments have begun to blur demarcations among different types of information (e.g., primary and secondary information, different media) and have made the information-seeking process more interactive, fluid, and parallel. These changes offer challenges to information seekers not to lose the content in the seeking or become overloaded by information, and to designers to create systems and interfaces that balance user control and system help or suggestions. Third, the notion of interdisciplinarity pervades the book. Information and technology have become inextricably intertwined as information has led to new technologies and technologies have in turn allowed more information to be created, stored, manipulated, and communicated. Cognitive science has drawn together scholars from diverse fields, and human–computer interaction is similarly emerging as an interdisciplinary field drawing ideas from psychology, computer science, information science, philosophy, sociology, and education. One cannot discuss interfaces or interaction styles without considering the human users, the tasks they perform, and the context in which information seeking takes place. Information-seeking tasks are increasingly important to and dependent on technology, and so a variety of disciplinary perspectives are needed to advance our state of knowledge and to develop better systems.

This book is aimed primarily at two communities: information scientists, graduate students in information science, and practicing information specialists who wish to gain a human–computer interaction perspective for information seeking; and human–computer interaction researchers, students, and practitioners who want to gain insight into information seeking and information science in order to build the next generation of information retrieval and processing systems. My goal in writing this book is to present a user-centered perspective of information seeking in electronic environments that serves as a bridge between these communities. Depending on which side of the bridge you start from, my hope is to present an integrated view that informs the reader about a related literature base and provokes thoughtful reactions to the state of our evolution.

# Acknowledgments

Many people shaped my thinking about information seeking and human–computer interaction (HCI) and have influenced the development of this book. Ben Shneiderman inspired me to look beyond the data of user studies to the more global implications of HCI. Other members of the Human–Computer Interaction Laboratory at the University of Maryland, especially Kent Norman and Catherine Plaisant, were helpful participants in discussions and projects. Christine Borgman and Nick Belkin were most influential in helping me understand a new view of information science that melds communication theory with organizational theory. My colleagues in the College of Library and Information Services, especially Dagobert Soergel and Delia Neuman, also contributed to my thinking in many ways. The chapter on browsing benefited from lengthy discussions in November 1992 with Marcia Bates, Shan-Ju Chang, Barbara Kwasnik, and Ronald Rice.

I am grateful to the talented students with whom it was my privilege to work over the past decade. Peter Liebscher, Xia Lin, Peter Evans, Valerie Florance, Xianhua Wang, Deborah Barraeu, and Susan Boerner worked with me on numerous user studies as we learned a great many things about human information seeking and system design and evaluation. Thanks are due to Kristi Mashon whose precision search appears in Figure 5.1 and to Elizabeth Brown and D. Timothy Burall whose Hyperties project screen display appears in Figure 6.3.

Helpful comments were provided on drafts of chapters by Christine Borgman, Peter Liebscher, Charles Meadow, Ronald Rice, Ben Shneiderman, and Dagobert Soergel. I am grateful to Julia Hough, Editor for Psychology and Cognitive Science at Cambridge University Press for encouraging and advising me and to Tom Landauer, a series editor, for reviews and suggestions. Thanks are also due to Edith Feinstein, Production Editor, and Margaret Yamashita for making the book much more readable. Finally I thank my wife, Suzanne, and children, Brian and Deanna, for putting up with missed dinners and moody ramblings about information seeking at those we did share.

# 1

# Information and information seeking

*For knowledge, too, is itself a power.*

Francis Bacon, De Haeresibus

*Where is the wisdom we have lost in knowledge?*
*Where is the knowledge we have lost in information?*

T. S. Eliot, The Rock

Our world continues to become increasingly complex, interconnected, and dynamic: There are more people and institutions; they engage in more relationships and exchange; and the rates of change continue to grow, largely because of developments in technology and the importance of information to human and technical development. We live in an information society[1] in which more people must manage more information, which in turn requires more technological support, which both demands and creates more information. Electronic technology and information are mutually reinforcing phenomena, and one of the key aspects of living in the information society is the growing level of interactions we have with this complex and increasingly electronic environment. The general consequences of the information society are threefold: larger volumes of information, new forms and aggregations of information, and new tools for working with information.

First, we find ourselves dealing with more information in all aspects of our lives. More of us are "knowledge workers," generating, managing, and communicating information to produce and provide goods and services for an increasingly global economy. In addition to the often-noted trend toward more people managing more information in the workplace, people must go beyond the workplace to learn new skills and acquire new knowledge to do their jobs. But new knowledge is no longer acquired only to prepare for a career but, rather, is now an essential part of "knowledge work." As Zuboff (1988, p. 395) noted, "To put it simply, learning is the new form of labor." Lifelong learning as part of the job has long been an important part of professional responsibilities and has spread to all venues of the labor force. More than 57 million adults participated in some form of adult education in 1990–91, of which almost 13 million were professionals (*Statistical Abstract of the United States 1993*).

Not only are we required to continually seek and acquire information, but increasingly more sources and larger volumes are available. Consider the magnitude of the following examples: In 1993 there were 11,296 newspapers and 10,857 periodicals published in the United States alone (*Statistical Abstract of the United*

*States 1993)*; there were 5500 new book publishers and 136,400 new books added to the 1.5 million books in print *(Books in Print, 1993)*; and the U.S. Government Printing Office offered over 20,000 titles and the National Technical Information Service offered 2 million titles *(Informing the Nation: Federal Information Dissemination in an Electronic Age)*. Not only are the volumes astounding, but they also are growing rapidly. For example, 90 billion pieces of first-class mail were handled by the U.S. Postal Service in 1991 versus 60 billion in 1980 *(Statistical Abstract of the United States 1993)*; in 1986 there were 378,313 research articles published worldwide in science and engineering alone, versus 267,354 in 1976 *(Science and Engineering Indicators – 1991)*; there were 2490 cable television systems serving 4.5 million subscribers in 1970 and 11,075 systems serving 57.2 million subscribers in 1992 *(Statistical Abstract of the United States 1993)*.

These large volumes of information are organized into many collections that require secondary and tertiary indexes and directories that in turn are growing in size and complexity. The growth of directories and indexes is reflected in the competition among different companies that offer phone directories and bibliographic databases. The development of new and alternative organizational structures for dealing with large volumes of information in turn demands more information management skills. In our personal lives, billboards, newspapers, mail, telephone, and television serve as vehicles for the incessant information assaults on our senses. To cope with these large amounts of information in our lives, we have developed complex personal information infrastructures, which require time and effort to build, maintain, and use. These structures include conscious and unconscious filtering and finding strategies for achieving our immediate goals and protecting ourselves from information overload. There is a tension between the goals and plans we make and the information resources necessary to achieve them; we travel a narrow road toward our goals with a sea of seductive information to distract us on one side and a spiraling abyss of confusion and information overload on the other. Technology accelerates the rate at which we are able to travel toward our goals, but it also increases the scope and peril of the two sides.

Second, we deal with information in new forms, especially electronic digital forms that are more abstract, more dynamic, and more malleable than is printed or painted information. Much more information is becoming available in electronic form. The number of publicly available databases grew from 400 in 1980 to 8400 in 1993; the number of database producers grew from 221 to 3260; and the number of online services rose from 59 to 825 during this same period *(Gale Directory of Databases, 1993)*. In addition, more than 3500 CD-ROM titles were available in 1993 *(CD-ROMs in Print 1993: An International Guide)*. Although much of this information is also available on paper or microfiche, there is a burgeoning amount of information available only in electronic form. The collection of more than 31,000 computer networks *(Communications of the ACM, August 1994)*, known as the *Internet,* reaches 20 million users worldwide and is growing exponentially. For example, 7.5 billion packets were sent over the Internet in the month of May 1991, and this monthly volume had grown to 26 billion packets by February of 1993 (*Merit/NSFNET Link Letter* 6(1), p. 12) and to 56.2 billion packets by March 1994 (Merit Network Inc., personal communication, May 24, 1994).

Information in electronic digital form is both enabling and complicating. On the one hand, electronic digital information is more accessible – available from anywhere in the world with a few computer keystrokes or mouse clicks. On the other hand, it is less accessible because it is not directly perceivable to humans unaided by technology. We are dependent on machines to express this information in forms that we can perceive. Electronic digital information is manipulable – it allows us to use the computational power of computers systematically to aggregate, classify, compare, change, and transmit information. Electronic digital information forms allow copies to be made perfectly and recursively, unlike analog or physical forms that degrade over generations of copies. Electronic digital information is simple because it is fully expressed by only two elements (bits), but it is complex because many levels of coding schemes must be used to map the enormous variety of structure and meaning in the world into binary form. The many sets of codings necessary for humans to "make sense" out of digital information allows the same digital code to be represented in many ways; for example, the set of bits 1001101 can be expressed on a display as an uppercase "M" or as a set of black and white pixels in a larger image, or as part of a note value for a compact disk recording. Standard coding schemes (e.g., American Standard Code for Information Interchange – ASCII, Tag Image File Format – TIFF, Digital Alternative Representation of Musical Scores – DARMS) facilitate communication and exchange of information, but the many possibilities support a kind of information alchemy in which words, numbers, images, and sounds can be interchanged – for better or worse. Given the sound and graphic editing tools available, it is no longer possible to believe that digitally recorded sounds or images represent reality. The implication for humans is that additional levels of learning and cognitive effort are necessary to use, interpret, and validate information based on electronic digital expressions.

Third, we find ourselves using new tools to manage information – tools that we must learn to use, pay for, and maintain. The primary tool of the information society is the computer.[2] Microprocessors are used to improve the performance of other technologies, and computers are increasingly used to control and integrate other kinds of information technology (e.g., TV, radio, telephones).[3] Computer literacy has become a component in primary and secondary school curricula in all industrialized countries, and billions of dollars a year are spent on training and upgrading workers' computer skills. As more computing technology is created, more new learning and retraining will be needed, placing demands on our time and financial resources. The computer industry accounts for an increasingly large share of the gross national product of the industrialized countries, and the massive personal computer market has driven the invention of new software tools that fit the needs of a great variety of users. The need to produce products that can be used by the general population has in turn spurred advances in human–computer interface research. Although much progress has been made in making computers easier to use, the evolution of hardware and software and the rapid pace of information creation and manipulation mean that for the foreseeable future, significant material and intellectual resources must be devoted to acquiring, learning to use, applying, and maintaining electronic tools. At the very least, it is obvious that more and more of our time and financial resources must be spent using computers, and we will become even more dependent on them in the future.

An important aspect of these effects is that more of our professional and personal lives will be spent interacting with complex systems. Interactions with other people are physiologically natural, psychologically necessary, and culturally expected. These interactions became increasingly mediated as communications technology developed, and computer technology is another step toward intermediated personal communication. This trend is illustrated by use of electronic mail, which had 9.2 million users in 1992 and is projected to have 38 million users by 1995 (Reinhardt, 1993). Individual people also interact with a variety of institutional systems such as government agencies, businesses, and other organizations. These interactions were traditionally mediated by other people, but information technology is finding increasing application. Consider, for example, the automatic teller machines, phone menu systems, and information kiosks at shopping malls or museums.

As more of these systems are connected, many of our interactions with the institutions of civilization and with other people will take place through electronic workstations rather than through personal contact. Working from one's workstation saves time and resources, and the computational power facilitates the execution of multiple tasks concurrently. The implications of mediated communication, high rates of exchange, and parallel processing of tasks are considered under the topic of interactivity.

Information is a valuable resource in an information society; thus acquiring and using information are critical activities. The process known as information seeking is therefore becoming more fundamental and strategic for intelligent citizenship. In addition, the information-seeking process is more and more dependent on electronic technology. This book examines the physical, cognitive, and affective consequences of electronic environments on the increasingly important process of information seeking and provides a framework for designing systems that support information seeking. It takes the point of view that information seeking depends on the interactions among information seekers and other people and systems for representing information. It argues that highly interactive electronic information systems are causing incremental changes in how we seek, acquire, and use information. The high volume and diverse forms of information demand better tools, which in turn change our behaviors, expectations, and attitudes. At this stage in the evolution of the information society, we need designs that place users in control of highly interactive environments that focus on content rather than on forms and tools.

## What is information?

The word *information* is used to refer to several different concepts in this book. Buckland (1991) distinguished information-as-process (the communication act), information-as-knowledge (an increase or reduction in uncertainty), and information-as-thing (the objects that may impart information). In this vein, he also distinguished the actual knowledge in a human mind (what one knows) from the artifacts of the world that represent knowledge. Most generally, *information* is anything that can change a person's knowledge. This sense, according to Belkin (1978), admits reflection on one's memory traces, the objects that convey information, and the ideas and knowledge contained in other minds. Thus, information is used in this book in a general manner that includes objects in the world, what is transferred from people or objects to a person's cognitive system, and as the components of internal knowledge in people's minds. To seek information, people seek to change the state of their knowledge and also physical representations (e.g., ink on paper, sound waves, electronically charged phosphorus) that represent abstractions (e.g., words, numbers, images, concepts, melodies) that can cause this change.

Because there are many manifestations of information-as-object, there are many terms that can be used to describe those objects. Terms such as bit, data, record, text fragment, graphic, document, utterance, database, book, and library all are used to label particular information units. Although these terms are typically associated with different media or information systems, the terms *document* and *information object* are used in this book in a general way to represent information-as-object. Thus, documents may be considered as a single numeric value, a database record, a distinct image, or a video segment, as well as the more typical textual collection of words related to a topic.

## Information seeking

Much of human existence is characterized by the notion of search; we seek and pursue material objects such as food or shelter, sensual experiences such as adventure or ceremony, and ethereal objects such as knowledge or justice. We are concerned here with the search for information that we will call *information seeking*, a process in which humans purposefully engage in order to change their state of knowledge. The term *search* is used to mean the behavioral manifestation of humans engaged in information seeking and also to describe the actions taken by computers to match and display information objects. The term *information seeking* is preferred to *information retrieval* because it is more human oriented and open ended. Retrieval implies that the object must have been "known" at some point; most often, those people who "knew" it organized it for later "knowing" by themselves or someone else. Seeking connotes the process of acquiring knowledge; it is more problem oriented as the solution may or may not be found. For example, seeking spiritual enlightenment makes sense, but retrieving enlightenment does not. Retrieval is applicable to database management and most applied problems, but seeking is closer to answering questions or learning.

Information seeking is a fundamental human process closely related to learning and problem solving. Nature has evolved tools and methods to support information seeking, resulting in physiological and psychological abilities that are well suited to information seeking. Our perceptual organs gather massive streams of environmental data; our muscles aim these organs and carry us closer to the objects of search; and our cognitive and emotive engines direct muscles and organs and process the incoming data. Our cognitive processors adopt various organizational structures and systematic strategies for filtering, comparing, and storing information in a variety of media. Our emotive selves derive stimulation and pleasure from seeking and integrating information. Information seeking is thus a natural and necessary mechanism of human existence.

The information-seeking processes needed to survive and prosper have become more complex as social organizations have developed. The ability to locate and apply information is an important component of what it means to be literate. Just as nature has evolved physiological and psychological tools and methods to support information seeking, so culture has evolved tools and methods to support information seeking. Information-processing technologies from the abacus to the zoetrope help us generate, manipulate, and represent information. As social and economic organizations have become more complex, so has the information necessary to work in these organizations, and this has led to new, more powerful technologies for managing information. Today, the generation, storage, and communication of information are inextricably linked with technology – it is virtually impossible to conduct business in many markets today without technology to help manage the generation, storage, and flow of information. Likewise, an enormous amount of information is necessary to select from entertainment options and to make good consumer decisions. Thus, one of the key changes in the information society is that information seeking has become a fundamental skill for larger portions of the population – more people must regularly manage more information in order to survive and prosper and they must use an expanding array of technologies to do so.

Information seeking, like learning, is a fundamental and high level cognitive process. Information seeking is often part of learning or problem solving, but it is also distinct. Information acquired during learning is stored so that it can be recalled and used at a later time, although information acquired as a result of information seeking may be useful for a specific task and then discarded. Intermediate or temporally relevant information often should be discarded so that it does not take up storage space or complicate the organization of stored information and subsequently interfere with retrieval functions. Information seeking at the level of scientific research is accumulative, with each new finding supporting or questioning theories and principles. Information seeking at the operational level often uses the results quickly and directly, archiving or discarding the information as soon as it is applied rather than making it part of the corporate memory. Because humans cannot selectively erase their memories, much of the information processed as part of information seeking is remembered, regardless of whether we think we will ever use it again. As we depend more on the external augmentation of our memories, especially through electronic technology, we should decide whether and how to store information. We must consider information from a life-cycle perspective in which destruction options are developed along with generation, acquisition, and storage options. As we seek, evaluate, and acquire information, we must consider integratability with respect to our existing private or corporate knowledge and reusability for future problems. Technology can surely help us be more selective about what information we store and thus use our mental and external resources better, but we must balance optimization against our abilities to spout trivia at parties or make disparate connections that spark intellectual breakthroughs.

Learning takes place in directed and incidental ways, but information seeking as defined here is a directed (purposeful) activity. There are, however, two ways that information can be acquired incidentally. First, our physical survival depends on our senses' constantly gathering information about the environment to alert us to dangers and possible gratifications. This kind of automatic search for information is important to survival but is beyond the scope of our definition of information seeking. Second, as we purposely seek information, we encounter many prospective units of information that we filter and compare. We remember much of this irrelevant information automatically in spite of our efforts to ignore it, and so we should be concerned with ways to minimize and label such information. The focus of this book is on intentional information seeking, a process driven by an information problem. The information problem can be a mild curiosity, the desire to occupy 30 minutes, an ongoing passion about a hobby, or a desperate quest with life-critical consequences, but it must initiate a conscious activity to move toward a goal.

As with learning or problem solving, we develop strategies to guide our progress. We use a variety of gross strategies in information seeking, including consulting our own long-term memory; asking friends, colleagues, or experts; consulting personal collections of books, periodicals, and files; conducting empirical investigations; and applying formal systems. Formal systems include libraries, research firms, government agencies, electronic networks, and the growing collection of information services that make up the information industry. The main focus of this book is on information seeking using formal systems, although as we shall see in later chapters, electronic technologies are blurring the distinctions among personal, informal, and formal information systems.

In addition to strategies defined by what sources are used for search, there are strategies for how one should search. A fundamental distinction is made between analytical and browsing strategies (Liebscher & Marchionini, 1988; Marchionini & Shneiderman, 1988). *Analytical* strategies depend on careful planning, the recall of query terms, and iterative query reformulations and examinations of results. *Browsing* strategies are heuristic and opportunistic and depend on recognizing relevant information. Analytic strategies are batch oriented and half duplex (turn taking) like human conversation, whereas browsing strategies are more interactive, real-time exchanges and collaborations between the information seeker and the information system. Browsing strategies demand a smaller cognitive load in advance and a steadier attentional load throughout the information-seeking process. Analytical strategies can be applied by intermediaries for the benefit of the person requesting information, whereas browsing strategies are conducted by the ultimate user of the information. In practice, people apply different mixes of analytical and browsing strategies, but electronic environments have severely limited what strategies information seekers can use. Although people have an inclination to browse, analytical strategies are more efficient in large document collections. Early computer systems required analytical strategies, and some present-day systems require browsing under the guise of ease of use. Both these developments have influenced how we seek information, and this book distinguishes between these strategies and argues for a new generation of designs that support both strategies.

Figure 1.1 illustrates the relationships among learning, information seeking, information retrieval, and analytical and browsing strategies. Information seeking is often a type of learning, because the goal in both cases is to change knowledge. Information seeking differs from learning according to the degree of retention desired; learning demands retention and information seeking may use the information for a temporary task. Much of information seeking may require identifying and retrieving previously stored information. Thus, information retrieval is one type of information seeking except when it is conducted by a machine – machines cannot seek information but they can retrieve information. Information may be retrieved by people in order to support learning. Browsing is often a type of learning and is not usually driven by well-defined goals or does not usually proceed according to a systematic plan as information retrieval does. Analytical search is sometimes a type of learning and is most closely associated with retrieval. As will be demonstrated when these strategies are characterized in later chapters, browsing and analytical search do have some similarities.

Other strategies that we explore are applying filters or templates to search and to minimize overload, broadening or narrowing the scope of search, and rationalizing results regardless of relevance. Electronic environments have begun to affect the

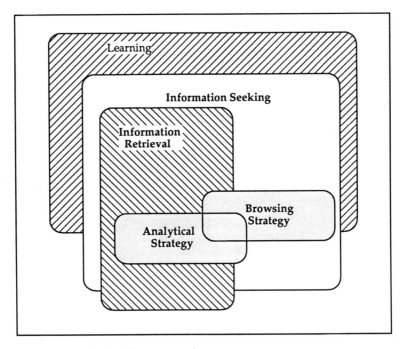

Figure 1.1. Relationships among key processes.

strategies we use in information seeking, and these effects are considered in the chapters ahead. For example, because planning and query articulation are difficult, electronic systems that depend on recognition and interaction have become popular. We take a user-centered perspective on information seeking in this book and argue for systems that amplify such strategies.

## Preview

In the following chapters, we consider how electronic environments affect information seeking and how interface design can support information seeking. Chapter 2 presents the perspective on humans and technology that serves as the context for this book. A general framework for information seeking is constructed in chapter 3 and is examined in subsequent chapters with respect to the effects of electronic technology. This framework is analogous to a computer program in that it contains a set of interrelated factors (data structures) and a network of processes (procedures). These factors include an information seeker, an information need manifested as a search task, a domain, a setting, search systems (information sources and interfaces, including people, books, computer systems), and search outcomes (the products and traces of information seeking). These components are managed by the information seeker as the information seeking progresses. Information-seeking processes are the actions taken during information seeking and include problem recognition and acceptance; problem definition and clarification; source selection; query articulation; query execution; result examination; information extraction; and reflection, iteration, and termination. Chapter 4 focuses on the human factors that drive information seeking and facilitate information-seeking strategies. The framework is used in chapters 5 and 6 to illustrate how information seeking in electronic environments compares with information seeking in manual environments and to examine analytical and browsing strategies in detail. The main differences that we discuss are related to speed of access, the scope of access (amount of information available), provision of interactive assistance and help during information seeking, flexibility and choice in representing information, availability of powerful retrieval techniques such as string search and relevance feedback, physical constraints of using electronic equipment, changes in expectations, and overall high levels of interactivity that invite browsing and heuristic strategies (Marchionini, 1987). Analytical strategies for online searching are considered in chapter 5, and browsing strategies are demonstrated in chapter 6 with interfaces from end user–oriented systems. Chapter 7 looks at the directions for interface design that supports both types of strategies. Chapter 8 summarizes the effects on information seekers, including physical changes such as decreased movement from place to place and more focused hand, eye, and muscle activity; cognitive effects such as cognitive amplification and augmentation; emotional effects due to increased interactions with systems replacing interactions with other people; and social and economic effects such as the evolution of personal information infrastructures and the costs of systems, training, and the information itself. It also discusses the constraints on the continued evolution of information seeking. The final chapter asks the reader to think about how information seeking should continue to evolve.

# 2

# Information seekers and electronic environments

*Physics does not change the nature of the world it studies, and no science of behavior can change the essential nature of man, even though both sciences yield technologies with a vast power to manipulate their subject matters.*

B. F. Skinner, *Cumulative Record*

Throughout our lives we develop knowledge, skills, and attitudes that allow us to seek and use information. This chapter introduces the notion of personal information infrastructure, which will be used to describe this complex of knowledge, skills, and attitudes. It also introduces the notion of interactivity, a key characteristic of computer technology that allows information seekers to use electronic environments in ways that emulate interactions with human sources of information. The chapter also provides an overview of the technological developments that underlie information seeking in electronic environments.

## Personal information infrastructures

The primary activities of scientists, physicians, businesspersons, and other professionals are gathering information from the world, mentally integrating that information with their own knowledge – thus creating new knowledge – and acting on this new knowledge to accomplish their goals. Most often, this knowledge and the consequences of using it are articulated to the external world as information. All humans develop mental structures and skills for conducting such activities according to their individual abilities, experiences, and physical resources. An individual person's collection of abilities, experience, and resources to gather, use, and communicate information are referred to as a *personal information infrastructure*. A personal information infrastructure is a collection of interacting mental models for specific information systems;[1] mental models for events, experiences, and domains of knowledge; general cognitive skills (e.g., inferencing, recognizing salience) and specific cognitive skills related to organizing and accessing information (e.g., filing rules, reading); material resources such as information systems, money, and time; metacognitive resources for planning and monitoring thought and action; and attitudes toward information seeking and knowledge acquisition. Figure 2.1 shows the main components of a personal information infrastructure. The level of development of a person's information infrastructure is roughly analogous to the level of his or her information literacy. Note that the term *personal information infrastructure* as used here is much broader than the way that *information in-*

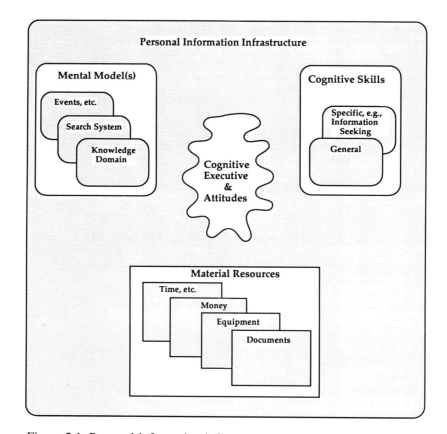

Figure 2.1. Personal information infrastructure components.

*frastructure* is used in the electronic networking literature in which the focus is on the physical and computational resources (e.g., Kahin, 1992).

Cognitive psychology has posited many levels of cognitive processes to explain human mental activity. Theories of memory, decision making, and problem solving include explanations of how knowledge is represented at different levels of granularity. For example, cognitive scientists offer theories for short-term and long-term memories (Estes, 1982; Wickens, 1987), semantic networks (Quillian, 1968), frames (Minsky, 1975), scripts (Schank & Abelson, 1977), and mental models (Johnson-Laird, 1983). *Mental models* are dynamic mental representations of the real world (Johnson-Laird, 1983; Norman, 1983). People construct and then draw on mental models to predict the effects of contemplated actions; that is, they make inferences based on running particular mental models. Information seekers develop and use mental models for a variety of mental and physical objects, including information objects and different domains of knowledge. A mental model for a particular information object such as a book allows one to base one's expectations about how to begin and proceed in reading and to estimate how much effort will be required. A mental model for the domain (topic area) related to the book's content allows the reader to integrate information (understand) as his or her reading progresses. Mental models account for expectations and therefore learning and change in behavior. A personal information infrastructure includes the various mental models that a person has constructed for different information systems and domains of knowledgc.

Experience with a variety of information problems and systems leads us to develop both a general knowledge of how information is organized and the skills needed for facilitating access to it. We learn to recognize the advantages and limitations of general organizational structures such as lists, arrays, hierarchies, and networks and the ways to leverage the advantages and mitigate the limitations. At the most basic levels, such skills include memory processes such as rehearsal, association, and chunking (Lindsay & Norman, 1977) and strategies such as the use of mnemonics. At more formal levels, they include the strategies and relationships we learn and develop throughout our lives. Greeno (1989) distinguishes symbolic or abstract knowledge from mental models to account for these types of knowledge. For example, we learn filing rules such as alphabetical, chronological, or positional orderings that facilitate subsequent retrieval. These rules are generic and serve as defaults for orderings when we encounter a new domain. Particular domains (e.g., biological classes, library classifications, chemical structures) use specific orderings that must be integrated into mental models for the domain. As we will see in chapter 4, recognizing the distinctions and overlaps between generic and specialized knowledge is the characteristic we call *expertise in a domain*. Well-developed personal information infrastructures allow people to look for organizational rules in new domains before applying default rules. The organizational rules become defaults for experts, and thus organizations in our personal lives reflect the domain organizations in our professional lives.

We also learn about information sources such as books, journals, encyclopedias, and indexes. Our general knowledge about what is typical about these generic type of systems overlaps with our particular mental models for those systems. Furthermore, the formal strategies for using particular information sources (e.g., use of a back-of-the-book index) that are part of our mental models for those systems are generalized and serve as the basis for heuristic or analogical strategies when we encounter new systems. We acquire knowledge about areas of personal interest and relationships with others with expertise in those areas so that we can exchange information when needed. As we gain experience with information problems, we strengthen our general information-seeking knowledge and skills, just as we develop our knowledge and skills in other general cognitive processes such as listening, reading, writing, speaking, reasoning, and decision making.

Many cognitive theories include an executive process that controls and monitors the various perception, memory, computation, and motor processes. A popular view of this executive process is termed *metacognition* (e.g., Flavell, 1985). Metacognitive activity refers to our ability to reflect on our own thoughts and actions in the past, monitor them as they proceed, and plan which ones to use to meet our needs. Our personal information infrastructure is guided by metacognitive activity directed at meeting situated information needs. Metacognition determines that we need information; it enables our general information-seeking knowledge and our mental models for systems and domains; and it monitors our progress. Metacognition is influenced by affective states such as motivation and attitude and by physical states such as fatigue and comfort levels.

Material resources that make up the personal information infrastructure include people, books, computers, telecommunication lines, and all the other tangible things we use to gather, generate, manage, and communicate information. Material resources also include the money and time we have available to use and maintain these resources. These physical components of our personal information infrastructures are most readily affected by sociological and technological developments. To augment our memories, we accumulate huge collections of paper covered with relatively permanent, visually accessible symbols and marks. To organize these collections of paper, we use drawers, cabinets, shelves, libraries, and archives. To replicate and distribute items from these collections, we use copiers, mail and courier services, and telefacsimile. To acquire new information, we maintain personal reference collections, hire clerical support staff, nurture networks of colleagues, contract with research companies, and visit libraries. All these objects, people, communication channels, and strategies are part of a personal information infrastructure that we use to accomplish our goals. We support many layers of personal information infrastructure to serve long- and near-term goals and many intermediate goals within the infrastructure itself.

### Influence of electronic digital technology on personal information infrastructures

Electronic technology affects personal information infrastructures at all levels. Most obviously, technology affects the material resources of our personal information infrastructure by presenting new objects (e.g., computers, disks) to purchase and manipulate. To acquire new information, we use online databases, electronic bulletin boards, and local magnetic or optical databases. Indeed, sources of information are increasingly made available only in electronic form. The physical changes that electronic technology bring are highly dependent on material wealth and moderately dependent on individual ability.

Electronic environments are also affecting the cognitive and affective components of our personal information infrastructures. Long-term memory is augmented by magnetic media and digital signals; magnetic, optical disks and backup systems store information organized in files, databases, and hyperdocuments; and information is copied and shared through local and global communications networks. We must develop new mental models for different systems so that we can use them and construct new experience bases that allow us to apply them appropriately. Technology augments our cognitive skills in several ways: by providing online assistance in selecting and using information sources (e.g., context-sensitive help, online reference manuals, spelling and grammar checkers, thesauri and encyclopedias, cut-and-paste tools); by broadening the proximity of personal networks (through electronic mail and bulletin boards); by extending our personal knowledge; and by changing the strategies we use for seeking and acquiring information (e.g., browsing, string search, relevance feedback).

Adding electronic technology to our information infrastructures can have significant impacts on our cognitive activity. Electronic technology generally can amplify and augment our abilities and performance (Engelbart, 1963) as well as disorient and confuse us (Mantei, 1982). Computer applications such as electronic text are changing the fundamental processes of writing and reading (Bolter, 1991), and electronic spreadsheets have enabled iterative decision making for individual persons and businesses. High-performance computing and scientific visualization techniques are offering new insights into complex scientific, medical, and engineering problems, and are enabling new discoveries and speeding progress. Calculators and computers have changed the K–12 mathematics curriculum by legitimizing systematic guessing – students are now taught iterative "guess and check" strategies for solving problems as well as formal analytic strategies.

In addition to amplifying and augmenting our cognitive activity, electronic technology affects our metacognitive activity by changing our expectations. When we are using a word processor with spell checking, we expect the system to find spelling errors and consequently type with abandon; likewise we have come to expect laser-quality output. Using database systems for managing lists leads us to expect to be able to display information in a variety of sorted forms with the press of a key, and we are disappointed when we look at a printed list that is not ordered in a manner that is optimal for our immediate needs. We expect rapid response and comprehensive scope when searching for information. We come to expect to use string-search capabilities to locate words or phrases and often incorrectly expect that string search will locate concepts or ideas rather than literal words or phrases. Novices often expect that information obtained from a computer will be more exhaustive and more accurate. Such expectations change the actions we take as we seek information as well as the way we create and use information. These changes are viewed as cognitive laziness or sloppiness by some and as mental emancipations by others.

The material resources that comprise personal information infrastructures maintained by professionals today are physical and virtual, static and dynamic, proximate and global. In fact, managing the material resources has become complex and expensive, requiring unique skills and technology. More and more, the material resources are managed and used from computer workstations connected to global networks rather than through personal contacts and physical manipulation of objects. Because we have limited short-term memory resources, any cognitive resources devoted to managing the personal information infrastructure itself are not available to the information problem at hand. Because the information problems we face are increasingly complex, they demand maximum perceptual and cognitive resources. We can ill afford to devote significant mental resources to managing the material resources; instead, we require easily manipulable interfaces.

Electronic augmentations of our personal information infrastructures can make us more productive and thus more emotionally fulfilled and happy. Moreover, these environments offer us the freedom to explore new areas of interest easily and rapidly. However, the complexity and ever-changing nature of the tools can cause stress and anxiety as well. Furthermore, we can come to feel dependent on the technology, requiring computers to access our written notes, files, and mail. These environments can also cause alienation if we have fewer and fewer personal interactions with people having common interests.

A key feature of living in an information society is managing the many resources that technology has enabled. We find ourselves interacting with complex, electronic environments to generate, store, manipulate, access, and use information resources. Electronically augmented personal information infrastructures affect us physically, cognitively, and emotionally. Physically, they cause us to use fewer large motor movements and more small motor movements; to be more sedentary – sitting, typing, reading from screens, subvocalizing – rather than actively moving from place to place, manipulating objects, and vocalizing commands and responses. In many ways, working with electronically augmented personal information infrastructures gives us a mechanical advantage, providing faster access to larger amounts of information, but the ergonomic consequences of such trade-offs are an active area of longitudinal research (e.g., Rohmert, 1987).

Cognitively, electronic augmentations of personal information infrastructures allow us to access, manage, and communicate more information and more varied types of information. We are able to handle more complexity and process information more rapidly. These changes have also led to requirements for new skills in organizing information and for using technology itself and, consequently, to additional cognitive pressures and stress. The interactions between cognition and technology are a central concern in this book.

Emotionally, technology has relieved some of the stress of communication in emergencies, but it has likewise caused new pressures for improving intellectual productivity. On the one hand, computers have broken down interpersonal barriers of race, gender, age, and culture; provided new modes of expression; and opened up new levels of communication. On the other hand, computers have given bullies new avenues for intimidation and control, exposed many technophobics, and provided yet another excuse for obsessive–compulsive perfectionists to avoid finishing their work. Although technological augmentations of personal information infrastructures obviously can empower disabled persons, they have also isolated people who strongly depend on interpersonal interactions for satisfaction and joy. Although powerful new environments must interact with human emotional evolution, very little attention has yet been paid to the nature and consequences of these interactions.

## People and electronic environments: Interactivity

Human existence is a series of interactions with the environment. Most of humankind's early history was surviving these interactions, and the purpose of our science and technology is to control the environment so that we can choose the interactions that serve our personal or social objectives. We master and value interactions with other people through a variety of natural communication mechanisms that have evolved over time. *Interactivity* – the propensity to act in unison with external objects or other people – is a basic human characteristic. The complexity of modern society forces us to interact with more institutions and systems, using limited and cumbersome communications mechanisms that we generally characterize by phrases such as *bureaucratic protocol*. Interactions with institutions are becoming less natural because electronic systems are slowly replacing human "front ends" to the overall institution. Thus, our interactions with the environment are constantly evolving.

Information seeking is fundamentally an interactive process. It depends on initiatives on the part of the information seeker, feedback from the information environment, and decisions for subsequent initiatives based on this feedback. Our personal information infrastructures serve to regulate and standardize our interactions with information. It is necessary to comprehend the interactive nature of information seeking, which is described in detail in subsequent chapters, for understanding why electronic environments are so conducive to information seeking.

Interactivity has become a central characteristic of computers. The essence of computer programming is to apply computation and memory to control physical devices according to inputs provided by the user at "run time." The speed of computers allows programs to compare inputs with stored responses and to execute those responses almost instantaneously, thus giving the illusion of interaction. Interactivity is what allowed the personal computer market to develop and is the key reason that computers are increasingly important tools for group work and decision making. The electronic spreadsheet is a success not because it serves as an editor for numbers but because it enables the interactive process of "what if" analysis (Kay, 1984).

Human activities that are inherently interactive in nature are strongly affected by computer technology, and information seeking is one such process. In addition to design principles such as giving the user control of a system through interface options, we advocate maximal interactivity in interface design. As a simple illustration, consider a system such as Perseus (Crane, 1992), which provides access to multiple images of objects such as vases. When a user has identified a vase of interest, a descriptive window is displayed that includes a list of all the views available for that vase. Rather than inviting the user to select a number of views (e.g., 1, 2, 7, 34) to see in advance, maximal interactivity suggests that the user select a view so that then he or she can go easily and quickly back to the vase description to select another view. This keeps the user engaged in concurrent viewing and decision making rather than batching the decision making first and then the viewing. Of course, the option to make multiple selections could also be provided, but the default should be to invite interactivity.

Psychological and sociological investigations of interactivity have been spurred by the development of computers and have helped define the field of human–computer interaction (HCI). HCI explores theories that explain the interactions among humans and computers and the interfaces that support these interactions. One view of HCI is based on communication models. According to this view, the human and computer are senders and receivers of messages relayed along communication channels. The communication channel is called the *interface,* and the goal of design is to develop high-bandwidth channels that reliably facilitate the flow of messages. This view is a useful one, although it is necessary to augment it by considering the context of the overall communication system. From this point of view, interface design is based on understanding the fundamental features of humans and systems. Such features include physical constraints such as memory capabilities, information transfer limits, computational ability (logic more than arithmetic), and conceptual constraints such as knowledge of the task domain and mental models for objects and processes in the world (especially mental models for the other receiver/transmitter and the communication process itself).

Using this HCI perspective, it is natural to study human–computer interactions by first considering human–human and computer–computer interactions. An implicit bias in most HCI research is that human–computer interaction should be based on models of human–human interaction. Human–human interactions are multimodal and complex, and there are rich traditions of evidence from the fields of communications, psychology, sociology, and physiology. However, human–human interactions are also ambiguous, are situated in that they depend on awareness of context, and depend on redundancy in order to be effective.[2] Computer–computer interactions are well defined and fully understood from a technical perspective, but the many layers of translation needed to represent ideas as binary signals lead to the ultimate example of "losing something in the translation." As a result, computer–computer communication is best for explicit, discrete information transfer rather than complex or creative expression. A crucial design decision for all HCI is determining the degree of mix between human–human and computer–computer models. Consider some of the following differences between humans and computers with respect to information-processing features.

Human memory is believed to be made up of working memory and long-term memory (e.g., see Wickens, 1987). The size of working memory is severely limited (5 to 9 units or memory-chunks), but that of long-term memory is infinite. Human memory is thought to be associational and episodic and allows us to make direct connections between memory traces. But human memory also is unreliable, and so we cannot always recall information on demand. Computers have random access and mass storage memories as analogs of human working and long-term memories. Computer memories are highly reliable (as long as physical requirements like electrical power or the absence of electromagnetic disturbances are maintained), and their size has been increasing steadily. Computer memories are not associational but, rather, depend on pointers and indexes that specify exact addresses for information units. Also, all computer memory is stored in binary code, and thus far we have been unable to represent in binary code the full richness of events, let alone ideas. This severely limits the range of practical expression, especially with respect to nuance and impression.

Human computational ability has been estimated as 10 cycles (operations) per second,[3] with each cycle being able to recognize or select a chunk of information. Determining what a chunk is, is an open problem in cognitive psychology. Computers have excellent computational power, capable of making millions of computational cycles per second. Computer cycles are able to execute arithmetical steps or to compare items in memory. Whereas humans can execute a wider range of processes on a wider range of information units than computers, computers can execute more well-defined processes with much smaller information units at much faster rates of speed than humans.

Humans can receive and transmit information using a variety of channels. Output channels include voice, gesture, facial expressions, and a host of muscle movements that control devices such as pencils, keyboards, musical instruments, and pointing devices. Input channels include sight, hearing, touch, smell, and taste. All these channels have associated bandwidths to meet environmental and intentional conditions. Humans can integrate these channels in parallel, although each channel may have strict sequential limitations. Bandwidth varies greatly,[4] and the rich array of channels that humans use is referred to as *high fidelity*. Computers are able to transmit at enormous rates of speed. For example, Sumner (1990, p. 14) predicted that in a few years, it will be possible to send all recorded knowledge past your house in only one second. However, computers currently offer only low-fidelity communications. A goal of HCI research is to develop input–output devices and mechanisms that map more naturally onto human channels.

Humans acquire highly integrated knowledge about areas of interest. Knowledge can be based on experience, acquired vicariously and symbolically or created internally through computation, inference, and imagination. Human knowledge is dynamic. It grows according to conscious activity and ebbs according to a variety of physical and psychological states. Computers have highly rigid knowledge bases provided by the external world. Although computer knowledge bases may be huge, how well they will perform in application tasks is an ongoing problem.

Humans are learning systems. We apply our cognitive power of reflection to our continuing life experiences and try to understand the environment – we think about what is currently occurring and what happened to us in the past and learn to improve our performance in the future. We construct mental models for objects, events, and activities in order to benefit from subsequent interactions. Users of computers construct mental models that allow interaction, with these mental models varying in accuracy and depth. Although models for machine learning have been proposed, machine learning remains very much a long-term goal (Carbonell, 1992). Computers are given knowledge about the world by programmers. This knowledge includes primitive models for users that facilitate the human–computer interaction process. User-modeling research attempts to characterize human task performance and to introduce these characterizations into the design of systems, but currently these models are quite crude and coarse (e.g., Allen, 1990; Daniels, 1986).

Clearly, because of such differences, communication between humans and computers is more difficult than is either human–human or computer–computer communication alone. A major goal of HCI is to develop new devices and interaction styles that take advantage of the respective strengths of humans and computers so as to build new mechanisms and languages for human–computer interaction and collaboration.

Communication is perhaps a better metaphor for human–computer interaction than a precise model, and a variety of alternative viewpoints are possible. Some people believe that communication is strictly a human-to-human activity and object to the anthropomorphic implications of human–computer communication. One possible human-centered design consequence would be to consider computers as prosthetics for humans. Interaction would be limited to control and manipulation by the human, although preprogrammed actions could be initiated by specific sets of conditions dictated in advance. Quite a different viewpoint assumes that computers are a new type of entity, with intelligence and evolving volition. One possible communication viewpoint is to assume that humans and computers should have equal authority for initiation and action. Still another viewpoint is task oriented, in that humans and computers are viewed as components of a larger system. Interaction may be viewed as collaboration between humans and computers, in which the task determines how best to take advantage of strengths and minimize weaknesses.

Two issues that emerge from these considerations of models and metaphors for interactivity between humans and computers are related to autonomy and adaptability. Consider, for example, the degree of autonomy that should be built into robots and intelligent agents. Should a robot under the sea or in space be controlled through telepresence, or should it be capable of making autonomous decisions based on environmental conditions? Setting aside the technical problems of both capabilities and acknowledging that some combination of each is desirable, there still are fundamental philosophical differences between arguing for autonomous versus directly controlled robots. In any case, robots will be designed and built, and decisions about levels of control will be made on the basis of technology, cost, and task analysis. Similarly, those agents that are proposed for helping humans explore information spaces will be designed using both autonomous and direct control perspectives.

It is naive to believe that any single interface can serve the needs of all users for all tasks. We go to people with special skills and knowledge to help us solve problems (e.g., physicians, attorneys, librarians), and we go to physical places to take advantage of special features (e.g., spectacular scenery, healthy climate, commercial activity). Interfaces should also vary according to the information-seeking task and personal characteristics. Some argue that an interface should automatically adapt to the user, based on user profiles or records of past experience; others contend that all adaptations must proceed from the users' conscious actions. Just as with autonomy, systems will be built that reflect both viewpoints. Rather than interfaces that "act human," we should develop interfaces that improve performance by reinforcing the characteristics that bring us to the system to begin with – we need more reality, not more virtual reality! For example, speech interfaces would be much more commonly used today if the quest for humanlike continuous speech had not drained away so much talent and resources. Short, commandlike speech can be quite effective for many common tasks and can be easily provided in most interfaces as an inexpensive option.

HCI research has significant implications for information seeking because information seeking is critical to an information society and because our personal information infrastructures are becoming increasingly dependent on computer technology. Although many of the issues of general interest to HCI research also apply to interfaces that support information seeking, particular requirements and conditions must be considered. The objects of information seeking are ideas and their many representations. These abstractions are distinct from manipulating physical objects and typically are less well defined than is manipulating numeric or factual data. Interfaces will most likely need to be more personalized and flexible because information seeking depends so heavily on interactions among complex information-seeking factors.

Interactivity that depends on such interfaces introduces new variations on old problems. Just as information sources vary in validity and reliability, so do interfaces, and users must establish evaluation and selection standards for interfaces just as they have for information sources. Whether these interfaces ameliorate or exacerbate the problems of information pollution (overload) remains to be seen. There is a tension between redundancy and memory – we need redundancy and context to remember information. When does context become information pollution? If our filtering agents become so efficient that we eliminate most redundancy and context, will we "know" anything?[5] What levels of adaptability are appropriate and "comfortable" for humans also are an issue of concern for researchers and designers.

HCI research is critical to meeting the challenges of information seeking in electronic environments. Devices and interaction styles must be developed that match the physical, conceptual, and emotional activities of accessing, assessing, and extracting information from electronic sources. To construct such interfaces, models of information seeking must be taken into consideration as the basis for design.

Of course, before these long-term interfaces are built, a host of specific design problems must be solved. Screen display layouts, interaction styles, mappings of information-seeking tasks to levels of representation and mechanisms for controlling those representations, and mappings of physical devices to tasks are examples of immediate problems in the larger context of interfaces to support information seeking. A general problem with today's interfaces that support information seeking is that support is strong for some of the subprocesses but is weak or nonexistent for others.

In the next chapter, we look at the subprocesses in detail and discuss interface issues. The main problem is that today's interfaces focus on query formulation and results examination functions but ignore problem identification/clarification and information extraction (Marchionini, 1992). Much of what needs to be done in information-seeking interface design relates to perceptual versus cognitive processes. This book argues for systems that support active browsing and that minimize memory-intensive activities. Such systems amplify perception by maximizing interactivity and augment cognition by freeing cognitive resources to focus on filtering/judging/interpreting information rather than attending to query formulation and system manipulation.

## Developments in electronic environments: Systems, data structures, and algorithms

Interactions with electronic devices have increased in all aspects of knowledge work, including information seeking. Developments in hardware, data structuring, and algorithms had early influences on information seeking by forcing experts to formalize information-seeking strategies. The computer systems of the 1960s and 1970s led mainly to analytical strategies that were based on the careful explication of steps taken in manual environments and that took advantage of the power of electronic computation and storage. As we will argue in subsequent chapters, electronic environments of the 1980s and 1990s have ushered in a new wave of expansion in electronic information seeking by allowing broader classes of information seekers to use highly interactive browsing strategies. Thus, the continued evolution of electronic environments promises that the full range of information-seeking strategies used in manual environments will be applied and augmented. Today's storage, computation, and communication technologies allow full text and multimedia databases to be accessed rapidly by masses of end users in a variety of physical locations. The results of all these efforts are coming together to support the highly interactive information seeking described in this book. A brief overview of the developments most specific to information seeking follows.

Hardware developments have been dramatic and will likely continue as efforts in the United States such as the High Performance Computing Initiative (U.S. Office of Science and Technology Policy, 1991), the many projects related to developing digital libraries and the National Information Infrastructure, Europe's ESPRIT Program (Smeaton, 1992), and Japan's Fifth Generation Computing Initiative (Feigenbaum & McCorduck, 1983; Fuchi et al., 1993; see also the large-scale Japanese efforts to develop interfaces known as the FRIENDS21 Project; Nonogaki & Ueda, 1991) evolve. Computing power has grown from thousands of floating-point operations per second (kiloFLOPS) to megaFLOPS to gigaFLOPS in the last decade, and parallel architectures are beginning to increase actual throughput for complex processing.[6] Most significantly, these dramatic increases in high-end computing have been accompanied by the general availability of personal computers and workstations that provide substantial computing power to offices, schools, and homes. In addition to central processing unit power, developments in magnetic and optical technology make it possible to distribute large libraries of text and growing collections of images, sounds, and multimedia documents. Companion advances in display technology and data compression techniques allow electronic digital displays to surpass analog video displays and rival photographic technology. Optical scanner technology has become fast, accurate, and cheap enough for a cost-effective conversion of archival or esoteric paper-based documents to electronic form, and video-capture technology offers similar capabilities for video.

Research on interfaces for online systems has made these systems more easily available by improving both learnability and usability. Advances have been made in user–system dialogues, that is, by viewing computer use as a communication process; ensuring the consistency and clarity of messages, prompts, and feedback; studying and improving command and interaction languages from the user's perspective; developing natural-language processing; considering documentation and instruction from the initial stages of design rather than as afterthoughts; using metaphors such as the desktop to aid learning; developing and testing of graphical user interfaces (GUIs) and window-icon-mouse-pointing systems (WIMPS) that enable data to be manipulated more easily; and establishing alternative rules and mechanisms for query specification and feedback.

The combined effects of hardware and interface research have yielded new kinds of systems such as hypermedia that provide user-centered control of multimedia databases by means of powerful hardware and highly interactive software. These technical developments have not been made independently but represent the more general trend toward a more efficient and effective automation of information work. Perhaps less dramatic but equally important ultimately is the research on how information is collected, stored, and organized for eventual retrieval and use by information seekers. Research in document representation and retrieval techniques has been spurred by hardware and interface progress and is essential to the overall development of systems that support information seeking.

The traditional way to represent information documents in large collections such as libraries is to support search through indexing. Each document is assigned one or more index terms selected to represent the best meaning of the document. These index terms are then searched to locate documents related to queries expressed in words taken from the index language. In the simplest cases, the index language is a set of dates, names, or identification numbers that serve as entry points to the database. This is the basis for database management systems in which the documents are called records (tuples) and the index language is simply the set of possible values for key fields (attributes). The most important and difficult cases involve accessing information by "subject," and for this purpose, well-defined indexing languages that delineate concepts are used. There are generic indexing languages for library access (e.g., Library of Congress Subject Headings), but specialized indexing vocabularies for specific literatures (e.g., Association for Computing Machinery Classification system for computer science, Medical Subject Headings for medicine) have been devised to index information in those areas better (see Soergel, 1985, for a full treatment of indexing).

The main technique used by today's large commercial information retrieval systems is to index each document by a number of terms (these range from a few to dozens) and create an "inverted file" for the database. The inverted file contains each word in the index language and pointers to each document indexed under that term. This technique usually is accompanied by algorithms that allow searchers to enter Boolean combinations of words as queries and to combine document hits appropriately and automatically. In the case of some online databases and most full-text CD-ROM databases, the index language consists of all words contained in the entire collection of documents.[7] Each document is then indexed by all words that occur in it. Full-text indexing is one way of supporting what is generally termed *string search* (because any string of characters can be located), which is one of the most significant differences between manual and electronic searching.[8] These techniques allow information seekers to find every document that contains any word they specify. The assumption underlying all these forms of indexing is that the "meanings" of documents and queries can be and are captured in specific words or phrases (see Frakes & Baeza-Yates, 1992, for a collection of readings related to these and other information retrieval techniques).

Alternative approaches to representing documents have also emerged, including knowledge-based indexing languages that capture deeper and richer meanings of individual documents and the relations among documents. Humphrey (1989) invented a frame-based indexing system for medical literature that augments the existing MESH and helps indexers assign valid and useful terms. In addition to improving document representation, such systems may also be used by information seekers to augment terms specifically identified in a query with those implicitly related by the frame structures.

Another set of approaches to document representation treats the documents and queries as vectors (Salton, 1989; Salton & Buckley, 1990; Salton & McGill, 1983). Each cell in the vector corresponds to one term in the index language, and in the simplest case, each value represents the degree to which that term occurs in the document. These values can be simple binaries (e.g., $1 = $ yes, $0 = $ no), a raw number of occurrences, or a raw number of occurrences weighted according to the document's length and/or normalized according to the frequency of occurrence in the entire collection. Queries are likewise represented as vectors, and a variety of similarity measures can be used to match queries and documents (e.g., the cosine of the angle between the query vector and each document vector can be used as a semantic proxy metric to rank documents). The vector approach has a significant advantage over traditional indexing methods for end users, because the retrieved sets of documents can be ranked, thus eliminating the "no hits" result so common in exact-match systems. Experimental systems that provide ranked output have proved highly effective, and commercial vendors have begun to offer ranked output features. Ranked output also provides a reasonable entry point for browsing.

Extensions of this statistical approach to information retrieval include models based on clustering techniques. Some clustering approaches compare vector representations in pairwise fashion to form groups of similar documents that subsequently are combined to form a smaller number of still larger groups. Alternative approaches begin with one or more key documents that focus on a topic or concept and then process the remaining documents by comparing similarity values and assigning them to the concept group most closely matched (see Rasmussen, 1992, for an overview of clustering techniques).

A model known as *latent semantic indexing* has also been used to automatically process documents and queries. It assigns terms based on frequency to a term-document matrix, as in the vector-based approach, but also uses correlational metrics to augment co-occurrences across documents. LSI uses singular-value decomposition, an algorithm related to factor analysis that collapses a large matrix into a smaller set of distinct factors (Deerwester et al., 1990; Dumais, 1988). These factors are vector representations for concepts – the "latent semantics" of the document collection. Queries may return documents that do not contain any of the query words but have similar vector representations.

Relevance ratings are based on information seekers' judgments about a document with respect to an actual problem. Because the query expressed in any search is a surrogate for the problem, models that match queries to documents assume accurate problem-to-query mappings for query to document comparisons. Probabilistic models acknowledge that there are degrees of relevance and are based on some estimated probability of document–query relevance. These models rank documents according to system-estimated probabilities for the relevances of queries and documents or query classes and document classes. User probability estimates also can be used as the basis for relevance feedback to the system (see Bookstein, 1985, for an overview of probabilistic retrieval models and Larson, 1992, for empirical comparisons of vector and probabilistic models).

In addition to matching based on vector similarities or probability rankings, connectionist models of pattern matching have been proposed. Models based on supervised neural network algorithms (Belew, 1986) or unsupervised algorithms (Lin, 1993) have been tested (see Doszkocs, Reggia, & Lin, 1990, for a review of connectionist techniques for information retrieval). These approaches use vectors as inputs and provide clustered sets of outputs. The main idea is to process the document collection by comparing an input vector (e.g., a randomly selected document vector) with all document vectors to determine the best match. The vector weights for the "winning" document are then adjusted to reflect more closely the input vector, as are its proximate neighbors. This process, called *training,* proceeds for thousands of iterations until the document vector space stabilizes (few weight adjustments are made between subsequent iterations). This space then represents documents in neighborhoods where proximity depends on document similarity.

All these techniques provide a basis for ranking documents that provides a good entry point for a user-centered, interactive model of human information seeking. Relevance feedback is a technique that has proved highly effective for improving retrieval (Harmon, 1992). Users examine results and indicate those that are most useful. The system then locates more documents that are similar, and the process continues iteratively. Relevance feedback requires an interactive setting in which information seekers select relevant items and the system reformulates the search. The reformulation may be based on simple matching of index terms used in an exact-match Boolean system, or on new query vectors adjusted according to a variety of adjustment techniques. Together, ranking and relevance feedback support highly interactive information seeking. With continued developments in hardware and interfaces, these techniques offer the potential for new generations of highly interactive systems to support information seeking.

Most operational systems apply one combination of these approaches, and users must learn the best strategies to use for that system. Some systems are more hybrid, offering information seekers choices between exact match Boolean and ranked approaches. As this trend continues, information seekers will need more guidance in selecting the best strategy to use for specific problems. As the next generation of analytical and browse strategies evolves to accommodate such systems, our personal information infrastructures will be enlarged as well.

# 3

# Information-seeking perspective and framework

*Any piece of knowledge I acquire today has a value at this moment exactly proportional to my skill to deal with it.*

Mark Van Doren, *Liberal Education*

Information seeking involves a number of personal and environmental factors and processes. In this chapter we identify these factors and processes and see how they work together to define and constrain information seeking. Before reading further, stop and consider the many information-seeking activities you perform each day. Suppose you have a well-defined information need such as finding a phone number for a business in a foreign city. What do you need to know to begin? What things do you already know about telephones, businesses, and information seeking that will help in your search? What sources could help? How can you determine whether they are available? How do you use them? What are the costs in time or money? How will you know when you have found the correct number? What kinds of questions can you imagine for a more openended but better-focused information problem such as understanding the implications of the European Common Market's trade agreement with Japan on what investments to make for a child's college trust fund? How would your strategies differ for a fuzzy problem like gaining information to improve one's knowledge of a domain of interest? Clearly, we encounter many varieties of information problems and apply varied information-seeking strategies to solve these problems. To understand this variety, it is useful to have a framework that explicates factors and processes common to information seeking in general.

## Information-seeking perspective

The perspective on information seeking taken in this book has its roots in the work of scholars in information science, psychology, education, communications, and computer science. The perspective emerges from three beliefs about human existence: Life is active, analog, and accumulative. The active view of life implies that we learn by "bumping into the environment." This experiential and biological view was expressed in the learning philosophy of John Dewey and the psychological theory of Jean Piaget. Our actions may be classified as reactive or proactive. Reactions require perceptive inputs of information and relatively rapid recall of information from memory. We perceive the situation at hand through our senses and determine our reactions according to existing mental models. Proactions are guided by plans, employ outputs of information (e.g., trial balloons) and active information gathering (e.g., hypothesis testing), and require synthesis of information. The balance between reactive and proactive actions is determined by individual characteristics such as age or experience and by the stability and organization of the environment. Thus, highly organized social and political environments allow those who have experience to manipulate more information in imaginative and reflective ways to plan their actions. The information society and its highly organized work environments demand highly developed personal information infrastructures to guide its members' many intellectual and physical actions.

Life as an analog process means that it is continuous and periodic. The continuity of individual lives implies that information incessantly flows from the environment, regardless of how we are able to process and store it. This continuity forces us to develop mental and physical apertures as part of our personal information infrastructures so that we can control information flow. Periodicity describes the "ups and downs" of our physiological, psychological, and spiritual lives. These periods are both internally determined and influenced by the environment, and they affect our abilities to seek, accept, and process information.

Life as accumulation is a corollary of continuity in that it is difficult or impossible for us to selectively and purposely forget the effects of information we have processed during our lives. As information affects our knowledge structures, these structures are extended, reinforced, or altered. This accretional process not only broadens our understanding of the world but also bolsters our biases and affects our subsequent expectations. This belief implies that organization of our information resources is critical to effective future actions and that we must not only control the amount of information but also must create evaluative filters to minimize inaccurate or low-quality information.

Life requires us to plan and execute actions (actions can be mental activities as well as physical). To do so, we need to have plausible mental models (understandings) of the world. To have such mental models, we need information – anything with the potential to change a mental state (Belkin, 1978). Thus, information seeking is a process driven by life itself. More specifically, information seeking is a process driven by humans' needs for information so that they can interact with the environment.

This view of information seeking has paralleled developments in our thinking about psychology, sociology, and technology. Rather than focusing exclusively on the representation, storage, and systematic retrieval of information or on information systems, the current view of information seeking emphasizes communication and the needs, characteristics, and actions of information seekers (Dervin & Nilan, 1986). This focus has followed the development of cognitive psychology, which goes beyond the stimulus–response (input–output) constraints of behavioral psychology to examine human cognitive processes. It has been reinforced by developments in communications and computing technology and their attendant problems related to acceptance, behavioral changes, and potential abuse. As discussed in the previous chapter, these developments have led to more interactions among people and systems.

### Human-centered models of information seeking

Attention to users of information systems and consideration of their needs from a communications perspective are well represented in the literature. Dervin (1977) was particularly influential in focusing attention on users' needs through her model based on people's need to make sense of the world. The model posits that users go through three phases in making sense of the world, that is, by facing and solving their information problems. The first phase establishes the context for the information need, called the *situation*. People find a gap between what they understand and what they need in order to make sense of the current situation. These gaps are manifested by questions. The answers or hypotheses for these gaps are then used to move to the next situation. This situation-gap-use model applies to more general human conditions than information seeking but has been adopted by researchers in information science and communications as a framework for studying the information-seeking process.

Belkin and his colleagues (Belkin, 1980; Belkin, Oddy, & Brooks, 1982) constructed a model of information seeking that focuses on information seekers' anomalous states of knowledge (ASK). In this model, information seekers are concerned with a problem, but the problem itself and the information needed to solve the problem are not clearly understood. Accordingly, information seekers must go through a process of clarification to articulate a search request, with the obvious implication that search systems should support iterative and interactive dialogues with users. This model was designed to explain generally open-ended information problems and does not directly apply to fact-retrieval problems or to accretional information seeking by experts in a field. The ASK model serves as a theoretical basis for the design of highly interactive information systems.

In a much more specific context, Kuhlthau (1988) devised a model of how students search for information as part of the writing process. Her model extends to both cognitive and affective perspectives and was developed through observations and interviews with students over long periods of time. The model crosses feelings, thoughts, and actions through seven stages: task initiation, topic selection, prefocus exploration, focus formulation, information collection, search closure, and the starting of writing. The model is robust across different age groups of learners (Kuhlthau, Turock, George, & Belvin, 1990) and addresses the affective states of information seekers.

These and other models of information-seeking behavior share perspectives on information seeking as a problem-solving activity that depends on communication acts. This perspective is accepted by researchers and practitioners in information science but has only begun to influence designers and engineers who implement electronic retrieval systems. Because this perspective does parallel the user-centered philosophy dominant in human–computer interaction research, it is likely that electronic retrieval systems will eventually exhibit interfaces that support active, problem-oriented information seeking. The perspective shared by these models is also the basis for the framework developed in this chapter. Before describing the components of the framework and the processes associated with them, we offer an overview of three types of user studies that motivate and provide examples for this framework.

### Studies of users of electronic retrieval systems

A number of researchers have studied people using electronic retrieval systems in order to characterize the search process from a user perspective. These studies have concentrated on professional intermediaries who regularly use a system or on "end users" who may be novices or occasional users of the system. Often, these studies have been conducted using existing systems with design specifications that are typically information centered or system centered rather than user centered. Some more recent studies have taken the approach of formative evaluation in conjunction with actual system development. A few of these investigations are described here to illustrate the many factors that make up the information-seeking framework.[1] This overview is meant to provide a context for the framework, and in subsequent chapters, we will discuss user studies in detail in light of this framework.

Fidel's work with professional online searchers is typical of the studies of expert intermediaries (Fidel, 1984). She conducted intensive case studies of intermediaries conducting searches of online bibliographic databases. Based on her observations and interviews, she defined two searching styles: operationalist and conceptualist. An operationalist searcher devotes considerable effort to manipulating the system and conducts high-precision searches. A conceptualist searcher devotes more effort to the concepts and terminology and develops subsets of results that are then combined in various ways to yield high recall.[2] Fidel's work has been extended to address particular aspects of searching, such as how subject terms are selected and used by professional searchers in a variety of fields (Fidel, 1991).

Saracevic and his colleagues (Saracevic & Kantor, 1988a, 1988b; Saracevic, Kantor, Chamis, & Trivison, 1988) conducted the largest study to date of online searching by expert intermediaries using a framework of five variable classes: users, questions, searchers, searches, and items retrieved. Their findings indicate that end-user variables have little effect on outcomes as measured by the odds of retrieved documents being at least partially relevant and that recall and precision values were generally consistent across variables. Exceptions include the following: Well-defined problems increased relevance odds; estimates of public knowledge (the end user's expectations about what information is available in the system) increased relevance and precision odds; and user-defined limits on language and currency of documents increased relevance and precision odds. Various cognitive characteristics of searchers had mixed effects on their performance, with a preference for abstractness over concreteness as having significant positive effects on relevance and recall odds. Term selection overlap among intermediaries was low, as was overlap among retrieved document sets – reinforcing the view of online retrieval as more an art than a science. The studies reported many other results related to how searches were executed and what types of outcomes were obtained, but a key recommendation was to investigate the complex nature of the search process in context as well as in laboratory settings. In addition to the extensive portrait that these studies provide for intermediaries searching electronic databases, the framework for question classification and the application of quantitative and qualitative evaluation measures make these efforts seminal in the field.

Studies of end users are exemplified by Borgman's investigations of the cognitive activity of college students and children using various bibliographic databases (Borgman, 1986a; Borgman, Gallagher, Krieger, & Bower, 1990). She applied the psychological theory of mental models to explain learning and errors and made a case for instructional approaches that are conceptual rather than simply procedural. Her systematic user studies also provide the basis for the continued development and redesign of an online catalog customized for elementary students (Borgman et al., 1990). Borgman's early work was the basis for some of the studies that Marchionini conducted with K–12 students searching full-text electronic encyclopedias (Marchionini, 1989b; 1989c). In his work, elementary school children were able to use the electronic environment to conduct searches for simple subjects, and high school students had difficulties with complex queries and made mental models for the new system based on print metaphors and individual information-seeking skills and characteristics.

In some cases, studies of end users were part of overall development efforts for specific electronic retrieval systems. Formative evaluation examines how users interact with system prototypes to inform the iterative design process. Egan and colleagues (1989) studied users of their SuperBook hypertext system and used the results in making substantial improvements in subsequent versions of the system. Marchionini and Shneiderman (1988) likewise used the results of user studies for subsequent versions of the Hyperties hypertext system and various Hyperties databases. Ongoing end-user evaluations of the Perseus Project system also influenced subsequent releases of this hypermedia corpus (Marchionini & Crane, 1994). Generalizable results from these studies illustrate the usefulness of highlighted query terms, the use of tables of contents to provide content for users, and the high acceptance by users of interactive browsing.

Studies of end users concentrated on online public access catalogs in libraries. Early studies sponsored by the Council on Library Resources led to a better understanding of the types of searches that users conducted (e.g., over half of all

OPAC searches were by subject rather than title or author) and identified the wide range of results that users obtained (e.g., about 10% of commands resulted in errors, except in the menu interface of MELVYL, which produced 2% error rates) (Larson, 1983; Markey, 1984; Matthews, 1982). Studies of user error patterns (Janosky, Smith, & Hildreth, 1986) highlighted not only the interface defects of OPACs but also the fact that casual users have a poor understanding of libraries in general and exhibit naive and careless actions while searching. These results are cited as influential in the improved designs for second generation OPACs (Hildreth, 1989; Larson, 1991).

In sum, the results of studies of how users apply electronic retrieval systems to information-seeking problems reinforce the general theory of user-centered information seeking that focuses on highly active users with a broad range of information problems. They also illustrate the importance of task and system parameters. These results have led to new designs for retrieval systems and demonstrated the value of user testing and iterative design. More important, they have reinforced and extended the perspective of information seeking as a human-centered problem-solving activity.

## Factors of information seeking

Information seeking depends on interactions among several factors: information seeker, task, search system, domain, setting, and search outcomes (Marchionini, 1989a; Marchionini & Shneiderman, 1988). Figure 3.1. depicts these factors and the relationships that bind them. The setting is the situational and physical context for information seeking. The information seeker is central to the framework and exploits these factors as the information seeking progresses. The information seeker is motivated by an information problem or need that activates a variety of noumena – mental images or memory traces. These noumena and the relationships among them form concepts that define the problem and are in turn articulated as a task (e.g., a verbal statement of the problem or a set of purposeful actions related to solving it). The search system is the source of information and the rules for access. Search systems are selected by the information seeker or are made available by the setting as a default. Domains are fields of knowledge (e.g., chemistry, medicine, and anatomy may be activated in a health situation). Outcomes are the feedback from the system (e.g., document surrogates, images, system messages) and traces of the overall process. Information seekers reflect on outcomes, and this reflection in turn changes the seeker's knowledge and thus determines whether he or she should continue or stop seeking information.

All the factors are embedded in a setting; the domain and search system are interrelated; the information seeker perceives and interprets the setting, has mental models for the domain(s) and the search system, and turns an information problem into a task that drives his or her interactions with the search system; these interac-

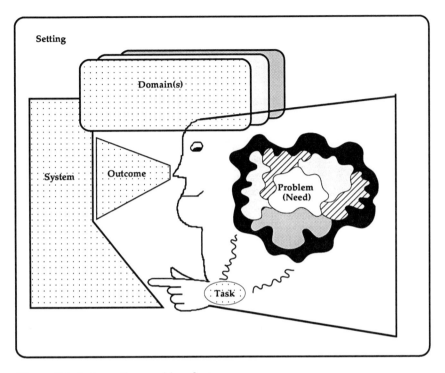

Figure 3.1. Information-seeking factors.

tions yield outcomes that in turn affect the information seeker and the problem. These factors are discussed in detail in the following sections.

### *Information seeker*

This framework for information seeking is human centered in that the information seeker defines the task, controls the interaction with the search system, examines and extracts relevant information, assesses the progress, and determines when the information-seeking process is complete. Each information seeker possesses unique mental models, experiences, abilities, and preferences. Experience with particular settings, domains, and systems generally allow more comprehensive and accurate mental models and thus more facility with these models. The information seeker's personal information infrastructure affects overall performance while solving information problems and executing tasks and continues to develop as information seekers accrue experience and knowledge. For every information problem, information seekers reinforce and extend their mental models for the various factors and subprocesses associated with information seeking.

Professional intermediaries who regularly conduct searches for others are familiar with many sources of information (search systems) and are able to apply various information-seeking strategies. They demonstrate expertise in information seeking through their knowledge of different search systems and strategies for assisting people in articulating tasks. Experts in a field of study have comprehensive vocabularies in the domain, know what types of sources are best applicable to problems, and are aware of alternative access points for finding information in the domain (e.g., personal, corporate, geographic). Our studies of professional intermediaries and domain experts in computer science, economics, and law suggest that although both types of experts have significant advantages over novices when conducting searches, each type of expert also exhibits specific advantages with respect to one another (Marchionini, Dwiggins, Katz, & Lin, 1993; Marchionini, Lin, & Dwiggins, 1990). Intermediaries focus on the information task as expressed in the question, on query formulation, and on the interface aspects of the system (e.g., structure of information) and are generally guided by matching questions to the database's structure. Domain experts seem to have an image of the answer and are guided by identifying possible answers in the database. Domain experts spend more time in scanning and reading text and less time formulating and modifying queries. Regardless of the specific advantages that either type of experts have, expertise clearly affects information seeking, just as it does other intellectual efforts such as chess (Newell & Simon, 1972) or medical decision making (Spiro, Feltovich, Coulson, & Anderson, 1989). The nature of expertise and its role in information seeking are examined in detail in the next chapter.

Individual differences among information seekers play a role in both specific instances of information seeking and the overall development of personal information infrastructures. Egan (1988) identified age and spatial reasoning as important factors in a variety of task performance areas, including information seeking. Other researchers studied cognitive style (e.g. Bellardo, 1985) and personal variables such as academic success, reading ability, field of study, and verbal and quantitative abilities in order to determine their relationships to information seeking (e.g., Borgman, 1989; Marchionini, 1989a). Because these individual differences are not independent, no single characteristic alone can predict information-seeking performance. However, cognitive, physical, and emotional differences between and within individual persons do influence specific behaviors and general affinities and abilities.

In addition to individual differences, information seeking is part of a person's ongoing effort to understand and act in the world. Each person is situated in a context that at any given instant influences all actions, including information seeking (see Suchman, 1987, for a theory of situated human activity applied to human–machine interactions). Situational personal variables such as physical, cognitive, and emotional health affect human performance and cannot be ignored. Commitments to a work group or other persons influence performance and how people perceive themselves fitting into an organization are part of the setting. Even more slippery is the motivation to initiate and continue information seeking. The motivation to initiate a search may be driven by external or internal needs, but the tenacity to continue the search may depend on personality factors such as perseverance and on external factors such as time and money.

The most basic situational factor for information seeking, however, is the information problem that causes the user to act. Taylor (1962) defined four levels of information needs: visceral, conscious, formalized, and compromised. The visceral level is the recognition of some deficiency, although it is not cognitively defined. At the conscious level, the information seeker characterizes the deficiency, places limits on it, and is able to express the problem, though not precisely. At the formalized level, the person is able to articulate the problem clearly (e.g., in English), and the compromised level refers to the formalized statement as presented in a form limited by the search system (e.g., in a database query language). The conscious and formalized levels correspond to the task in the framework presented here.

Taylor's visceral and conscious levels of information need correspond to what Dervin called a *gap,* and what Belkin and his colleagues refer to as an *anomalous state of knowledge.* Using a computational metaphor, Marchionini (1989b) characterized the information problem as emerging from a defect in one's mental model for some idea, event, or object. This state initiates a search in long-term memory, and if the defect cannot be mended (either correctly or through rationalized guessing), then information seeking is initiated by activating the personal information infrastructure and passing the contextual parameters to it. Marchionini defined the personal information infrastructure procedure by observing how people use manual and electronic encyclopedias, and he noted a significant difference in the electronic instantiations in that those systems often returned large sets of articles as outcomes rather than a single article or small set of "see also" articles in the manual case. By automatically involving the index in search, these electronic systems required additional explicit decision-making steps by users. This approach was useful in formulating the human–system interaction phases of the information-seeking process but mental model structures seemed badly suited to information needs, as they are elaborate and take time to develop.

To address this deficiency, consider the knowledge state of an information seeker at some instant as a collection of noumenal clouds. Each noumenal cloud represents a concept or idea composed of noumena (memory traces and impressions). These clouds are highly fluid; the noumena within a cloud come and go as thought progresses, as do the clouds themselves. A knowledge state consists of several noumenal clouds related by common noumena – analogous to valence bonds between atoms in a molecule. The knowledge state is well defined when the noumena within clouds are stable and the clouds have many noumena in common. In this case, new clouds are not formed, and active clouds remain active – there is relative certainty in the knowledge state. An information problem is a collection of noumenal clouds that is unstable; clouds come and go because there are not enough stable common noumena. In this case, the knowledge state has a high degree of uncertainty in the definition of noumena and clouds and thus a high potential for state change, that is, acquiring information. In the most common cases, greater numbers of noumena are needed for stabilization (simply activating more memory traces to define a cloud). In more complex cases, overlaps of noumena across clouds are needed for stabilization.

Information problems typically arise directly from the external world – inputs stimulate noumena and clouds. The information problem may also arise from a stable knowledge state when a cloud is deactivated or a new cloud is added to extend thought. As new clouds are activated, the knowledge state can stabilize quickly as many noumena from active clouds overlap (e.g., as one thought leads logically to the next), or the knowledge state can become less stable if noumena do not fit into active clouds. In the latter case, information is needed (e.g., finding out what one does not know may be a revelation that informs and guides one's subsequent action).

Note that each of these characterizations is based on information imparting some cognitive change, not on overt behaviors. There is a great range in the degree of cognitive change that a person may seek. For example, physicians often seek information to confirm what they believe to be the proper course of treatment. The need to confirm information does not change cognitive structure so much as reinforce it. Regardless of the terminology used and the motivation, the information problem is the trigger for information seeking and as discussed in sections ahead, it evolves and changes as the search and the overall situation progress.

## *Task*

As used here, a *task* is the manifestation of an information seeker's problem and is what drives information-seeking actions. The task includes an articulation, usually stated as a question, and the mental and physical behaviors of interacting with search systems and reflecting on outcomes. Tasks are composed of entity-relationship states and plans for expanding those states to some goal state. Although tasks are explicitly goal driven, the human element and the interactive nature of information seeking allow the goal and therefore the task to change or evolve as the search progresses. The balance between goal-driven initiation and data-driven progress and change are one measure of the browsing considered in chapter 6. As information seekers define the information problem, they identify concepts and relationships and assign terms[3] to the concepts in order to articulate a task. These concepts and terms vary in number (the number of noumenal clouds) and in degree of abstractness (the amount of variability possible when mapping noumena to specific objects or events), and these variations determine the complexity of the task.[4]

In addition to complexity, tasks may be characterized according to their goals or the answers expected. A key problem in information-seeking performance and information system design is clarifying different levels of the task's goal. For example, the goal from the system's point of view is to provide a document of some sort, whereas the goal from the information seeker's point of view is to extract information (make meaning) from some document and stabilize or advance his or her knowledge state. From the information seeker's point of view, answers to questions (goals for tasks) may be characterized along three continua: specificity, quantity, and timeliness.

The specificity of a goal can range from single fact to an idea to an interpretation or opinion. In the case of facts, information seekers are assured of a high level of certainty that they have accomplished the task and reached the goal. This is not to say that the answer is necessarily optimal but, rather, that there is typically a high degree of confidence in the result's validity. In the case of ideas, the certainty of attainment and therefore of terminating the search is less well defined. Such tasks may invite subsequent iterations of action and termination decisions based on factors such as time or resource constraints. In addition, these types of answers are often multiple in number, and so information seekers must choose or synthesize outcomes. Goals with very low specificity offer the greatest challenges to information seekers for they provide low levels of certainty about completing the task and require great efforts to develop confidence in the validity of one of possibly many interpretations.

Related to specificity is the volume of the answer as measured in either information bits or time for users to process the result. At one end of this continuum we have a single word, date, or image that satisfies the task. Such goals are often satisfied by ready reference services in libraries, telephone directory assistance, or traditional database management systems. Such answers can be transmitted and processed easily and quickly. Another level of volume requires one or more documents, and these answers take more time to transmit and process. Most important, these levels of goal volume traditionally require information seekers to process and extract information. This makes the information seekers' relevance judgments both more personal and difficult, with subsequent implications for evaluating the system's performance. In the most extreme case, such as the task of "keeping abreast of one's field," which we term *accretion of knowledge,* the volume of the answer reaches large subsets of a domain or domains. These goals are typically met by regular reading of periodicals, discussions and exchanges with colleagues, and participation in courses, workshops, and conferences.

Timeliness of the goal describes the expected time to completion. One of the common frustrations of information seeking is when expectations of timeliness are far out of sync with actual times to completion. Thus, regardless of how effective an information service is, if we expect the task to take 10 minutes and it actually takes 2 hours, we will be disappointed. At one end of the timeliness continuum are those answers that we expect to verify immediately or in a few minutes. We can have such immediate expectations only for high-specificity, low-quantity goals. These types of answers are not insignificant, however, because they are common and they highlight one of the distinctions between information seeking and learning. They are common in that they include things we once knew but have temporarily forgotten or things we need as an intermediate step in some larger task; thus we ask someone near us, or we quickly look them up in a reference book, dictionary, or service. In many cases, we have no intention of ever using the information again and so acquire it for immediate needs without making mental or external notes. This contrasts with learning, which always aspires to retaining the information acquired. Many tasks aim at goals that we expect will be achieved in some generally defined period such as minutes, days, or months. These tasks include most formal information retrieval such as database searching, interlibrary loan requests, and written requests to persons or institutions. At the most extreme, our expectations are that we will never fully achieve our task but will progress toward it. These accretion of knowledge tasks are part of expert learning and distinguish information seeking from information retrieval.

All these characteristics of task goals work together to define the cost of the task. The total cost is not composed simply of external costs such as connect and copying charges but also of personal costs such as time, as well as cognitive and emotional resources. Early estimates of the costs are computed by information seekers to determine whether tasks should be defined and executed. These estimates are strongly influenced by personal abilities and motivations, especially with respect to personal information infrastructures.

### Search system

The *search system* is a source that represents knowledge and provides tools and rules for accessing and using that knowledge. Here a search system includes, for example, people, books, libraries, and maps, as well as a variety of electronic information systems. A search system represents knowledge in what is called a *database*, regardless of whether the search system is a book, a computer, or a person. Thus, a database refers to the knowledge potentially available to an information seeker. The representations of that knowledge and the tools, rules, and mechanisms for accessing and manipulating it is an *interface*.

The search system supports information seeking by structuring knowledge and constraining access. The way that knowledge is organized and made available affects the way that information seekers are able to access this knowledge and thus their information-seeking performance. Information seekers construct and use mental models of search systems to execute information-seeking tasks.

Both the database and interface have conceptual and physical components as illustrated in Figure 3.2. The interface serves as an intermediary between the user

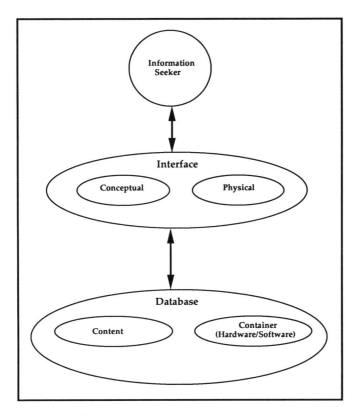

Figure 3.2. Search system components.

and the database. Conceptual elements include representations and mechanisms and physical elements include input and output devices. The database content may be in different containers (e.g., a paper and electronic version of a text), and the database and interface may be integrated or separated physically or conceptually. The interface should provide robust mappings between the database content and the conceptual representations that information seekers manipulate. In the sections that follow, we use three general types of search systems – a book, an electronic retrieval system, and an expert human – to clarify the characteristics of search systems.

*Database: content and container.* Information seekers are most concerned with the content of a database, which may be characterized by its topicality, aim, data type, quantity, quality, and granularity. The primary aspect of content is "aboutness," the domain represented by the database. Clearly, an information problem related to nuclear waste management will not likely be well served by a database concerning ancient Roman poetry. Books can be assigned subject headings that try to capture their primary topics; electronic retrieval systems have data dictionaries specifying what entities and relationships are included, and people develop expertise in specific domains.[5]

A second aspect of the content is whether it is primary or *n*-ary in nature. Secondary (e.g., bibliographic) or tertiary (e.g., a bibliography of bibliographies, database guides, directories of electronic servers) databases are important for locating primary databases, and information seekers must have clear images of the intermediate role they play. The classic disappointment in electronic environments is exemplified by students who use a CD-ROM index to conduct a search and then are dismayed that they must locate the periodical in the library. It is important that information seekers understand which level of access is most appropriate to reach the primary database relevant to their problem.

Another aspect of the database content is the type of information it contains, for example, text, numeric, graphic, verbal, kinesthetic, or mixed. These types of information determine how system designers organize, index, and display information. This in turn influences the strategies that information seekers use to locate, scan, and extract information. Books often include mixed forms; electronic multimedia databases are becoming more common; and humans offer a broad range of verbal and kinesthetic information.

The quantity and quality of database content also are important. It makes a great difference to an information seeker in terms of effort and expectations whether the database consists of a single book of 200 pages or an entire shelf of books on the topic. Likewise, an electronic system of 1000 records is treated quite differently by an information seeker than is a system with a billion records. Although human memory is, for all practical purposes, infinite,[6] different people have different degrees of experience and expertise on a topic. Experienced information seekers assess the accuracy of the content as part of search system selection and while making judgments about initiating and terminating the search. The authority of a book's author, the integrity of an electronic retrieval system, and the credibility of human experts each are taken into consideration by experienced information seekers. In addition to accuracy, the database content must be clearly organized and presented if it is to be considered a quality information source. Books can be well written or not, electronic documents can be well structured or not; and human experts can be logical and articulate or not.

Finally, the granularity of the database content affects information seeking. Books, databases, and people can represent knowledge at very specific or highly general levels, with the levels of variability differing according to the needs of the information seeker. For example, a book, electronic system, or person can represent information on dogs in general or be specific to the sleeping habits of a particular family of dogs. Although experienced information seekers expect an encyclopedia to provide generic information on a variety of topics, emerging electronic environments have yet to establish specializations and precedents for communicating granularity to users. For example, an electronic archive may indiscriminately mix highly specific commentary on minor points of an electronic forum with generic overview information on the topic.

Databases have physical attributes that affect information seeking. These attributes may be though of as the "container" for the contents and include the hardware, media, and physical organization of the system. For a book, the attributes are related to size and weight, printing (e.g., characteristics of paper, glue, and ink), typography, and the author's physical ordering of ideas. From a computing point of view, these attributes are related to computational power, storage capacity, coding mechanisms, display characteristics, and data structures. For example, computational power determines whether graphical interfaces can be used effectively or whether sophisticated retrieval schemes will operate in a timely manner. From a human point of view, physical attributes are related to mental and verbal capabilities, and training or biases.

A significant influence of the container is how it determines organizational presentation and the interface. Books generally invite sequential presentations and traversals, although there are many ways in which linearity can be disrupted (e.g., footnotes, citations, indexes, figures). Electronic systems can use networks, webs, and arrays to invite associational traversals – the basis for hypertext. In addition, the processing and structuring of data determines whether retrieval features such as ranking and relevance feedback are available. For example, an inverted index and a primary file together facilitate rapid exact-match retrieval; a file of vector values and a primary file facilitate ranked retrieval; and both leverage the preprocessing captured in the access files to outperform a simple primary file searched sequentially. Humans can present information in free-associational or in carefully sequenced fashion, and information seekers can "traverse" these presentations in random snatches or in sequence. Whether the linear organization and presentation of ideas is inherently more transferable by people or our culture has been conditioned by the limits of transmissional technology is a research topic that will continue to occupy generations to come.

*Interface: physical and conceptual.* The interface is a communication channel between a user and a machine. Interfaces have physical and conceptual components, and the concept of interface is evolving as people use computers as intermediaries for collaborative work (e.g., Grudin, 1993). Physical input and output devices, selection and feedback mechanisms, and retrieval rules characterize an interface and serve as portals to the content. The interface determines how learnable, usable, and satisfying a search system is, and therefore, it affects information-seeking performance. The "look and feel" of a book, electronic document, or person is dependent on assumptions made about the information seeker's needs and abilities. For books, these assumptions are stable, and for humans, the assumptions are dynamic and may be personalized to each individual information seeker.

For most electronic systems, these assumptions (the user model, Allen, 1990; Daniels, 1986) are, in practice, fairly stable and depend on a set of default conditions that reflect the system designer's view of typical information seekers and their information problems. Some systems have adaptable user models that can be controlled by the user (e.g., allow information seekers to use command or menu modes), and research proposals for automatically adaptive interfaces continue to find support (e.g., Hefley, 1990). Interfaces for electronic search systems have received substantial attention, and developments in end-user interfaces have contributed to the adoption of information retrieval technology by a variety of groups and organizations.

The physical interface is composed of objects that facilitate input and output and that control interaction. For books, input to the system is limited to using separate tools such as pencils or highlighters to mark text or write notes. For electronic retrieval systems, input is typically through keyboards, although mice and touch panels are common, and speech recognizers, eye trackers, data gloves, and other devices are finding more applications (Jacob, Legget, Myers, & Pausch, 1993). Input to another person is via the entire range of the human communication spectrum, including voice, body language and gestures, and intermediated channels such as paper and chalkboards.

Output is limited by the database's container. Output from books takes the form of clear, systematic arrangements of ink on paper illuminated by a light source. Many qualitatively distinct techniques have been developed in the hundreds of years that books have been produced. Output from an electronic system is typically through a visual display unit,[7] although printers are common, and speech synthesizers are finding wider use. Output from a human expert may come through any of the channels listed for human input.

Objects that control interaction are dependent on the physical containers discussed under databases. There are physical constraints on exchange between the information seeker and the search system. Books are static in that the author makes all the decisions about what it is possible to see, and the information seeker makes all decisions about how to see it, with no exchange between the two. In electronic systems, authors can provide many alternative views of the material, and information seekers can add, modify, or delete information. Moreover, the electronic system can offer usage-sensitive help or error diagnosis that depends on the information seeker's actions. Human information systems are the most interactive, allowing control through interpersonal dynamics. Physical interfaces for electronic systems have made dramatic progress and have significantly improved the interactivity of information seeking. This trend will likely continue as alternative devices and the coordination of multiple devices evolve.[8]

The conceptual interface of a search system limits the rules and protocols for information transfer. The main categories of the conceptual interface are interaction style, representational structure, and search mechanisms. Interaction style encompasses the mode of communication, including selection and feedback mechanisms. In the case of books, this communication is simplex;[9] that is, the book acts exclusively as the source and the information seeker as the destination. Electronic systems have four types of interaction style: commands, form fill-ins, menus, and direct manipulation (Shneiderman, 1992).

Command-driven interfaces depend on the information seeker's knowing a specific language in order to manipulate the system. Most information retrieval systems are either strictly command driven or provide a command interface as an option. Command-driven interfaces are generally preferred by experts as they are efficient to use (once they are learned) and often can be extended to facilitate short cuts or highly specialized tasks. Command languages are so pervasive that international standards committees are working to establish a common command language for computer-to-computer communication, thus allowing information seekers to use familiar command languages available on their local machines (NISO, 1989).

Form fill-in interaction styles prompt the user with blank forms to complete. Although all the slots to fill in are defined in advance, users have wide discretion as to what they put in the slots. Form fill-ins are thus a cross between command and menu styles. Menu-driven systems have become increasingly popular and allow novice or casual users to execute information-seeking tasks without knowing a command language. Menu systems fully limit the actions an information seeker may take and thus do not allow the expressiveness of command styles. Menu-driven systems are half duplex, in that users make selections and the system provides feedback and then another menu.

Direct manipulation styles provide the information seeker with explicit mappings between their physical activities and system responses. Direct manipulation demands rapid, reversible selections and feedback (Shneiderman, 1983). Sliding a mouse along a pad and watching the cursor slide along the screen in the same direction and at a proportional rate is an example of direct manipulation. Direct manipulation interaction styles make the system "transparent" in that users are able to focus on the task at hand rather than manipulating the system as an intermediary between themselves and the database contents. Direct manipulation is one of the key components to highly interactive, advanced information-seeking systems. Direct manipulation systems are more closely full duplex than other interaction styles are, as selections and feedback are nearly simultaneous. Another person as a search system is the ultimate in a directly manipulable interface. Although verbal language is mostly half duplex, the multiple modes of interaction that occur as humans communicate provide rapid and reversible stimulus-feedback. Direct manipulation is most obviously applicable to tasks with physical analogs, but examples of direct manipulation interfaces for abstract tasks such as information seeking have begun to emerge (Shneiderman, 1992, especially chap. 11).

Another characteristic of interaction style is the metaphor of action supported by the search system. Books emulate verbal activity, often a lecture or argument in the case of nonfiction. The metaphor of narration or thought (stream of consciousness) is often used in fiction. Electronic search systems often use the book as a metaphor, displaying screens of text or tables of data. The desktop has become a popular metaphor for today's variety of applications, and new metaphors such as agents and theater stages (Laurel, 1991) have been proposed. People do not need metaphors for other people, because other minds are ultimately the source of all information and the assumption that facilitates communication is that other people's minds work in basically the same fashion as one's own does.

The representational structure of an interface refers to the organizations of information and the physical mechanisms required to manipulate the structure. It is here that domain experts offer valuable contributions to interface design, because they know how the content should be partitioned and aggregated in order to answer the broadest range of questions. In the case of books, themes may be presented hierarchically or interwoven in webs or spirals throughout what may be a primarily linear set of physical pages. Alternative or supplemental representations such as tables or figures may be used to augment key concepts. Links among physically disparate words, phrases, and concepts are found in footnotes, tables of contents, and indexes and as anaphora within sentences or documents and as allusions and metaphors beyond documents. The physical mechanisms to manage these links depend on alphabetical-ordering principles, parentheticals, page numbers, and citations. Conceptual links are based on the reader's knowledge and experience in the domain.

Electronic search systems support linear, hierarchical, or network structures for content, as does paper, and have the potential of providing alternative representations according to users' needs. This potential for providing many levels of representation or alternative representations is an essential distinction between manual, static environments and electronic, dynamic environments. This point is illustrated and discussed in detail in chapter 7. The cost of flexible representations is in the various mechanisms for controlling them. Today's systems are strictly limited to three management mechanisms: paging, scrolling, and jumping. Systems often provide scroll bars, sliders, pop-up menus, and displays in windows that may be resized or overlapped – requiring users to develop new strategies for manipulating the information's physical structure. One result of such representational structuring is the common complaint by novices that it is difficult to know how large a specific document is. Another is the additional attention that must be given to managing multiple windows on the screen.

One approach to simplifying representation problems is to separate the representations that the information seeker manipulates in the interface from the representations that the interface manipulates in the database. In database management systems, logical and conceptual schemes serve this function. In these systems, the logical scheme for a database is distinct from the physical scheme that defines data storage. The logical scheme makes it possible for different users to have different views of the database according to their specific requirements and access privileges. The logical scheme also determines how queries must be specified (e.g., in SQL language); that is, there are explicit mappings between the conceptual interfaces provided by the query language and the physical scheme of the stored data. This distinction between logical and physical data organization enables end users to use database management systems. Another example is what is known as the client–server model, in which a local interface (client) can be used by an end user to access a remote system with its own logical and physical interface by means of an automatic network intermediary that transparently facilitates the exchange (Lynch, 1991).

People are capable of all types of organizational structures, although teachers and information specialists try to present information consistently and directly according to the perceived needs of the learner or information seeker.[10] Moreover, human intelligence allows instant repairs to be made when communication breaks down.

All search systems offer specific features that define and constrain search. Books provide tables of contents, section headings, citations, and indexes to support direct search for specific information, and they encourage scanning and linear reading. Electronic search systems can support these same types of search features, but they also can allow string search, Boolean logic queries, ranking of results, and relevance feedback. A grand challenge for interface designers is to create new features that take advantage of the unique characteristics of the electronic medium. People are constrained only by their knowledge and ability to articulate their ideas. Paper, electronic, and human search systems will continue to be used, and well-developed personal information infrastructures will allow information seekers to decide which features are most appropriate to the task and to select the system that best supports those features.

### *Domain*

A *domain* is a body of knowledge (e.g., history or chemistry) composed of entities and relationships.[11] Domains vary in complexity, number of entities and relationships, specificity, similarity of the entities and relationships, evolutionary status, clarity of definition of the entities and relationships, and their rate of growth and change. These characteristics determine the type and amount of information and the level of organization for a domain. Most domains depend on textual representations of information, but some are dominated by graphical (e.g., art, architecture), audio (e.g., music), kinesthetic (e.g., dance, sports), or multiple information forms (e.g, film, journalism). The amount of information and level of organization vary immensely across domains. Some fields have enormous and diverse bodies of rapidly growing literature that spawn dozens of subdomains (e.g., medicine), whereas others are fairly contained and growing slowly (e.g., classics). Some fields have inherent ordering relationships that provide important access points for information seeking. For example, history leverages chronology and geopolitical units; anatomy takes advantage of subsystems of the body; and the arts depend on individual artists.

The domain is important because it affects several of the subprocesses that make up the information-seeking process. For example, domains employ different mixes of search systems and search strategies. A domain like hematology offers substantial online information from various vendors in various forms, from abstracts to full texts. On the other hand, a domain like contemporary music offers little online information and limited access through such common entry points as subject headings. Differences between information in the sciences and humanities are well known. For example, information in the humanities typically does not go out of date, whereas scientific and technical information ages rapidly; humanities publications are less likely to have multiple authors; the humanities make equal use of books and journals, whereas the sciences favor journals; and abstracting standards apply more readily to technical literature than to historical literature (Corkill & Mann, 1978; Tibbo, 1989). These characteristics affect the way that search systems are organized and how information seekers access them.

Scholars in all fields use a wide array of information sources, especially colleagues; however, distinct domains have sources that are frequently used. For example, business practitioners mainly use trade journals, trade associations, and word-of-mouth rather than libraries and books (Arthur Little Inc., 1967); physicians mainly use desk reference sets, textbooks, journals, and other professionals, especially colleagues (Connelly et al., 1990; Covell, Uman, & Manning, 1985). Studies of these and other professionals (e.g., clinical psychologists, Prescott & Griffith, 1970; professors, Kwasnik, 1989) agree that information seekers prefer interactive sources of information to static sources. Conversations with others who may have the information they need, conferences, workshops, and symposia are always listed as highly important sources of information in these studies, and some have expressed a desire for more active forms of information such as audiotapes and videotapes or computer programs and simulations.

### Setting

The setting in which information seeking takes place limits the search process. *Setting* here is regarded as having physical and conceptual/social components, including whether the task is done in collaboration or alone and the information seeker's physical and psychological states. As such, it corresponds to the context or situation described by Suchman (1987). This perspective of situated action was applied in education by Brown, Collins, and Duguid (1989), Garner (1990), and Bransford, Sherwood, Hasselbring, Kinzer, and Williams (1990); and in human–computer interaction by Carroll (1990) and Suchman (1987).

The physical setting determines physical constraints such as the amount of time allocated, physical accessibility, comfort, degree of distraction, and cost. It makes a considerable difference whether one is seeking information in a private office or in a public place with a line of impatient people nearby. Physical features such as lighting requirements for paper and electricity and hardware for electronic information are often assumed in modern environments but are basic setting characteristics nonetheless. Economic constraints such as cost and time are situational and influence whether and how tasks are initiated, executed, and terminated. The proximity of sources is a well-documented factor in information seeking, with personal collections and proximate coworkers the most commonly used information sources (e.g., Allen, 1977). Electronic networks have begun to have a significant influence on information proximity, by providing access to catalogs and primary materials from one's home or office workstation. In addition, electronic networks offer new opportunities for group collaboration on information-intensive tasks (see Grudin, 1991, for an overview). The physical setting also includes the type of access and procedures for obtaining access. Whether the information is accessed in a personal or shared work area and in paper form or electronic form affects overall information seeking. What forms must be completed, permissions secured, or identification cards shown also influence overall willingness to seek information and its costliness.

Conceptually, the setting includes the psychological and social ecology of information seeking. The cognitive aspects of this ecology were described in Dervin's (1977) situation phase of her sense-making model. These aspects may be considered to be the state of a person's working memory at any given time. Other psychological factors include a person's self-confidence in an environment. Self-confidence typically depends on familiarity with a situation or expertise in the problem area and influences how ready the information seeker is to take intellectual risks and to persevere in spite of intermittent failures. The social ecology of a situation relates an individual person to other persons or groups and to organizations. A person's role in an organization determines his or her self-image and influences self-confidence, alertness, and, ultimately, productivity. For example, people with low status in an organization may be less able or willing to use organizational resources to seek information. The organizational structure and procedures as described in the physical setting also influence how participants interact with the overall organization and other people, including how they seek information. Social considerations for information seeking become increasingly important as groups use technologies to collaborate on information-intensive projects.

### *Outcomes*

Outcomes for information seeking include both products and a process. As products, outcomes are the results of using an information system, that is, feedback from the system. Eventually, if all goes well, an outcome or set of outcomes will be attainment of the task's goal of answering a question and, on reflection, the solution to the information problem. These products range from individual words, phrases, or images provided by a source, to intermediate sets of document surrogates, to complete documents that are organized and displayed to aid the information seeker in interpretation and use. Most outcomes are intermediate stages in the information-seeking process that provide information to further the overall process. Thus, outcomes affect the task and subsequent iterations of information seeking. Outcomes affect the user as well, for they change the state of the information seeker's knowledge; that is, they impart information.

Outcomes also serve as objects of evaluation to assess the search's or system's effectiveness. Typical measures of search products include assessments of relevance or utility during or after search – including such quantitative measures as recall and precision, structured or informal subjective evaluations, and examination of the resultant products or artifacts (e.g., documents or abstracts). The behavioral moves made by information seekers also help evaluate performance, because evaluators assume that searcher behaviors manifest internal information-seeking strategies, which are themselves "runs" of the searcher's mental models for the search system.

Outcomes can also be viewed as mental reflections on information-seeking episodes. As such, a trace of the search process is itself an outcome, as information seekers consider the mental and physical actions taken during information seeking and adapt their personal information infrastructures accordingly. Thus, the experience itself becomes part of the searcher's knowledge for dealing with future information problems. Because of the powerful roles that outcomes play in information seeking, consistent and effective management and manipulation of outcomes are critical to the design of information systems.

### Summary of factors

Information-seeking factors are not mutually exclusive and are linked by relationships that vary in complexity and importance. The relationships can be considered in pairwise fashion for simplicity, but ultimately, the full interactions among the factors determine information-seeking activity. The framework is human centered, and the information seeker is responsible for integrating all the factors.

- The information seeker's problem considered in light of the personal information infrastructure manifests the task; the information seeker's mental model for the search system strongly influences performance, and the system influences this by presenting a user model that represents the designer's view of generic information seekers; the information seeker may have highly developed or novice understandings of the domain; the information seeker is influenced by the setting and may have some control over it; and outcomes are determined by the information seeker's actions and likewise themselves determine subsequent actions.

- The task influences which system is selected, and the system determines how the task can be operationalized; the task rarely influences the domain, but the domain can influence the nature and result of the task; the task and setting are weakly related in both ways; and the task determines the outcomes as they are incremental goals for the task and in turn may lead to modifications of the task.

- The search system is dependent on the domain for its content, but examples of how the search system may have an impact on the domain have just begun to emerge;[12] the system is a part of the setting, and in extreme cases (e.g., power outages) the physical setting can influence the system; and the system is a determinant of outcomes, and given the present state of system development, only in the case of human search systems does the system learn or change based on outcomes.

- The domain and setting have little influence on each other, and the domain has a weak influence on particular outcomes.

- Finally, the setting weakly influences the outcomes, but the outcomes only rarely and then indirectly influence the setting. These relationships are admittedly subjective but are useful to gain an overall sense of how the information-seeking factors interact. Of course, information seeking is determined by the concurrent interactions among all these factors. The main idea is that the framework is user centered and action oriented, as described in the process presented in the following section.

**Information-seeking process**

The information-seeking process is both systematic and opportunistic. The degree to which a search exhibits algorithms, heuristics, and serendipity depends on the strategic decisions that the information seeker makes and how the information-seeking factors interact as the search progresses. The information-seeking process is composed of a set of subprocesses, as depicted in Figure 3.3. Information seeking begins with the recognition and acceptance of the problem and continues until the problem is resolved or abandoned. In the figure, the likelihood of a subprocess calling another subprocess is represented crudely by three types of arcs. Bold, solid arcs represent the most likely (default) transitions from one subprocess to another; dashed arcs represent high-probability transitions; and solid arcs represent low-transition probabilities. These subprocesses may default to phases or steps in a sequential algorithm, but they are better considered as functions or activity modules that may be called into action recursively at any time, that may be continuously active (types of sentinels or demons), that are temporarily frozen while others

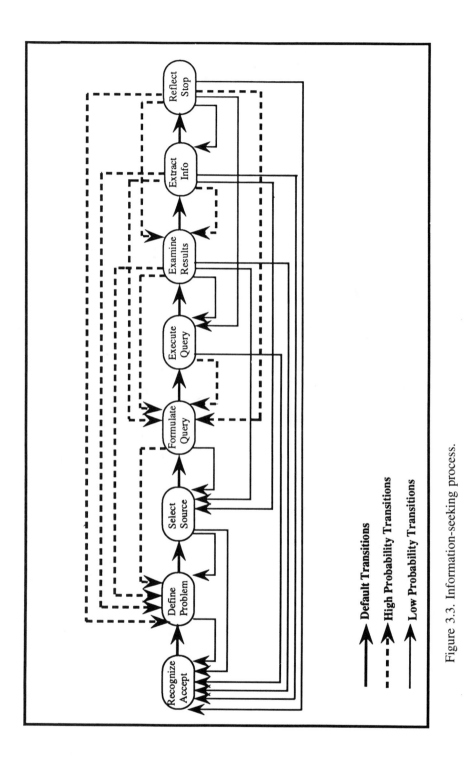

Figure 3.3. Information-seeking process.

proceed, and that may make calls to other subprocess. Thus, the information-seeking process can proceed along parallel lines of progress and take advantage of opportunities arising from intermediate or random results. The degree to which the information-seeking process deviates from a top–down, sequential default provides a basis for characterizing browsing and analytical search, and the number of iterations (cycles) per unit time serves as a gross measure of interactivity.

### Recognize and accept an information problem

Recognizing and accepting an information problem can be internally motivated (e.g., curiosity about the details of immediate thought) or externally motivated (e.g., a teacher asking a question or making an assignment). The problem may be characterized as a gap (Dervin, 1977), a visceral need (Taylor, 1962), an anomaly (Belkin, 1980), as a defect in a mental model, or as an unstable collection of noumenal clouds, but it is manifested as a resource demand on the perceptual or memory systems – the person becomes "aware" of the problem. At this point, the problem may be suppressed or accepted. Suppression is influenced by setting and the information seeker's judgment about the immediate costs (physical and mental) of initiating the search (e.g., "This is not worth the effort; I'll worry about this later"). If the information seeker judges the situation to be appropriate, he or she will accept the problem and begin to define it for the search. Acceptance is influenced by knowledge about the task domain, by the setting, by knowledge of search systems, and by the information seeker's confidence in his or her personal information infrastructure. Recognition and acceptance are typically ignored by system designers, as they are viewed as user specific and thus uncontrollable. However, systems that invite interaction and support satisfying engagement lead users to accept information problems more readily. Attention to this subprocess also reinforces the users' control and volition in any intellectual activity. Problem acceptance initiates problem definition.

### Define and understand the problem

Problem definition is a critical step in the information-seeking process.[13] This subprocess remains active as long as the information seeking progresses. Note that in Figure 3.3 most subprocesses have high-probability transitions back to the problem's definition. Understanding is dependent on knowledge of the task domain and may also be influenced by the setting. The cognitive processes that identify key concepts and relationships lead to a definition of the problem that is articulated as an information-seeking task. For intermediated information seeking, the intermediary conducts a reference interview (Auster & Lawton, 1984; White, 1985). For end-user searching, this step is often assumed or abbreviated – a major cause of end users' frustration and failure.

To understand and define a problem, it must be limited, labeled, and a form or frame for the answer determined. The problem may be limited by identifying related knowledge or similar problems or by listing what specific knowledge is not related. Concepts, words, phrases, events, or people related to the problem can be listed and grouped into categories that serve as the basis for assigning labels and problem statements (giving names to noumenal clouds). This process represents what Taylor called the *conscious need*. The information seeker may hypothesize what the answer will be but at least creates an expectation of what the answer will "look like," for example, will be a date, a fact, a route, an idea, an interpretation, or an expression. An expectation of the physical form of the answer (e.g., texts with tables, an image with an annotation, ideas shaped from interactions with various people and documents) may emerge that, in turn, strongly influences the selection of a search system. These expectations about outcomes ultimately guide (and bias) action. The limiting, labeling, and framing of solution properties lead to the artic-ulation of an information-seeking task, what Taylor referred to as the *formalized need*. While defining the problem, the information seeker represents the problem internally as a task with properties that allow progress to be judged and then determines a general strategy to use for subsequent steps.

### Choose a search system

Choosing a search system is dependent on the information seeker's previous expe-rience with the task domain, the scope of his or her personal information infrastruc-ture, and the expectations about the answer that may have been formed while defining the problem and the task. Domain knowledge is a powerful variable in selecting a search system and focusing the search. Experts in a domain have experience with the primary search systems specific to the domain. Economists in our studies were able to make spontaneous judgments about whether information required for assigned information problems was likely to be found in one or another journal. Likewise, attorneys were readily able to determine whether infor-mation in their assigned searches would be found in case law, statutes, or treatises. In both these cases, some professional intermediaries who regularly conducted searches in these domains were also able to predict where relevant information could be found (Marchionini, et al., 1993).

The information seeker's personal information infrastructure is dependent on past experience with information problems in general, their general cognitive abilities, and experience with particular systems. It is well known that information seekers prefer colleagues or human sources to formal sources and then proximate sources of information and easy-to-use systems. These preferences are powerful factors in information seeking and reflect natural human efforts to minimize costs, especially to seek the path of least cognitive resistance (Marchionini, 1987). Naive information seekers have default search systems that they turn to for many tasks.

For example, Marchionini (1989c) found that high school students used books and encyclopedias as default sources for a variety of information problems. When experienced information seekers are faced with tasks in foreign domains, they often seek general background information in reference systems that can help refine the problem and point them to primary search systems.

Given the constraints of domain knowledge, general cognitive conditions, and previous search experience, information seekers try to map the search task onto one or more search systems. The mapping process takes into consideration the type of task (e.g., complexity, specificity of answer) and the characteristics of available or familiar search systems. In practice, information seekers consult several search systems as they move toward solutions to their problems. For example, in libraries, information seekers may ask a reference librarian where to begin searching, or they may consult an index or a card catalog and eventually one or more journal or book primary sources. As electronic search systems and network access proliferate, more and more potential sources will become available to information seekers. It is becoming increasingly important to use secondary or *n*-ary systems to limit the time and effort spent locating and using primary systems. With a few exceptions,[14] today's electronic systems are specific to one or two particular levels of search (e.g., bibliographic records) rather than providing a common interface to many levels of systems. For example, there are expert systems that emulate a reference service, thousands of online bibliographic databases, and hundreds of online or CD-ROM full-text databases. Filtering, ordering, and selecting the collection of sources become increasingly important to mapping tasks onto search systems.

### *Formulate a query*

Query formulation involves matching understanding of the task with the system selected. In many cases, the first query formulation identifies an entry point to the search system and is followed by browsing and/or query reformulations. Query formulation requires two kinds of mappings: a semantic mapping of the information seeker's vocabulary used to articulate the task onto the system's vocabulary used to gain access to the content, and an action mapping of the strategies and tactics that the information seeker deems best to forward the task to the rules and features that the system interface allows.

Semantic mapping is similar to moving from Taylor's formalized need to the compromised need (1962) and is highly influenced by earlier mappings from the sensation (visceral need) that forces attention to a problem (conscious need) and the mappings while defining the problem from fuzzy noumena and general concepts into specific terms and concept classes (formalized need). In general, this mapping takes as its domain the entire set of identifiers (possible expressions) available to an individual information seeker and the complete set of identifiers (recognizable expressions) available to a system as its range. The mapping function most commonly takes words (rather than phrases or concepts) associated with the task onto the set of words that serve as entry points (indexed words or controlled vocabulary) to the system content. For static search systems such as books, the information seeker has total control (and responsibility) for the mapping and tries to match words or phrases from the task statement itself (or terms related to them), with words or phrases in the title, index, table of contents, headings, list of keywords, and text. For dynamic search systems such as people, the intelligence of both parties can be applied to enrich the mapping function, as the controlled vocabulary of a human is both large (in fact, is the same as the entire content vocabulary) and more associationally connected. Thus, experts in a domain not only know more terms that directly relate to the information seeker's query formulation, but they also can add additional terms and interact with the information seeker to clarify and verify the query. In the case of professional intermediaries, the process of formulating a query is part of the reference interview and has been shown to be an important determinant of intermediary performance.

In the case of electronic search systems, the query formulation is partially dynamic and system designers have used a wide range of techniques to assist the information seeker. Such techniques include expert system intermediaries (Croft & Thompson, 1987; Marcus, 1983), online suggestions (Meadow, 1988), query-by-example (Zloof, 1977), dynamic queries (Shneiderman, 1992), and hypertext (Croft & Turtle, 1989; Frisse, 1988; Marchionini & Shneiderman, 1988). An electronic system may have a strictly controlled vocabulary (e.g., field names in a database) or a full-text vocabulary (e.g., inverted file), each clearly affecting the cardinality of the set of items retrieved as a result of applying a mapping. The problem of representing concepts in document sets is fundamental to information science and is considered from several perspectives in subsequent chapters.

Action mappings take possible sets of actions to the inputs that a search system can recognize. If semantic mappings are thought of as "what" or declarative in nature, then action mappings are "how" or procedural in nature. Just as a search system limits the vocabulary that an information seeker may use in query formulation, search systems also limit how queries may be expressed. For example, humans recognize spoken or written expressions, but books do not, and electronic systems so far can recognize only a few expressions. Electronic systems may support Boolean expressions and provide a special syntax for how they may be formed. Electronic systems may allow users to enter any terms they wish, offer a menu that specifies all possible terms, or provide traversable links among various partitions of the database. At even more detailed levels, the system demands that users specify terms or previous sets using explicit characters, cases, or punctuation.

Marchionini (1992) argued that electronic systems made many of their greatest contributions to information seeking at the query formulation phase. These advances have been significant in the area of action mappings thus far, in that electronic systems provide a much broader range of ways to articulate queries, even though these ways are spread across different systems rather than being generally available in a single system at the discretion of the information seeker. Progress in augmenting information seekers' mapping of task vocabulary to system vocabulary has been more difficult, but human–computer dialogues and machine inferencing have yielded promising directions for aiding semantic mappings.

### *Execute search*

Execution of the physical actions to query an information source is driven by the information seeker's mental model of the search system. Execution is based on the semantic and action mappings developed while formulating the query. Looking something up requires actions like articulating a question verbally, picking up a volume, or pressing a key. For a card catalog, execution may entail selecting proper drawers and using alphabetical ordering rules; for an online database, execution may entail typing the query and sending it with a special keypress (e.g., return); for a hypertext, execution may entail browsing the database by following the links provided by the author. Communication and computing technology has greatly affected how searches are executed (and consequently if or when they are executed), by altering the physical actions necessary. Phone calls, telefacsimiles, and electronic mail make the execution of a search with a human search system much more feasible, and electronic networks allow direct queries of remote collections from a home or office. Although interfaces for these devices are often complicated and frustrating, the effects of performing information-seeking tasks in physically proximate space cannot be overestimated. Search execution is one of the most obvious changes wrought by electronic environments, as information seekers perform many fewer physical actions at workstations than they do in libraries or offices.

### *Examine results*

Executing a query results in a response from the search system. This response is an intermediate outcome and must be examined by the information seeker to assess progress toward completing the information-seeking task. This examination is dependent on the quantity, type, and format of the response and involves judgments about the relevance of information contained in the response. Responses are provided by information systems in units specific to the type of database, for example, numeric values, bibliographic records, fixed-length fields, entire documents, specific images, or verbal expositions on a topic. A response to a query may contain zero, one, a few, or many of these units, often referred to as *hits*.

The information problem and the user's personal information infrastructure determine the information seeker's expectations about the number of units required to complete a task, although these expectations often change as the information seeking progresses. For example, information seekers typically expect zero or one hit when searching a card catalog for a specific title, and zero, one, or many for a query about a topic (subject search). Users of print encyclopedias typically expect to find zero, one, or a few articles on a topic and may be quite surprised to find hundreds of hits when using a full-text electronic encyclopedia for the same topic. A significant difference in printed and full-text electronic encyclopedias is that electronic systems often retrieve many articles, thus requiring another major decision in the examination of results (Marchionini, 1989c).

When multiple hits are returned, they are usually presented as a set made up of document surrogates such as titles, bibliographic records, or descriptive identifiers. The way in which these sets are organized and presented affects how information seekers examine individual units, make relevance judgments, and decide what steps to take next. In a library, a set of catalog cards on a broad topic are ordered alphabetically according to the main entry for that document.[15] In a set of bibliographic records retrieved from an online search system, the items are often ordered in chronological order, beginning with the most recent. In more advanced electronic retrieval systems, items may be ranked according to query-term frequencies. In hypertext systems, explicit links to other units and implicit links such as next page, previous unit, or index lookups are provided by the database designer. The ordering of resultant sets becomes more important as the size of the set increases, and the ability to manipulate orderings of sets of items is recommended for all electronic search systems. The propensity of electronic systems to report large sets of documents significantly affects the examination of results subprocess, complicating the decision making associated with selecting relevant items of information.

The information seeker must judge the relevance of individual retrieved units with respect to the information-seeking task at hand. Relevance is a central theme of information science and has been considered from both theoretical and practical perspectives. Cooper (1971) defined logical relevance as a formal basis for evaluation of retrieval systems, and Wilson (1973) described situational relevance as dependent on the particular information problem at hand. Situational relevance is more specific to the relevance judgments that information seekers make as they examine intermediate results of search (see Saracevic, 1976, for a review of the literature related to relevance in information science and the April 1994 issue of the *Journal of the American Society for Information Science* for a series of articles). From a practical perspective, relevance serves as the main criterion for computing performance measures such as recall and precision.

From an information seeker's perspective, relevance may be considered as the decision about what action to take next in the information-seeking process. Alternatives include terminate search because the goal has been achieved; pursue the document more fully, that is, examine it again or more exhaustively; pursue the document later, that is, note its existence and location and continue examining other results; pursue implications of the document to the continuation of search (e.g., identify terms to use in subsequent queries); and continue examining other results in this iteration, formulate a new query, or redefine the problem; reject the document completely and continue examining results; or reject the document and stop seeking information without completing the task. Note that the examine-results subprocess in Figure 3.3 is a major decision point, with many arcs to other subprocesses.

The examination of specific items for relevance is obviously affected by the type (primary, secondary, numeric, graphic, textual) and the quantity (number of units or documents) of information in the retrieved set. For small sets of results, items can be scanned quickly, browsed systematically, or inspected comprehensively. For large sets of results, the set may be reduced by reformulating the query, or semantically related surrogates (e.g., titles, abstracts, thumbnail images) can be scanned to identify those that suggest a more comprehensive relevance assessment. Marchionini and his colleagues argued that information seekers are willing to scan substantial sets of textual or graphic documents if they are given appropriate display and control mechanisms (Liebscher & Marchionini, 1988; Marchionini, 1989c).

As with query formulation, electronic systems have made substantial progress in supporting the examination of results. Ranked output and alternative orderings of output offer substantial advantages to experienced information seekers because they assist in managing large result sets. Examination is also aided by display techniques such as highlighting query words in retrieved documents, presenting different levels of organizational details (e.g., table of contents and full text – Egan et al., 1989), fisheye views that cluster potentially relevant items in a spatially ordered manner (Furnas, 1986), and high-resolution graphic views of information in hierarchical displays (e.g., Card, Robertson, & Mackinlay, 1991).

### Extract information

There is an inextricable relationship between judging information to be relevant and extracting it for all or part of the problem's solution. Assessments about relevance cause information extraction actions to be taken, although information can be relevant to the problem but not fully meet the conditions of the task's goal. If a retrieved document is judged relevant, the information seeker may choose to continue assessing its relevance by extracting and saving information or to defer extraction and continue examining results. In the latter case, the document will eventually be reexamined, and a revised relevance assessment made based on what other documents were added to the relevant list and what events the information seeker experienced since the previous relevance judgment.

To extract information, an information seeker applies skills such as reading, scanning, listening, classifying, copying, and storing information. In the case of secondary databases, extraction may entail copying or printing bibliographic citations to facilitate retrieval of actual documents. In the case of verbal questions to human experts, listening skills, clarification requests or restatements of the information in one's own words aid in extracting the information relevant to the task. In full-text systems, basic reading skills, scanning skills, use of structural features such as headings and outlines, and jumping from section to section aid in extracting relevant information.[16]

As information is extracted, it is manipulated and integrated into the information seeker's knowledge of the domain. As more information is extracted and stored, new items may not be as relevant as they would have been before other items were manipulated and integrated. Information extraction often includes some physical action such as copying onto paper or another medium and saving those copies in larger structures according to well-defined organizational rules. For electronic systems, some of the techniques for ordering and display mentioned in the previous section on examination help users by allowing them to cut and paste items easily, including the contextual components that may appear in other windows on the screen. Thus, saving a section outline from a table of contents, the paragraphs around the most relevant information, and a path or query statement that retrieved the document all can be extracted and aggregated easily. Electronic tools for cutting and pasting already offer substantial advantages for extracting information from texts, static and moving images, and sound.

### Reflect/iterate/stop

An information search is seldom completed with only a single query and retrieved set. More often, the initial retrieved set serves as feedback for further query formulations and executions. Deciding when and how to iterate requires an assessment of the information-seeking process itself, how it relates to accepting the problem and the expected effort, and how well the extracted information maps onto the task. Monitoring the progress of information seeking is crucial to browsing strategies that are highly interactive and opportunistic. Determination of a stopping function may depend on external functions like setting or search system or on internal functions like motivation, task-domain knowledge, and information-seeking ability. Stopping decisions in full-text electronic systems are more complex because retrieval is both physically easier and yields more robust outcomes.

### Summary of subprocesses

The information-seeking process is dynamic and action oriented. The concurrent activation of some subprocesses is not captured in Figure 3.3. But Figure 3.4 illustrates some of this parallelism and also depicts three classes of subprocesses: understanding, planning and execution, and evaluation and use. Note that defining

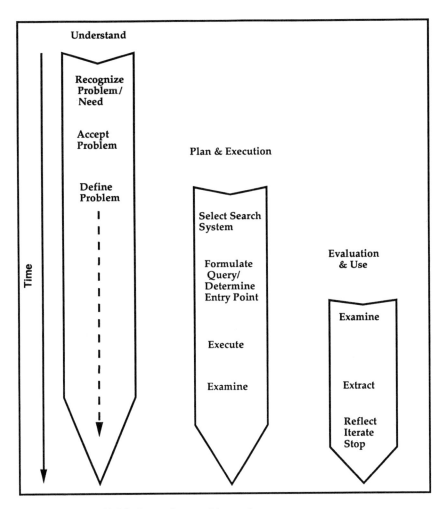

Figure 3.4. Parallel information-seeking subprocesses.

the problem and examining the results act as bridges across these three classes of action. The understanding subprocesses are mainly mental activities, and the planning, executing, and evaluation subprocesses are both mental and behavioral.

Because these subprocesses are controlled by the information seeker, they most often take heuristic or opportunistic paths according to skills and experience. These paths depend on ongoing judgments about the costs and benefits of the progress being made, redefinements of the task goals, and relevance judgments about the retrieved information. Electronic search systems have had a substantial impact on several of the subprocesses, especially the query formulation and examination of result subprocesses. Highly interactive search systems and full-text databases have begun to blur the boundaries separating the subprocesses and tend to decrease the linearity of their progression.

The information-seeking framework is composed of factors that affect information-seeking behavior and this dynamic, information seeker–centered process. In the chapters ahead we will examine more specifically how electronic environments affect information seeking and the information seeker. In the next chapter we revisit the information seeker and consider the building blocks for personal information infrastructures.

# 4

# Foundations for personal information infrastructures: Information-seeking knowledge, skills, and attitudes

*Knowledge is recollection.*

Plato

*The best way to stay young is to have a bad memory.*

Miles Davis

Information seeking, like learning and problem solving, demands general cognitive facility and special knowledge and skills and is influenced by attitudes and preferences. General cognitive facility – what is commonly called intelligence – includes our abilities to remember, make inferences, and monitor our intellectual activity. Special knowledge and skills of three types also interact to determine information-seeking performance: knowledge and skills related to the problem domain, knowledge and skills specific to the search system and setting, and knowledge and skills related to information seeking itself. Attitudes such as motivation, confidence, tenacity, tolerance for ambiguity and uncertainty, curiosity, and preferences for social interaction and media influence when and how we apply information-seeking knowledge and skills. Taken together, these types of knowledge, skills, and attitudes compose our personal information infrastructures. Information problems are always embedded in a context that determines which facets of our personal information infrastructure are brought to bear in a specific situation. Personal information infrastructures develop as we gain knowledge of the information-seeking factors and skills in managing the information-seeking process. Information professionals apply their general cognitive abilities to building knowledge and skills concerning sources and systems that contain information, techniques for mapping users' needs to tasks, and strategies for seeking and representing information. Knowing what knowledge and skills are useful in manual environments and today's electronic environments will lead to better designs for future information systems and to better training for professionals and end users alike.

This chapter considers these various types of expertise, with particular emphasis on knowledge and skills related to information seeking. It examines how people seek information using existing information systems and the various knowledge, skills, and attitudes that constitute information-seeking expertise. We begin with the general cognitive skills that are important to information seeking and then consider domain, system, and information-seeking knowledge as types of expertise. The final section outlines four levels of cognitive and behavioral activity specific to information seeking. These discussions set the stage for the following two chapters, which examine analytical and browsing strategies.

## General cognitive facility

Information seeking can be characterized as a set of behaviors controlled by interacting levels of conscious (logical) and unconscious (intuitive) mental activity. At the most general (pattern) level, humans demonstrate intelligence, preferences, and styles. Defining and understanding these qualities are central goals of cognitive psychology, and many theories and models of cognitive facility have been proposed, with most of the emphasis on the notion of intelligence (see Sternberg, 1982, for a taxonomy of theories of intelligence and a collection of views). A classical view of intelligence proposed by Guilford (1967) identifies three dimensions of intelligence, each with several factors that interact to produce 150 discrete components of intelligence. The operation dimension has five factors: cognition, memory, divergent production, convergent production, and evaluation. The content dimension has five factors: visual, auditory, symbolic, semantic, and behavioral. The product dimension has six factors: units, classes, relations, systems, transformation, and implications. Sternberg (1985) proposed a triarchic theory of intelligence made up of three subtheories. In addition to a components subtheory similar to the components view of Guilford and others, he added a sociocultural setting theory that considers how we adapt to and change the environmental context. The third subtheory considers experience, knowledge, and our ability to deal with novelty. Regardless of the theory adopted, any human activity is influenced by general cognitive abilities, especially complex processes such as information seeking.

At the strategic level, people use many perceptual and cognitive processes to plan, solve problems, make decisions, monitor progress, and reflect on past activity. These processes may be rooted either in belief or logic, but in practice, most intellectual activities – including information seeking – depend on interactions among various logical and intuitive actions. A fundamental form of logical reasoning is making inferences – "the process of deriving new information from old information" (Davis, 1990, p. 3). Clearly, information seeking can support inferencing by delivering the old information. However, the process of information seeking requires many types of inferences to be made as the information seeking progresses. For example, we make inferences to assign meaning during problem definition, to determine which system best matches the problem, to choose query terms and map queries to database structure, to judge relevance, to monitor progress, and to decide when to terminate. Inferences can be deductive, inductive, or adductive.

Deduction yields conclusions that are precise and certain, because each step in the process is validated by logical combinations of known facts or generalizations.

For example, all men are mortal; Socrates is a man; therefore, by the *modus ponens* rule of inference, Socrates is mortal. Thus, if the premises are true and one accepts the axioms of the logical system used, then truthful conclusions must follow. Unfortunately, most plans, decisions, and problems do not yield to these assumptions, and pure deduction cannot be applied. Consider, for example, whether the term *profit* captures all aspects of the concept *economic gain* or whether a given document is completely relevant to a topic. Deduction is applied at the tactical level but is rarely applicable at strategic or pattern levels. For example, deduction allows us to conclude that if we have retrieved two sets of documents for two specific terms, then joining these two sets with an AND operator will yield a set with cardinality (number of elements) less than or equal to the smallest cardinality of the two sets. Relational database management systems apply deduction and the relational algebra to ensure that records matching precise specifications are retrieved. This is advantageous to support the most basic types of information seeking and retrieval but cannot be used for the more general types of information seeking of interest in this book.

Induction yields general conclusions based on specific examples or cases. Inductive reasoning is closely related to empirical methods that draw conclusions based on testing controlled cases. For example, if there are several telecommunications carriers from which to choose when going online and carrier A is selected five times and found to be busy each time, induction leads to the conclusion that carrier A is not a good service to use as a default. Of course, induction may lead to incorrect conclusions if antecedent information is not accurate or representative, and systematic validity checks should be conducted to maintain confidence. Induction leads to many of the defaults that information seekers use at all levels of activity.

Adduction is the most common kind of inferencing in all but the most technical situations.[1] Adduction is plausible reasoning, for example, providing examples, arguments, or appeals to authority in order to increase the probability of some truth. All but the most rote forms of information seeking require adduction. Plausible reasoning has many forms and is influenced by different intuitive beliefs. Various heuristics or forms of plausible reasoning have been identified, and information seekers are well advised to reflect on which heuristic is used at various phases of information seeking.

Simon (1979) defined "satisficing" as a psychological form of the law of diminishing returns – we do not seek optimal solutions to certain problems because the costs are too high, so we settle for solutions that are satisfactory given the cost. This principle is clearly demonstrated in libraries, whose users show high levels of satisfaction because they are able to find at least some relevant items with minimal investments of time and effort. This result is even more common in electronic environments because time and effort can be minimal and the scope of sources can be broader. Satisficing is essential to most information seeking because all pertinent information for open-ended problems can seldom be assembled and assimilated optimally.

In contrast with the conscious application of satisficing, people often engage in "wishful thinking" when using complex reasoning. People sometimes neglect relevant information if it leads to conclusions that counter their beliefs, and they sometimes give high weights to information that reinforces stereotypes and low weights (or totally forget) information that disproves them. People selectively recall information to explain events or make decisions and reinforce beliefs with redundant information rather than seek additional new information. People are biased toward "first impressions," giving too much weight to initial hypotheses and too little weight to new evidence (see Kahneman, Slovic, & Tversky, 1982, for a collection of papers related to biases in decision making). These biases are not themselves inferences, but they do influence plausible reasoning.

In addition to biases, people take actions to protect themselves from discomfort and danger. In fact, there is often wisdom in selective ignorance. For intellectual activity, this tendency leads them to protect themselves from information overload and from topics that are beyond their knowledge or grasp. In the first case, people purposely ignore bodies of information or systems to avoid taxing or diverting their memory, time, or financial resources. In what may be thought of as the "installed base syndrome," experienced users of computer systems resist upgrading to the latest iteration of an operating system because they understand the many ramifications of such changes. They recognize the integrated nature of their systems and that special peripherals, old but reliable software, well-established databases and archives, and well-learned procedures may be affected as a seemingly straightforward change in one part of the system propagates throughout the system. Likewise, institutions resist upgrades and changes in application packages because of the heavy investments in employee training in existing systems. In the second case, people avoid overly technical information if they are not experts in the area, or they simplify information so that they can manipulate it more readily. They also may avoid formal information systems and instead turn to informal systems such as colleagues or ready-reference handbooks or services.

Davis (1990) provides a set of types of plausible reasoning and develops probabilistic models to represent plausible reasoning in a computer. Issues that affect plausible reasoning include degree of belief, strength of argument, the application of rules of general but not universal validity, the avoidance of all qualifications of a problem, inference from the absence of information, a limitation on the extent of inference, inference using vague concepts, the discovery of an expected utility, the inference of an explanation, scheme-based inference, analogy, and the inference of a general rule from examples. Degree of belief and strength of argument are dependent on experience and knowledge of the world. For information seeking, inferring the best selections of vocabulary at the proper level of granularity may use such knowledge. The application of general but not universal rules is the basis for default values and is a kind of inference that may be made automatically. For example, a specific database has been useful in finding information related to legal aspects of business practice in the past and is the first source used for similar problems in the future. The avoidance of all qualifications of the problem is a way of broadening the problem so that it can be approached. This heuristic is used to isolate the essential features of a problem when defining a problem.

Inference from the absence of information is important to information seeking. Davis illustrates three ways of assuming that a statement is false based on not knowing it to be true. First, he uses world knowledge about the probability of truth, for example, to assume that a particular dermatological disease is not fatal because it is believed that most dermatology diseases are not fatal; that is, classes inherit non-properties from superclasses as well as properties. Second, (autoepistemic inference) he assumes that a statement is false based on the fact that one does not know it to be true, for example, to assume that a communication package does not support macros because one has expert knowledge of the package and has not encountered such a facility. Third, he assumes that a statement is false because it is not present in an authoritative report; for example, because malaria is not discussed in a document describing travel procedures for a developing country, one should assume that malaria is not a health risk to worry about. In fact, some searches are conducted to determine explicitly that something has not been done (e.g., in developing a significance argument for original research or patent searching for a new chemical structure). Stielow and Tibbo (1988) termed this the *negative search*. At a tactical level, queries for specific terms may be executed to ensure that all facets of a concept have been considered.

Limiting the extent of inference refers to recognizing when an inductive inference has gone too far, and using vague concepts allows us to assign items to multiple classes in gradations – the basis for fuzzy reasoning. Finding expected utility refers to our abilities to do "back-of-the envelope" cost–benefit analyses, for example, to determine whether to consult a second source after extracting information from one source. Inferring explanations points to the human characteristic of justifying or rationalizing events, for example, assuming that someone picked up the phone extension when one is disconnected from a system while using a modem. Scheme-based inference allows us to infer more general or more detailed information based on world knowledge and relationships. For example, if a menu has an edit choice, we infer a variety of delete, insert, cut, and paste operations according to the specific operating system we are using. Analogy is a powerful heuristic that allows us to transfer our knowledge or skills to other settings and may be helpful in using our experiences with past problems or systems to solve immediate problems at hand. Analogy is related to the final heuristic addressed here, inferring a general rule from examples. This is a loose application of induction, leading us to jump to conclusions; for example, erroneously assuming that there are no documents related to Rocky Mountain spotted fever in a bibliographic medical database because the explicit term *fever* does not appear as a text word in any of the citations.

These examples demonstrate how adduction and other forms of inference influence information seeking. In most cases, specific inferences and heuristics are used as information-seeking tactics either spontaneously or by design as part of a larger information-seeking strategy. There is promise in exploring ways that systems can help users recognize biases and adductions and to select and apply them judiciously while seeking information.

## Domain expertise

Expertise in a domain requires knowledge and skills that allow the expert to solve problems in the area quickly and effectively. Studies of expertise typically focus on the distinctions between novice and expert within a content area or on descriptions of what constitutes expert behavior (see Chi, Glaser, & Farr, 1988, for a collection of papers on expertise). Several important characteristics of expertise have been identified. Experts perceive large meaningful patterns in their own domains (Chase & Simon, 1973) that reflect the organization of a knowledge base rather than superior perceptual skills (Glaser, 1987). Experts see and represent problems according to fundamental principles that structure the domain knowledge, whereas novices tend to represent problems at a more superficial level. When they begin to solve a problem, experts typically spend a great deal of time qualitatively trying to understand a problem, thereby building a representation of the problem from which inferences can be drawn (Glaser & Chi, 1988). This mental representation allows the expert to "see things differently" and to guide behavior in purposeful ways. For example, in a study of experts' and novices' diagnoses of x-ray pictures, Lesgold and colleagues (1984) found that the experts had a truly different perception of what they saw, which enabled them to discard unimportant information and quickly make a correct diagnosis. Studies of skill transfer among experts show little evidence that one domain can be transferred to another domain. In fact, experts in one domain solve problems in much the same way as novices do when confronted with problems outside their own subject domain.

In studies of computer scientists, economists, and attorneys searching full-text databases specific to their expertise, experts demonstrated how their facility with the information-seeking factors guided their searches (Marchionini et al., 1993). They were able to identify and critique types of information typically found in journals or databases (e.g., technical reports vs. reviews vs. news reports) and match information problems to those sources. They were able to identify key facets of the information problem and use technical terminology in formulating queries, and they could rapidly make relevance judgments about the results, in which they expressed high levels of confidence.

Through experience, workers in a field develop information-seeking expertise for information problems in that field; they are familiar with the various sources and systems devoted to the field; they have extensive knowledge of the domain and its major concepts, problems, organizational schemes, and vocabulary; they are comfortable in the settings in which work in the field takes place (e.g., laboratories, classrooms); they are skillful in solving typical classes of information problems; and they are able to differentiate between relevant and irrelevant information. Domain experts form hypotheses about answers and focus their information-seeking activity on testing those hypotheses. Thus, experts in a domain have greater facility and experience related to the information-seeking factors specific to the domain and are able to execute the subprocesses of information seeking with speed, confidence, and accuracy.

## System expertise

To be successful, information seekers must have a basic facility with the physical interface to a search system. For example, the abilities to read, use an index, and physically turn pages, as well as knowledge of alphabetical and numeric orderings are essential to finding information in printed sources. Likewise, some fundamental abilities are required to use electronic systems. These include the abilities to begin and end, to read from a screen, to scroll and page, to use keyboards or a mouse, to make selections from various types of menus, to recognize the difference between prompts and commands, to get help, and to manage windows (e.g., move, resize, hide/show). The minimal expertise needed to use electronic search systems can be acquired quite easily with a few minutes of demonstration, depending on the system interface. Remote online systems typically require more skill to use because they require knowledge about establishing network connections. These additional requirements can be minimized by interfaces that automate the connection process once the local parameters have been set. For example, the Grateful Med system automatically connects end users to various medical literature databases once the phone numbers and account codes have been set up.

Expertise with a system goes beyond these minimums and includes the ability to customize the system and use most of the system's features. More significantly, online systems require users to understand how the database is organized, what level of coverage is provided, and how documents are structured. Organizational considerations include how the database is indexed (e.g., alphabetical, conceptual), and what indexing policies apply (e.g., the most specific concepts assigned), and how morphological variations, abbreviations, and special codes are handled. Coverage includes sources and selection criteria, and document structure includes how records are fielded or how objects are defined.

System expertise is less important to information-seeking success than is domain or information-seeking expertise. Results with elementary school and high school students searching full-text electronic encyclopedias demonstrate that only very brief introductions are necessary for users to be able to apply minimal search system features to find information. Although these information seekers did not apply all the power of the system and used naive information-seeking strategies, they were able to use these powerful search systems to find information relevant to their needs (Marchionini, 1989b, 1989c). In studies of students using the Perseus hypermedia corpus, previous computer experience and experience with the Perseus system were less influential in determining performance than interface effects were (Evans, 1993; Marchionini & Crane, 1994; Marchionini, Neuman, & Morrell, 1994). On open-ended responses, only those students with no previous computer experience at all reported significant problems in completing assignments and dissatisfaction with their experience. These results suggest that the system interface was more important to user confidence and satisfaction than was previous computer experience or the actual use of Perseus itself. These results parallel those of Kahn and Robertson (1992), who found that previous computer experience and training had little effect on job satisfaction and motivation for workers in travel agencies. In fact, the actual job tasks were by far the best predictors of satisfaction and motivation.

Although basic familiarity with electronic systems appears to be a requisite for completing various information-seeking tasks, well-developed mental models for specific systems are far less important to information-seeking outcomes than are more salient factors such as task, domain knowledge, and setting. See Nardi (1993) for a summary of studies that support system design rooted in task and domain knowledge.

## Information-seeking expertise

All humans develop some degree of expertise in general cognitive abilities such as problem solving, learning, planning, decision making, and information seeking. In the case of information seeking, our personal information infrastructures develop as we gain expertise in various domains and operate in an information-intensive world. Note that expertise in a general cognitive ability applies across all domains of knowledge; we make specific adjustments and select particular parameters for instantiation when applying our mental models for information seeking to specific problems and domains. This contrasts with domain knowledge that does not transfer to other domains. Expertise in information seeking can be characterized by a person's general knowledge of information-seeking factors and his or her skills and attitudes for executing the information-seeking process.

Knowledge of how various domains are organized helps an information seeker to determine how the domain of the problem at hand may be organized. The value of specific domain knowledge clearly aids information seeking (the basis for professional intermediaries specializing in particular domains), but general experiences with how different domains are organized provide important clues to the organization of an unfamiliar domain when seeking information in that domain.

As with all intellectual activity, individual cognitive and perceptual characteristics influence information-seeking performance. People who have more experience with making inferences and recognizing the appropriateness and limitations of plausible reasoning should be more effective information seekers. Greene, Gomez, and Devlin (1986) found reasoning ability to be a determinant of information-seeking success and Vincente, Hayes, and Williges (1987) reported that spatial visualization was a determinant of successful database searching. It seems reasonable that capabilities such as superior memory and visual scanning abilities interact to support broader and more purposive examination of text. One goal of human–computer interaction research is to apply computing power to amplify and augment these human abilities.

In addition to knowledge and skills with a variety of search systems, expert information seekers recognize that every information-seeking activity is guided by the particular information problem at hand.[2] Recall that the information problem is manifested as an information-seeking task that drives the information-seeking process and may change as search progresses. Both the task as stated by the information seeker and the "answer" or solution to the problem may be defined in detail or anomalously. Consider the following cases that vary according to how well-defined the tasks and solutions are: To retrieve or verify a fact, an information seeker has an explicit and well-defined image of both the task and the solution – this is a production task that does not involve the information seeker in learning. Rather, it is a task typical of database management applications, in which the object is to recover a specific object previously stored in a systematic fashion. The task requires minimal decision making and reflection during the search. In the case of finding information to write an assigned essay, a student may have a well-defined task statement but few expectations about what the literature will hold. This is a learning task and requires significant decision making and reflection during the search process. In another case, an information seeker may come across an interesting concept incidentally and look for a task to which it applies. This is a solution in search of a problem, a different type of learning that requires less decision making and reflection and more open-ended, synthetic hypothesis generation. Finally, an information seeker may initiate a search without a specific task or preconceptions about what solutions may emerge, for example, a scholar examining literature to monitor progress in a research area. In this case, the information seeker must use both synthetic and analytic cognitive strategies to determine the information need (topic) and find information relevant to the topic that may change and emerge as the information seeking progresses. This last case – which we term *accretional information seeking,* in which both the task and the solution are ill defined – includes much of the information seeking we do to stay abreast of fields of interest or to develop new interests.

Naturally, the ways that problems are recognized and accepted and how people articulate them as information-seeking tasks depend on the individual person's characteristics and the specific context and setting. The point is that information seeking is highly variable, more like general problem solving than it is like word processing or statistical analysis, which are complex and challenging but also circumscribed. In spite of these variations, humans have developed both general-purpose information-seeking strategies and highly specialized strategies for specific classes of tasks or systems. We all learn general-purpose strategies during our basic education and learn specialized strategies through our advanced education or our professional work. Electronic information systems have begun to make some specialized strategies more generic and have led to new general and specialized information-seeking strategies.

Journalists, librarians, detectives, and other professionals devoted to information seeking build collections of approaches and actions for their work. Journalists learn interviewing techniques, nurture relationships with sources, and monitor their information seeking with the goal of organizing results for formal dissemination. Librarians also learn interviewing techniques, although to elicit questions rather than answers, learn about and use a large number of reference sources and indexing techniques, and monitor information seeking with the goal of organizing the results for presentation to an end user. The results depend primarily on the librarian's ability to elicit and clarify the information problem, experience with similar questions, and knowledge of various indexes and reference sources. Katz (1987) outlines a general manual strategy that focuses on the reference interview, using reference sources to identify potential primary sources, retrieving and assessing potentially relevant information, and including additional exchanges with the end user. These general steps are influenced by the librarian's personal creativity in matching the problem to sources and by time constraints.

Information specialists must be acquainted with a wide variety of information systems and have skill in using the most representative systems. Much of the training in reference that librarians receive, for example, is devoted to the many types of bibliographic sources and indexes that point to primary information sources (see, e.g., the chapter headings for reference textbooks such as Katz, 1987). Likewise, much effort in the field of library and information science is aimed at creating compilations and organizations of information sources. Thus, librarians and information specialists have assumed important roles in the development of electronic networks (Buckland & Lynch, 1987; Dillon, Jul, Burge & Hickey, 1993; McClure, Bishop, Doty, & Rosenbaum, 1991). Likewise, information specialists must be able to apply new hardware and software as electronic information systems become more widespread.

Expert information seekers possess substantial knowledge related to the factors of information seeking, have developed distinct patterns of searching, and use a variety of strategies, tactics, and moves. Because electronic environments have been used most extensively by professional intermediaries, studies of professionals using such systems have produced valuable insights into the information-seeking process.[3] Because the earliest and still the most common electronic systems are bibliographic, studies of intermediaries searching bibliographic online databases provide the bulk of our knowledge of expert information seeking in electronic environments. These results must be tempered by our understanding that they are based on the experience of professionals who are accustomed to primitive and specialized search systems. They define a collection of analytical information-seeking strategies and are considered in detail in chapter 5.

The development of electronic search systems led the information industry to provide new services and products and caused significant changes in how professionals seek information and how librarians and other information professionals work and are trained. Changes in how information is accessed and managed subsequently changed the users' expectations, thus affecting subsequent system development and use. These changes in information systems and user behavior reflect the larger ongoing evolution of actions and expectations that affect the behavior of users and the design of new systems in general. For example, patent searches for new pharmaceuticals take significant time and effort in manual systems but are necessary in order to make investment decisions. The ability to do patent searches online and by way of chemical structures leads to more searching because researchers come to expect routine searches to check and verify developments as work progresses.

The earliest systems provided secondary information (e.g., bibliographic data), and many of today's online systems still separate secondary information from primary information. Furthermore, these systems are usually complex and difficult to use, requiring significant training for the users. The value of specialized systems that support the practice of medicine, law, business, and engineering has changed the way professionals in those fields work and what expectations they have about information access, but the complexity of using such systems has led to increased dependence on information specialists as collaborators in the information-seeking process. Although this state of affairs has begun to change toward end user–oriented systems that contain primary information, the early experiences with developing online systems and training professional intermediaries to use them has led to numerous studies of information-seeking behavior and the identification of strategies for efficient and effective use. An important transition in electronic environments that is currently under way is the augmentation of analytical information-seeking strategies by end user–oriented browsing strategies.

## Patterns, strategies, tactics, and moves

Our thoughts and behaviors related to information seeking can be viewed from four levels of granularity, to show how early electronic systems have affected how experts seek information and what these effects should have on emerging end user–oriented systems. Electronic environments first affect the most finely grained activities such as the physical actions taken when executing searches (e.g., pressing keys or a pointing device instead of turning pages) but eventually will affect all levels of information-seeking activity.

At the coarsest level, people exhibit information-seeking patterns. *Patterns* are sometimes conscious but most often reflect internalized behaviors that can be discerned over time and across different information problems and searches. Patterns may be caused by chunked strategies or tactics that people internalize through repetition and experience. Psychologists have described automatic information processing for specific skills and tasks (e.g.,"skilled memory"; Ericsson & Staszewski, 1989), and automatic information processing has also been studied for complex skills such as reading (Schneider & Shriffrin, 1977; Shriffrin & Schneider, 1977). Automaticity for groups of related actions may aggregate as default actions for general classes of problems; for example, the high school students in our studies most often reported books and encyclopedias as their primary sources of information for a variety of search problems (Marchionini, 1989c). There is ample evidence in a variety of fields that people tend to use proximate sources (e.g., colleagues, personal collections) before libraries or other formal sources. Note that default patterns need not reflect accurate or efficient performance but do serve to reduce immediate cognitive load. As more secondary and primary sources become physically proximate owing to network access from homes or offices, new default patterns for source selection will emerge.

Patterns are also caused by personality traits, attitudes, or cognitive style. Some people are highly tolerant of ambiguity and uncertainty, whereas others demand specificity and completeness. Likewise, some enjoy social interactions and adopt information-seeking patterns that maximize interactions with colleagues or experts, whereas others prefer the challenge of personal discovery and immerse themselves in books or electronic systems (e.g., see Turkle, 1984, for characterizations of computer hackers' personalities). Bellardo (1985) identified professional intermediaries according to field dependence/field independence measures and compared their searching behavior but found no statistically significant differences in their searching. Fidel (1984) conducted case studies of professional intermediaries and described operationalist and conceptualist styles. Operationalists tend to manipulate the search system to search further and to aim for high precision. Conceptualists tend to manipulate concepts and vocabulary and aim for high recall. Patterns are highly individual, dependent on complex interactions, difficult to identify and classify, and resistant to change. The introduction of electronic systems has clearly affected the behavioral aspects of patterns and eventually will change the underlying cognitive and affective determinants as well. Patterns are mainly information-seeker specific but are also influenced by domains and search systems.

A *strategy* is the approach that an information seeker takes to a problem. *Strategies* are those sets of ordered tactics that are consciously selected, applied, and monitored to solve an information problem. Thus, strategies are concerned with

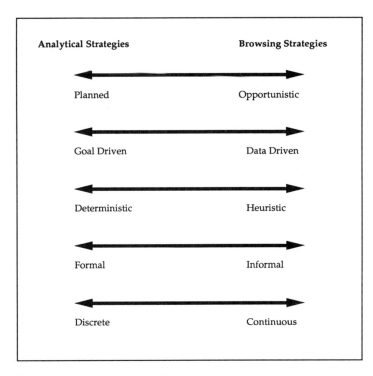

Figure 4.1 Information-seeking strategy continua.

multiple subprocesses of the information-seeking process and are applied to specific information-seeking tasks. Strategies can be general and flexible or highly specialized and well defined. Belkin, Marchetti, and Cool (1993), for example, define very broad strategies that are closely related to information seekers' goals. They propose a user-centered system that supports a variety of strategies. Because electronic systems operate according to well-defined algorithms and many systems charge fees on time-based schedules, expert information seekers have adopted information-seeking strategies that are systematic and specialized. These formal, batch-oriented approaches to information seeking are called *analytical strategies* and are distinguished from *browse strategies* that are informal and interactive. These two classes of strategy are the extremes of continua, as illustrated in Figure 4.1.

Analytical strategies tend to be more goal driven, whereas browsing strategies proceed according to cues that arise in the data as the search progresses. Analytical strategies require planning and thus are appropriate when information seeking is highly time sensitive. On the other hand, browsing strategies are opportunistic, beginning with an entry point and proceeding according to what occurs along the way. Well-defined goals and planning make analytical strategies more deterministic, whereas browsing strategies tend to be heuristic. Analytical strategies are more precise and methodical, and browsing strategies are informal and depend on interaction. Expert information seekers typically choose analytic strategies, and novices choose informal strategies, although I argue that this is mainly because of primitive search systems and setting factors such as time pressures. Electronic environments make the strategies used in manual environments more explicit and extensive and have enabled new strategies for information seeking. Strategies are mainly search specific.

*Tactics* are discrete intellectual choices or prompts manifested as behavioral actions during an information-seeking session. Tactics most often are applied in one or two information-seeking subprocesses. Tactics are thus more focused than strategies, for example, when restricting the search to a specific field or document type in order to narrow the search results. Tactics often apply inferences that advance information seeking; for example, asking a question that requires a binary answer that allows the search space to be limited – consider a physician who orders a specific test that does not solve the diagnosis problem but eliminates many possible diagnoses. Expert intermediaries have used numerous explications of tactics, most of which were influenced by Bates's (1979a, 1979b) taxonomy of search tactics and idea tactics. New tactics were made possible by electronic systems, and tactical skills with online systems most obviously distinguish between expert and novice users of those systems. Improving systems at the tactical level is one of the most practical and promising areas of interface design. Tactics are mainly task-system specific.

*Moves* are finely grained actions manifested as discrete behavioral actions such as walking to a shelf, picking up a book, pressing a key, clicking a mouse, or touching an item from a menu. Moves are manifestations of tactics, and although they are conceptually uninteresting individually, taken in context, they offer observable evidence for interface assessment and mapping the intellectual activity at higher levels of action. This level of study lends itself to electronic environments because discrete acts taken during information seeking can be automatically and unobtrusively logged by the computer, together with time and system status data. Computer-monitored data were first used for information retrieval by Penniman (1975); they were described by Rice and Borgman (1983); and they were used for comparing search strategies by Borgman (1986a), Marchionini, (1989b, 1989c, 1990), Lin, Liebscher, and Marchionini (1991), and Evans (1993). Clearly, the physical moves taken by information seekers are radically affected by electronic environments, because moves are mainly system specific.

These levels of information-seeking actions are not mutually exclusive, as a set of specific moves with a given system may be chunked (e.g., as a macro) as a tactic, and sets of tactics or strategies may be chunked as patterns by searchers regularly using the same system. These levels are partially analogous to the Goals–Operators–Methods–Selection Rules (GOMS) model of human–computer interaction (Card, Moran, & Newell, 1983). In this model of human–computer interaction, the users set the goals and work through a search space that consists of possible operators and methods for applying and combining operators. They try to reach the goal by judiciously selecting operators and methods in the space. GOMS operators are conceptually analogous to tactics and behaviorally analogous to moves; methods are analogous to tactics; and selection rules are guided by overall strategy.

The development of electronic environments that provide primary information via high-speed networks and that offer highly interactive interfaces requires new information-seeking patterns, strategies, tactics, and moves. A major goal of research and design in the human–computer interaction involved in information seeking is to determine what patterns, strategies, and tactics are useful and how they can be supported by new systems. This is an example of a chicken-or-egg problem of user-centered design: We cannot discover how users can best work with systems until the systems are built, yet we should build systems based on knowledge of users and how they work. This is a user-centered design paradox. The solution has been to design iteratively, conducting usability studies of prototypes and revising the system over time (e.g., Egan et al., 1989; Nielsen, 1989b).

One approach is to use the various online searching patterns, strategies, and tactics identified in studies of professional online searchers to create systems that optimize those activities. And in fact, this is what has occurred with today's systems. Early systems were cumbersome, but only experts used them and they devised workarounds to use the system efficiently. These workarounds became strategies and tactics over time and as end user–oriented systems were planned, they were designed to help novices use these strategies and tactics rather than supporting strategies and tactics appropriate to casual users. For example, the document set–oriented approach offered by Boolean-based systems lends itself to analytical strategies such as building sets that are then aggregated (building block strategy) or divided (successive fractions strategy). Preliminary experience with systems that provide ranked output suggests that new analytical strategies are needed when document sets are ordered (Marchionini, Barlow, & Hill, 1994).

Alternatively, systems can be designed to improve the naive patterns, strategies, and tactics exhibited by novice users, as those are presumably more natural and intuitive and computing power can be used to leverage and expand them. Clearly, the inertia of the marketplace and the user-centered design paradox will ensure that system design blends both approaches in iterative ways over time. We argue for starting with systems that amplify naive patterns, strategies, and tactics and then enhance performance with features that support expert patterns, strategies, and tactics. This approach addresses learnability first and usability second, a natural progression when both requirements have been met.

# 5

# Analytical search strategies

*Necessity is the mother of invention.*

*All things are difficult before they are easy.*

Thomas Fuller, Gnomologia, no. 560

The storage and retrieval of scientific texts were early applications of computers, and by the early 1960s, schemes for automatic indexing and abstracting had emerged (e.g., Doyle, 1965; Luhn, 1957, 1958; O'Connor, 1964; Tasman, 1957). As online systems emerged in the 1960s and 1970s, more databases and new search features were created to give professional intermediaries more power in searching for information. Searching in online systems was complex, and so intermediaries created systematic strategies for eliciting users' needs; selecting terms, synonyms, and morphological variants appropriate to the need and the system; using Boolean operators to formulate precise queries; restricting those queries to specific database fields; forming intermediate sets of results; manipulating those sets; and selecting appropriate display formats. The strategies and tactics that professional intermediaries use are meant to maximize retrieval effectiveness while minimizing online costs. These strategies are goal oriented and systematic and are termed *analytical strategies.* In this chapter, we describe several analytical strategies to illustrate how electronic environments have changed information seeking by allowing searchers to systematically manipulate large sets of potentially relevant documents. These strategies in turn influenced subsequent designs of online systems. Next we look at studies of novice users working with various online systems, showing how difficult analytical strategies are to learn and apply, and the need for electronic systems that support informal information-seeking strategies for end users.

## Online search strategies and tactics

Using an index to find target selections is the most basic example of an analytical search strategy. Such lookups depend on an ordered list of concepts that provide pointers to primary information. Textual indexes are often ordered alphabetically and depend on pointer anchors such as page numbers, file offset, and record number. The strategy is to start with index entry points and follow the pointers until the information is found or all entry points are exhausted. Electronic systems that are based on inverted files depend on this basic strategy. When Boolean-based query languages are added, users can create complex queries that allow multiple index entry points to be combined in one query. Likewise, users can create multiple sets of documents related to specific entry points and then combine those document sets to obtain the union, intersection, or difference of the sets. Various specific strategies have been developed for use in online systems.

The most widely used online searching strategy is the "building blocks" approach (Harter, 1986). When defining the problem, the information seeker identifies the main facets or concept groups associated with the problem. These facets then become the basis for specific query formulations that retrieve sets of document citations for each facet. After the individual sets are formed, they are systematically combined with Boolean operators (most commonly AND) to produce a document set relevant to the problem as a whole. Thus, the individual facet sets (blocks) are combined to build a solution set for the problem. For the building blocks strategy, various tactical options may be used to build queries for facets (e.g., using controlled vocabulary, ORing synonyms, limiting to specific fields) and to combine resulting sets (e.g., combine sets in pairwise fashion or all at once).[1] Which tactics to use depends on the information seeker's experience in using feedback from the system. For example, if a set for a facet is too small, the searcher may decide to combine it with another set or reformulate a broader query to increase its size. Inferences are then made about the combined document set in regard to precision and recall, and adjustments are made to individual facet sets or to how the facet sets were combined. Figure 5.1 presents an example search that uses the building blocks strategy. The original statement of the problem was used as the basis for a high recall search (the recall search formed 68 sets and was substantially longer than the high-precision search; see Marchionini & Barlow, 1994, for full searches), and then the precision search was conducted based on additional conversations with the end user. Note that a specific syntax is required and that some additional tactics such as sifting intermediate result sets are used in the overall building blocks strategy that identifies document sets for the two main concepts and then combines those sets with the AND operator.

The building blocks strategy is popular because it simplifies the process by breaking it down into manageable parts, for both the conceptual analysis of the problem and the technical specification and refinement of Boolean queries. Another strategy that finds common use is the "successive fractions" approach (Meadow & Cochrane, 1981), which begins with a large subset of the entire database and successively pares it down with facets specific to the problem. As with the building blocks approach, there are variations on the main strategy; for example, Harter distinguishes three successive facet strategies according to how the initial set is obtained and how the successive facets are ordered. Hawkins and Wagers (1982) note that the successive fractions strategy works well with problems that are vague or broad and cite its advantages for backtracking and monitoring the search's progress. As with the building blocks strategy, the successive fractions

**User Problem.** Adaptive gridding on structured grids. Other keys words I am interested in are *redistribution* and *truncation error*. Some key words that are not of interest are *unstructured grids* and *refinement*. (Based on an earlier search, with *computational fluid dynamics* removed.)

```
Set Items Description
--- ----- -----------
```

?ss grid?()generat?/de*               *Develop the grid concept.*
S1   4795 GRID?/DE*                              [Block 1]
S2  22734 GENERAT?/DE*
S3   1243 GRID?()GENERAT?/DE*

?ss finit?()different?()theor?/de     *Develop a computational theory subconcept.*
S4   47451 FINIT?/DE                             [Block 2]
S5   67381 DIFFEREN?/DE
S6  154251 THEOR?/DE
S7   16218 FINIT?()DIFFEREN?()THEOR?/DE

?ss finit?()element?()method?/de      *Develop a computational theory subconcept.*
S8   47451 FINIT?/DE
S9   54517 ELEMENT?/DE
S10 105570 METHOD?/DE
S11  29106 FINIT?()ELEMENT?()METHOD?/DE

?ss s7 or s11                         *Combine the two computational subconcepts.*
     16218 S7
     29106 S11
S12  43955 S7 OR S11

?ss s3 and s12                        *Combine the two main concepts.*
      1243 S3                                    [First Intermediate Result]
     43955 S12
S13    360 S3 AND S12

?ss ud=9001:9212b2                    *Create a date range.*
S14 205080 UD=9001:9212B2                        [Refine by Date]
    205080 S14

?ss s14 and s13                       *Restrict to a date range by combining the date range and two concepts.*
       360 S13
S15    236 S14 AND S13

approach is popular because it simplifies the search process by breaking it into a sequence of systematic and discrete steps.

A third general strategy is the "pearl growing" approach (Markey & Cochrane, 1981). This method begins with a specific document or document set that is known to be relevant (a pearl) and uses the characteristics of that document to successively grow a set of related (and presumably similarly relevant) documents. For an actual document or citation, the information seeker uses assigned index terms, title or text words, names, citations, publication data, or structural and statistical properties to formulate queries to retrieve subsequent sets. After locating the "pearl" to use, the most difficult problem with this strategy is determining when to stop forming and

```
?ss s7/de*                    Restrict the intermediate subconcept sets to the number of citations
   S16  6363 S7/DE*           pulled from major descriptors.
                                        [Refine Block 2 by Descriptors]
?ss s11/de*
   S17  16425 S11/DE*
         6363 S16
        16425 S17

?ss s16 or s17                Combine the sifted sets to form a concept.
   S18  22413 S16 OR S17
         6363 S16
         1243 S3

?ss s3 and s16                Combine the grid set with the sifted computation concept.
   S20    52 S3 AND S16               [Combine Block 1 and refined Block 2]
          52 S20

?ss s14 and s20               Apply the date range to a new combined set.
        205080 S14                    [Restrict Result by Date]
   S21    37 S20 AND S14

?ss s21 not computat?()fluid?()dynamic?  Remove variations of free text for computational fluid
        37 S21                        dynamics based on previous user experience.
   S22  82336 COMPUTAT?                       [Remove Unwanted Terms]
   S23  97938 FLUID?
   S24 171698 DYNAMIC?
   S25  26184 COMPUTAT?(W)FLUID?(W)DYNAMIC?
   S26     23 S21 NOT COMPUTAT?()FLUID?()DYNAMIC?
```

Figure 5.1. Example of high-precision search using building blocks strategy. (Search conducted by Kristi Mashon)

"growing" subsequent sets, as this requires more active engagement on the part of the information seeker. Hawkins and Wagers (1982) point out that this strategy is highly dependent on interaction between the searcher and the system and note that using indexing terms from the retrieved pearl is impossible in manual environments because indexing terms are seldom provided in printed indexes. Like the other strategies, pearl growing is dependent on searcher inferences and has many variations and extensions. Of particular interest in highly interactive environments are relevance feedback techniques based on the same underlying assumptions about relevant documents having common structural and semantic characteristics. Although this strategy begins with a well-defined and solid entry, it is less algorithmic than building blocks or successive fractions and requires more searcher interaction with the system.

A fourth general strategy was characterized by Hawkins and Wagers (1982) as "interactive scanning." This approach requires much user–system interaction and is less algorithmic and more like guided discovery. The idea is to begin with a comprehensive set of documents generally related to the problem area (e.g., retrieve a large set of documents using one or a few general terms). By scanning the documents, key features of the problem are noted (e.g., authors, terminology, methods), which are used to formulate and pose successive queries that further clarify the problem. As the problem becomes better understood, documents or sets are printed or saved as part of the final set. Clearly, this strategy requires continuous cognitive attention, changing criteria for judging relevance as the problem and its associated literature are better understood, and plausible reasoning about when to terminate search. Hawkins and Wagers note that this strategy takes more time than the others do but is useful for professionals conducting searches for high recall or for problems in domains unfamiliar to the end user or the searcher. It may also be used by professionals to explore a topic area before applying one of the more analytical strategies. The interactive scanning strategy is used by novices in many different environments and is much closer to browsing strategies than to other analytical strategies.

Other strategies have been described in the literature of online bibliographic searching. Variations of a simple strategy, known somewhat disparagingly by professional intermediaries as "quick-and-dirty" or "easy" searches, are often used by novice searchers and sometimes by professionals for background or intermediate information (*briefsearch* in Harter, 1986). Wagers (1989) outlines the steps in the easy search as follows: select a database, write a statement and divide it into concepts, compose a simple query using a few terms linked by AND or OR, display an abbreviated record, modify it with simple changes as needed, and print the complete records retrieved. He compared easy search strategies with sophisticated strategies (e.g., those that use field limitation, more synonyms, special codes) for the same search questions and found that the average precision was similar across all searches but that the sophisticated searches yielded higher recall on average. Not unexpectedly, the best easy search results were for problems with few concepts that could be expressed in a few words or phrases that were common in the literature. Modifying the original query made the search much easier and illustrated the importance of iterative and interactive searching, regardless of the type of strategy used. These results parallel those of Salton and his colleagues (Harmon, 1992; Salton, Fox, & Voorhees, 1983), who found that relevance feedback significantly improved retrieval outcomes. Overall, the end users judged the results of the easy search strategy to be acceptable.

Vigil (1983) described a strategy he called *closed-loop relevance clustering*, which uses the NOT operator to successively remove redundant documents from sets formed as a result of query modifications and combinations. Once a reasonable set is retrieved, a second set is formed by using a variation of the original query, and NOT is used to find the relevant items in the difference between the two sets (those relevant items in the second set but not the first). If the difference contains no (or few) relevant records, the search will terminate; otherwise, a third set will be formed, and NOT will be used to determine whether there are relevant records in the difference between the newest set and the union of the original set and difference of sets one and two. The process continues until no new relevant records are found in the successive differences. Although the preliminary results of these tests demonstrated that the strategy yielded reasonable retrieval, its main contribution was to remind intermediaries of the uses and limitations of the seldom-used NOT operator.

These strategies are often combined in practice. For example, interactive scanning or citation pearl growing may be used to generate terminology for facets that eventually are used in a building blocks strategy. These strategies are influenced by the characteristics of the online systems themselves. Boolean-based retrieval based on inverted file organizations, controlled vocabularies for bibliographic records, and charges based on connect time all deeply influenced the development of these strategies. For example, these characteristics lead to careful planning before going online. The strength of this influence is evident from consideration of how CD-ROMs have affected information seeking: End users are able to use informal strategies, and librarians who teach users how to search have difficulty convincing learners that planning in advance is helpful.

### Online search tactics

Research and practice in online searching have identified the tactical actions that experts use in conducting searches. Although many of the tactics can be used in manual environments, many are made manageable or practical by electronic systems. Bates constructed an early taxonomy of search tactics (Bates, 1979a, 1979b), identifying 29 search tactics in four categories plus 17 idea tactics. The search tactics include monitoring, file structure, search formulation, and term categories. They range in specificity from very general, strategylike suggestions (e.g., that break down complex queries into subproblems) to more specific guidelines (e.g., that use alternative affixes of a word) and include some commonsense but often overlooked suggestions (e.g., that see whether the search has already been done by someone else). Her idea tactics include a series of psychological suggestions to initiate and continue difficult searches, ranging from general tactics like brainstorming or consulting with a colleague to specific suggestions like concentrating on a broader or narrower formulation of the problem or stopping to do something else for a while. Bates's tactics highlight the psychological aspects of online searching and have influenced both the training of professional intermediaries and system design.

Harter and Rogers-Peters (1985) presented a more detailed taxonomy of tactics for online searching. They identified 101 tactics in six categories: philosophical attitudes and overall approach, language of problem description, record and file structure, concept formulation and reformulation, recall and precision, and cost/efficiency. Attitudes and approaches stress general tactics such as willingness to browse and learn and specific suggestions such as knowing one's terminal well. The 26 language problem tactics are divided into five subcategories (general development of search terms, acronyms and abbreviations, spelling and usage variations, compound terms, and codes) and include suggestions to use thesauri, to use index terms in retrieved records in reformulations, to begin with the most specific or relevant concept, to use antonyms, and to check spelling and morphological variants. These tactics closely parallel Bates's term category tactics. Tactics in the record and file structure category include the general recommendation always to question null sets and suggestions about field and record structures, stop word lists, default search fields, and parsing rules. Eighteen concept tactics in two subcategories (formulation and reformulation) include cautions about using the NOT operator carefully, using Venn diagrams, ordering facets from most to least relevant, saving queries and strategies for future searches, and browsing retrieved records to aid in reformulation. Twenty tactics in four subcategories (specificity of the concept's definition within facets and of whole facets, narrowing, and broadening) are presented for increasing or decreasing recall and precision. Many of these are specific statements for Bates's general search formulation and term tactics. For example, tactics for narrowing a search include limiting the search to specific fields; decreasing the use of truncation; using a classification code to limit to a subject area; limiting the search by date, language, or publication; and tightening the word proximity. Finally, 12 tactics to decrease cost or improve efficiency are provided, reinforcing the overall importance of time and cost pressures for professional intermediaries.

Harter and Rogers-Peters's taxonomy has an immediate practical value for professional searchers because it is more specific to Boolean-based, bibliographic systems than is Bates's more generic compilation. Both sets of tactics show how electronic systems have influenced both the theory and practice of information seeking, as so many of them are specifically enabled by electronic technologies. As with strategies, however, there are questions about how these tactics apply to full-text, interactive systems designed for end users. To what extent are the strategies and tactics artifacts of early, bibliographic database technologies? Which technological factors (e.g., retrieval techniques, interfaces, hardware limitations) and content factors (e.g., secondary or primary content, size, scope, and organizational structure) most affect learnability and usability? Are end users willing and able to learn and apply these approaches and techniques? Of the techniques best suited to end user–oriented systems, which should be automatically embedded in interfaces so that users need not learn them, and which should users master? As more systems provide ranked results and support relevance feedback, which tactics are useful, and what new tactics are needed?

These results emerged in bibliographic online systems. As full-text databases become more widespread, new strategies and tactics will be needed. Although commercial legal and other full-text databases support proximity limits and full-text queries, the economics of system development, the underlying data structures, and the retrieval algorithms remain the same, limiting the development of strategies more appropriate to full-text online databases.

### *Searching full-text online databases*

As full-text and other primary databases become more widely available, expert information seekers will adapt their patterns, strategies, and tactics. Tenopir and her colleagues have been foremost in studying full-text database searching by experts (Tenopir, 1984; Tenopir & Ro, 1990). She and her coworkers found that full-text searches yielded higher recall results than did searches limited to bibliographic records that included abstracts. Full-text searches were more costly, however, and yielded somewhat lower precision. She recommended using proximity rather than Boolean connectives to combine concepts and to combine both free-text and controlled vocabulary to gain good results in full-text systems. Thus, the tactics used in full-text databases as well as the outcomes appear to be distinct from those in bibliographic databases. Full-text systems may require experts to adjust their strategies and tactics and perhaps create new ones, although more experience with and study of these effects are needed.

Full-text systems may change information seekers' expectations. Tenopir reported that many information seekers noted that a significant difference between bibliographic and full-text searching was that full-text searching allowed immediate assessments of relevance to be made during a search. Full-text searching removes the step of locating actual documents, thereby increasing the probability that relevance judgments are accurate and stable. This characteristic should be a clear advantage for end users who can quickly make informed judgments and extract relevant information as they make those judgments. The balance between recall and precision may also change in full-text environments. For example, 20 pages (screens) of bibliographic citations may be far too much for users to examine, but 20 pages (screens) of primary materials may be far too little. These early results with expert intermediaries using full-text databases indicate that unique characteristics of primary search systems will require new strategies and tactics for experts and novices alike.

### *Lessons learned from professional online searching*

Much has been learned about information seeking in general from studies of professional users of online bibliographic systems. This experience base reveals how electronic systems differ from manual systems, highlights some of the special capabilities and limitations of electronic environments, and delineates the specific strategies and tactics used in information seeking.

Katz (1987) described four main advantages of online versus manual searching:

speed, convenience, depth of searching, and currency. First, searching an online database is clearly faster than searching a manual index, especially when the search spans several years and requires handling multiple index volumes. Second, searching online is more convenient because a variety of databases can be accessed from different sites, including offices and homes – the indexes come to the user rather than the information seekers going to them. Furthermore, traces and results can be more conveniently printed and saved with online systems. Third, the quality of searches can be better in online environments because a variety of entry points can be used, possibly including text words in abstracts. More important, the subject can be controlled better because terms can be combined with logical connectives. Also, searches can be automatically limited according to characteristics like date, type of publication, or language. Although many of these information-seeking tactics can be executed in manual systems, it is highly unlikely that they will be applied as extensively. Finally, electronic databases are typically updated more frequently than printed indexes are, and thus more timely information can be obtained with electronic systems.

Online systems offer other advantages over manual systems. They can provide more value and adapt to the individual needs of different information seekers. In one form of added value, electronic indexes may contain more information than their printed counterparts do. For example, the MEDLINE database, a bibliographic collection for the medical literature, is analogous to the printed *Index Medicus.* The online version of the database covers over 600 more journals than the printed version does and about 65% of all the citations includes abstracts, whereas none of the printed citations include abstracts (*Grateful Med User's Guide,* 1992). Electronic systems may also provide instruction and help for users. This assistance can be dynamic and context sensitive and so resemble specific advice. Online systems can also provide flexible or individualized interfaces for information seekers. For example, many systems allow users to specify commands directly or use menus to select options while searching. Information seekers with special needs can also be accommodated with alternative input (e.g., joystick or voice recognition) and output devices (e.g., large print, graphics, speech synthesis). Thus, electronic systems provide windows of opportunity for designers to go beyond the limitations of bulky and static manual search systems.

Electronic systems are not without costs and limitations. Specialized equipment and power are required; users must be minimally computer literate; display technology is often inferior to paper for text and graphics; and the costs of connection and access may be high. Nonetheless, these disadvantages are diminishing as computing pervades our work and economies of scale take effect. Regardless of their disadvantages, the advantages of online bibliographic systems over manual systems are rapidly extending to end user–oriented, primary information sources such as full-text, electronic databases, statistical and graphical databases, and electronic forums and publications available via high-speed, worldwide communications networks.

The most significant contributions of research in professional online searching are related to our understanding of information seeking itself. Studies of online searching have led to the identification and specification of information-seeking patterns, strategies, and tactics and illustrate the importance of underlying data structures, retrieval engines, interfaces, and user training for electronic systems. These studies have elucidated many interacting factors associated with information seeking and highlighted the complexity of various steps in the information-seeking process. We have learned that expert intermediaries benefit from knowledge of specific controlled vocabularies and database structures; become highly skilled in specific query languages and the use of Boolean, proximity, and truncation operators; and are strongly influenced by training and connect charges.

In many ways, professional intermediaries have adapted their behaviors and expectations to the search systems made available to them. As new systems are invented and competition among different systems increases, these new capabilities or the relaxation of existing constraints may influence behavior and expectations. The strategies and tactics of expert intermediaries are commonly emulated in instruction for intermediaries and end users alike and thus are perpetuated in today's more interactive and primary environments. It is important for researchers, designers, and users alike to ask: How do the strategies and tactics exhibited by expert users of online bibliographic systems apply to full text or other primary databases? Are they suitable for end users? Which end users? Are they appropriate for hypermedia environments?

As systems evolve to include primary information and improved interfaces, more professionals have chosen to do their own searching, which has led vendors and agencies to develop specialized products and marketing strategies. This, in turn, has led end users to expect more from the availability and use of information resources of all kinds. For example, medical students and law students typically take classes or workshops to learn about electronic search systems in their respective fields. These developments in end-user searching have begun to influence system design and the types of strategies and tactics information seekers use in their daily work. The early directions were to use training and to build interfaces that allow end users to apply analytical strategies. As more systems were created and end users' behaviors were studied, it became clear that the complexity of analytical search strategies often was frustrating. As a result, systems began to emerge based on models of naive users and informal information-seeking strategies.

## Naive models of information seeking

Driven by growth in the personal computer industry in the 1970s and 1980s, end-user computing became an active area of research and development. The information industry saw huge new markets for information products accessible by the increasingly large base of personal computers and thus explored ways to make

databases more accessible to novice users. Likewise, the computer industry supported the development of interfaces that allow users with little specialized training
to purchase and use computers. These forces allowed the human–computer interaction community to grow and promoted new innovations from designers and
engineers. Studies of novice users of various types of information systems have
begun to yield a more complete picture of information seeking in electronic
environments.

### Novice users of bibliographic search systems

Because the end users of early bibliographic search systems were professionals in
technical fields, investigations focused on how information seekers with much
domain expertise used these systems. Because medical information has life-critical
consequences, medical knowledge is growing rapidly, and significant funding has
been available, the field of medicine has figured prominently in these studies. In an
early study of the National Library of Medicine's MEDLARS search system,
Lancaster (1972), reported that after training, medical practitioners were generally
successful in locating information in the online system. Sewell and Teitelbaum
(1986) reported similar results based on 11 years of longitudinal data from various
medical databases and search systems. The essential point of these results was that
specific training was necessary to achieve appropriate results. To apply analytical
strategies, users were required to learn at least a minimal set of search commands,
simple Boolean logic, and some basic principles of database organization and
medical subject headings.

An alternative to training end users to use complex systems is to develop specialized interfaces called *front ends,* which typically support only primary system
features and offer users precise instructions and help (Meadow, 1992). Front ends
usually help information seekers employ analytical strategies. A front end
developed for professionals searching Department of Energy databases used iterative testing methods to develop and improve automated instruction and help
(Meadow, Cherry, Borgman, & Case, 1989). Evaluations of the end users of this
system demonstrated that they conducted successful searches using the interface,
although the searches were overly complex, and the users had difficulty selecting
terms (Borgman, Case, & Meadow, 1989). Thus, customized interfaces designed
for professionals who wish to access specialized databases have facilitated general
success, although more improvements are needed. These systems generally have
taken the approach that the judicious application of computational power (e.g.,
simplifying choices through menus or form fill-ins) will allow novices to apply
expert strategies and tactics.

In another domain, broader access to the medical literature by physicians has
been strongly encouraged by the National Library of Medicine (NLM) through its
development of the Grateful Med search software that runs on personal computer

platforms and automatically connects to the NLM databases through phone lines or the Internet. Grateful Med was introduced in 1986, and by late 1992 it had more than 40,000 users generating more than 200,000 sessions per month. Almost one-half of all searches of the Medline databases are conducted with Grateful Med rather than through direct connections using the MEDLARS language or other search front ends. Although this has been a highly successful effort to make medical literature more accessible to end users, there are ongoing efforts to improve the system to overcome some of the problems that users have with it. For example, almost one-third of all searches result in no documents. Incremental improvements in the Grateful Med system have been made over the years, and a recent effort by a University of Maryland Human–Computer Interaction Laboratory team focused on minimizing the number of "no hits" results and improving query reformulations. A case-based approach was used that provides different alternatives for continuing the search, depending on whether no hits or too many hits were found (Marchionini, Norman, & Boerner, 1992).

Another type of search system that has attracted attention is the online public access catalog (OPAC). Unlike online systems designed for domain specialists, OPACs must serve a diverse collection of novice and casual users. OPACs have allowed users more subject access, but many problems with OPACs have been discovered (Bates, 1986; Borgman, 1986b). OPAC studies indicate that 30 to 50% of all subject searches result in no hits, that many systems require users to use Library of Congress Subject Headings or other controlled vocabularies, and most systems offer no real browsing capabilities. Although aimed primarily at end users, OPACs have suffered from rigid underlying databases, primitive retrieval engines, and interfaces modeled on online bibliographic systems. This is beginning to change, however, as OPACs are designed to circumvent these constraints, to accommodate specific user populations, or to omit these constraints.

Rather than creating front ends for OPACs that lead users to learn and apply expert strategies and tactics, an alternative is to use a minimalist design approach (Carroll, 1990). This approach gives users the essential features for basic functionality and adds functions as the user gains experience and confidence with the system. The Library of Congress took such an approach in designing its touch panel–based interface for the combined LC catalog (Marchionini, Ashley, & Kortzendorfer, 1993). The ACCESS system assumed that its users were novices who wanted quick access to the collection and had little expertise in using library classification systems or finding aids. The interface guidelines were developed in cooperation with the University of Maryland Human–Computer Interaction Laboratory and provided single-point access (e.g., a single subject) via a graphical interface and touch panel selections. In the main reading room of the library, both ACCESS workstations and traditional workstations are available. The ACCESS workstations have been popular with patrons and with reference librarians who spend far less time helping patrons use the system than before the new interface was available. Users with expertise or with complex searches can use the sophisticated workstations, which require considerable knowledge but allow complex analytical strategies that can save time. The system has proved to be so popular that other reading rooms of the library have installed ACCESS workstations. This project is an example of an alternative front end that provides immediate usability but minimal functionality. Users who require more sophisticated access can move at their own comfort levels to the full-function workstations. In addition, more functions will be built into subsequent versions of ACCESS. Ultimately, the underlying databases must be changed to support more interactive end-user access, but providing distinct levels of interface for different types of users makes good sense in public areas serving a wide variety of information seekers.

A system developed for use at the Denver Public Library uses a highly interactive color graphics interface that provides multiple types of access to children. In addition to using a keyboard to enter subjects, users can select topics from menus for a specially constructed subject classification based on categories (e.g., animals, famous people, science) that children use and understand. Children can select categories such as new books or scary stories. In addition to bibliographic information, users can see the book cover to help them decide whether to get the book from the shelf. This type of design is much more user oriented than library oriented and is an example of a user-oriented design paradigm.

A similar system was developed at the University of California at Los Angeles for elementary school science collections (Borgman et al., 1990). This system uses an adapted Dewey Classification System to support subject searching, a bookshelf metaphor to support browsing, and locational maps to help children find the actual shelves in the library. Test results showed that all children were able to use a hierarchical browsing version of the system but that the younger children (ages 7 to 11) had difficulty using a command-driven keyword version.

A radical departure in OPAC design is represented by the OKAPI system (Walker, 1987), which ranks retrieved documents according to term frequencies and supports relevance feedback. It has virtually eliminated the "no hits" problem. Hancock-Beaulieu (1992) reported that the automatic query expansion feature of OKAPI improved its users' success and that as many as one-fourth of the searches would have failed in an exact-match Boolean system. As new OPACs are created, designers are well advised to build retrieval engines based on vector representations for documents so that ranked output and relevance feedback can be easily made part of the interface. Likewise, interfaces that are customized for particular user populations will also be more successful and satisfying.

Students and other end users without expertise in either specific domains or with retrieval systems have begun to use online bibliographic systems other than OPACs that assume that analytical strategies will be used. Borgman (1986a) studied how college students learned to use a search system for a subset of the OCLC bibliographic database, by comparing conceptual and procedural training methods. Her research demonstrated the superiority of conceptual training for complex search tasks but also noted how difficult learning and searching using Boolean queries was for novices. Huang (1992) studied college students who were trained to use an online search system to access various databases to find information about problems related to their own interests. Her research focused on the subjects' pausing behavior. Presumably, a pause in activity reflects mental activity, including wondering how to use the system. She found that her subjects were able to find information related to their problems and that their pausing behaviors grew shorter as they became more expert with the system. Her work illustrates the learning curve of end users and provides another metric that may be useful for adaptable interfaces, because such systems can automatically gather pausing data as users work. Neuman (1993) investigated how high school students learned and used an online search system to access various databases to find information for school projects. Her interviews and observations demonstrated the difficulty that students have in learning to use such systems and their frustration with not having easy local access to the primary articles and reports that their searches located. All these studies illustrate how difficult it is for novices to learn and use existing online bibliographic systems and demonstrate the need for simpler and more effective interfaces and better access to the primary information found through bibliographic searching.

These studies show that given time and effort, novice users can learn to locate pointers to relevant information by using online bibliographic systems and analytical strategies. This is especially true if users have expertise in the domain or are strongly motivated to persist. If novice users participate in training, they use behavior, strategies, and tactics that strongly reflect that training. With no or ineffective training, novices exhibit passive patterns by accepting defaults and applying informal strategies and tactics. Improved interfaces or "front ends" are somewhat effective in facilitating access and minimizing the technical details of query formulation, and more end users are using online bibliographic systems to locate potentially pertinent information. More improvements are needed, especially in light of the improved interconnectivity brought by wide area networks.

### Novice users of systems containing primary information

Because studies of professional intermediaries using full-text systems demonstrate that different strategies are needed in secondary and primary search systems, it is reasonable to expect that similar differences are true for end users. A brief overview of three technological developments is helpful to understand the results of the studies of end users that follow.

*Technological basis for primary search systems.* Although full-text, numeric, and other primary databases are available through traditional online services, there has been huge growth in primary search systems that are locally attached to end users' workstations. A *primary search system* is one that can provide direct answers to information seekers' questions or information that allows them to solve their problem. The most common example of a primary search system is a full-text database that provides firsthand rather than pointer (e.g., bibliographic) information. Other primary search systems provide statistical data, scientific data sets, images, video clips, or sound recordings. Growth has been spurred by developments in storage, display, computational power, and software advances that facilitate new types of electronic search systems. Increased computational power in the form of faster central processing units and expanded random access memories offers faster processing of large databases, supports highly interactive graphical user interfaces, and allows information retrieval techniques traditionally used in large-scale environments, such as fully inverted indexes and hypertext linking, to migrate to personal computer platforms. In addition to the retrieval methods discussed in chapter 2, three technologies are particularly important to primary search systems.

Mass storage in both magnetic and optical forms allows large data sets to be accessed through inexpensive personal computers. Reference collections were obvious first choices, and electronic versions were quickly produced for most basic collections such as dictionaries, encyclopedias, and popular directories. These were closely followed by textual collections (e.g., the Bible) and government data (e.g., the U.S. Census), and a host of multimedia databases aimed at the home market. CD-ROM databases have been particularly important to sparking the development of full-text databases. Access to primary information on CD-ROM has been popular with users, and libraries were the largest early market for CD-ROM databases; in turn, this has affected libraries in fundamental ways. Subscription costs, workstation costs, and space requirements compete with traditional collection development and patron service costs for shares of library budgets, and reference librarians are spending more time helping patrons use search systems. The most immediate impact on information seeking is that time pressures due to online connect charges have been removed, thus allowing more interactive strategizing. Although CD-ROM technology makes full-text searchable material available to end users, it is not an ideal technology. Optical access speeds are much slower than access from magnetic disks, and although the typical 600-megabyte capacity is large, many applications far exceed one disk, leading to awkward disk-swapping procedures for users.

Bit-mapped, color displays gave new dimensions of representation to designers and led to graphical user interfaces (GUI) that made primary search systems easier to use. In a single decade, the display technology of personal computers went from monochrome, 40-column-by-20-row text-only displays to high-resolution, color graphics displays that support multiple text fonts and styles and motion graphics. These developments have allowed designers to create direct manipulation environments for all applications, including information systems. Display technology continues to advance, driven by portable computers and progress toward large, high-resolution flat screens, although, these changes are costly to users who must upgrade or replace systems to take advantage of the new capabilities.

The confluence of work in text processing, human–computer interaction, and information retrieval led to the development of hypertext systems that permit users to move among various units of information (nodes) by following links. Hypermedia refers to hypertext systems that support multimedia nodes. See Barrett (1988), Berk and Devlin (1991), Jonassen (1989), McKnight, Dillon, and Richardson (1991), Nielsen (1990a), or Shneiderman and Kearsley (1989) for overviews of hypertext and hypermedia technology and Akscyn (1991) for an electronic version of the early research literature. Nodes can be small or large amounts of text, graphics, or any discrete object, and links can emanate from anchor points in a node to anchor points in other nodes. Although most systems allow any node to have many in-and-out links, any specific link typically points to only one node. Selection mechanisms such as iconic buttons or embedded menus denote links and let users follow links by pressing keys or mouse buttons. Hypertext gives more control (and responsibility) to the user by allowing moves among nodes in a nonlinear fashion. This technology gives users new ways to use primary materials and has been applied to a variety of problems in documentation, reference, education, entertainment, and data management. Some problems associated with hypertext are disorientation for users and additional overhead for authors in planning and organizing their work. Hypermedia technology is often used by designers to give users alternative information-seeking strategies that are informal and interactive.

*Studies of novices using primary search systems.* Search systems with primary information were aimed at the end-user market and first appeared in schools, libraries, and other publicly accessible sites. As part of the ongoing investigation of the interactions of novice information seekers with primary electronic search systems, I and my coworkers at the University of Maryland conducted studies with a variety of users and systems. Because they were instrumental in developing the information-seeking framework presented in this book, these studies, rather than a broader representative sample, are used here. A series of studies focused on fact retrieval tasks for full-text encyclopedias and hypertexts. In one study (Marchionini, 1989c), 28 third and fourth graders and 24 sixth graders conducted searches using a full-text, CD-ROM encyclopedia. After demonstration and practice sessions, the students were assigned a fact retrieval question and an open-ended question and were observed as they searched. Keystrokes were captured, and together with the observer's notes, formed the basis for analyzing information-seeking processes.

The results showed that the older searchers were more successful in finding the required information and took less time than the younger searchers did. Although no differences in the total number of moves were found between the two groups, transaction matrices of the two groups showed that older subjects favored examination moves and younger subjects favored query formulation and refining moves. Some subjects posed phrases or sentences as queries, indicating that although they were forming mental models for the electronic encyclopedia that were distinct from the familiar print encyclopedias, they tended to overestimate the capability and "intelligence" of the electronic system. Most subjects accepted the system's defaults and limited themselves to Boolean ANDs as connectives. An analysis of search patterns showed that all these novices used heuristic, highly interactive search strategies rather than carefully planned analytical strategies.

A later study (Marchionini, 1989c) focused on how high school students move from a print to an electronic encyclopedia. This investigation looked at how 16 students conducted simulated "mental" searches, as well as searches in print and electronic versions of an encyclopedia over three sessions. Before starting each search, the students were asked what they already knew about the problem and what they expected to find. The results suggest that for many of the subjects, encyclopedias were default search systems; that they knew and expected to find factual (what, when, where, who) rather than explanatory (how, why) information for various problems; that they were able to generate vocabulary for queries beyond that found in the statement of the problem; and that those students with less ability had generally higher expectations of the electronic system. One-third of the subjects simply used the electronic system like a print system, entering an article via its title and reading it in linear fashion. The other two-thirds of the students, however, took advantage of the full-text search features of the electronic version by adapting their print-based mental models to the new system.

Only half of the subjects in this study used AND connectives, and none used OR, NOT, or proximity features. They took almost twice as much time, posed more queries, and examined more articles in the electronic system than they did in the print system. The number of articles examined ranged from zero to six for the print searches and one to 10 for the electronic searches, although differences in the mean numbers of articles examined were not reliably significant across print and electronic searches. Equal proportions of print and electronic searches (20% and 19%, respectively) yielded no hits, and 10% of the electronic searches yielded too many hits, that is, when students immediately reformulated a query before examining any articles. The proportion of no hits in this study is below the 30% range found in OPACs and other bibliographic system studies, reinforcing the distinctions between searches in primary and secondary databases. Although few of these students were observed to use the highlighted query terms in articles as browsing aids, some of them commented on the usefulness of highlighted terms. Overall, these subjects performed somewhat perfunctory searches without taking full advantage of the system's interactive nature. They might have been influenced by the novelty of participating in an experiment and using what was then new technology. These results demonstrate that information seekers must be guided in adapting their mental models of manual systems if they are to take full advantage of the features of electronic versions. When introducing electronic analogs of manual systems, examples of how the new system is unlike the manual system are as important as examples of similarities to promote learning.

Based on these earlier investigations, a study was undertaken to compare how novices used highly interactive browsing strategies and formal analytical strategies with an electronic encyclopedia system (Liebscher & Marchionini, 1988). Twenty-six ninth-grade science students were randomly assigned to either a browse or an analytical treatment group and were assigned to write a short essay about the effect of the earth's rotation on climate and ecology. The browse group was trained to use a "scan and select" strategy, that is, to enter a simple query and scan the list of titles for potentially relevant articles, and to then use articles' outlines, headings, and highlighted query terms to reject them or extract relevant information. The analytic group was trained to use Boolean connectives to formulate precise queries to retrieve only a few article titles. The students conducted individual searches, and all their keystrokes were logged. The contents of the essays were analyzed by comparing numbers of prepositional phrases, numbers of relevant prepositional phrases, and grades assigned by a teacher.

Although no statistically reliable differences were found, predictable trends were apparent. Students in the "scan and select" group used fewer terms and retrieved more titles than did those in the analytical group, but there were no differences in the number of relevant articles retrieved by the two groups (both groups had similar but poor precision). The analytical group showed greater within-group variance on these measures and reinforced the observations that the analytical strategy was more difficult to learn than was the scan-and-select strategy. The essays written by the analytical group generally received almost one grade higher than did those written by the scan-and-select group. The scan-and-select group used more prepositional phrases per essay (26) than the analytical group did (23), but fewer relevant prepositional phrases (18 and 23, respectively). A large negative correlation was found between the essay's grade and the number of nonrelevant prepositional phrases. Students who used the scan-and-select strategy may have tried to incorporate more information as they scanned a great deal of text during their searches and were unwilling to give up large volumes of it. This may be related to the cognitive biases of representativeness and availability described by Tversky and Kahneman (1974). Another possibility is that the scan-and-select strategy may not have required students to organize facets of the problem when formulating their queries, thus leading to difficulties in discriminating between relevant and nonrelevant information.

Overall, this study demonstrated that both types of strategy were effective in identifying relevant information but that more attention must be given to finding ways to make scan-and-select strategies more discretionary. One approach may be to devise techniques to focus attention on how the problem relates to an entry point for browsing and then to continually relate the problem to text while browsing. The former technique is a type of query formulation step and the latter an examination step. Another approach is to train users. Alternatively, diagnosis rules may be discovered that could allow the system to point out biases to users. In any case, regardless of whether or not strategies are intuitive and easy to apply, information-seeking expertise should include knowledge of not only how to apply strategies but also their limitations.

These results with electronic encyclopedias led to subsequent investigations of novices using hypertext databases designed to invite browsing strategies (Marchionini, 1987). In an early set of investigations, paper and hypertext versions of a database and two hypertext access methods were compared (Wang, Liebscher, & Marchionini, 1988). The hypertext system (Hyperties) is distinguished by its intuitive interface and ease of use. In the first investigation, 24 graduate students were randomly assigned to one of three versions of a database consisting of 106 articles about the Holocaust. One version was a paper version; one was a hypertext database with only an alphabetical index for the article titles; and one was a full version of the hypertext with embedded menus (highlighted hypertext links) in the text as well as the index. All subjects conducted six searches. Because most participants were successful in finding relatively straightforward answers, there were no statistically reliable differences among the groups in accuracy of answers, mean number of articles viewed, and judgments of task difficulty. Subjects in the electronic groups judged the system to be slightly more difficult to use than did the subjects using the paper version, and they were generally less satisfied with the system, especially with respect to level of comfort and level of frustration. Subjects using the paper version were statistically reliably faster than the subjects in the electronic groups (means of 620 and 870 seconds, respectively). All but two subjects in the full-version treatment exclusively used the index rather than the hypertext links. Thus, users were not willing to adopt the novel hypertext jumps when the well-known index was available. This study illustrated some of the problems of using even a hypertext system optimized for ease of use when compared with a familiar paper-based text.

In the second investigation, 36 graduate students were randomly assigned to one of two access method treatment groups. Both groups used the same database and the full version of the hypertext system, but one group received training only in using the embedded menus and the other only in using the index. For the purposes of this study, use of embedded menus was considered as a type of browsing strategy, and use of the index as an analytical strategy. All subjects conducted six fact retrieval searches. The dependent measures were success, number of moves made, total time to complete searches, number of articles viewed, and number of screens viewed. Subjects in the index group performed marginally better than did those in the browse group on four of the five dependent measures (all but total time); however none of these differences was statistically reliable. When trends across the six questions were examined, differences in performance disappeared as more questions were completed. Thus, a learning effect was noted as subjects gained more experience with the browse strategy. These results may also have been biased by the subject population which consisted of library science students who had substantial experience building and using indexes. The subjects in the index group were generally more satisfied with the system, reliably so for ease of use, speed of use, and frustration level. They reported their computer experience before participating in the study and were assigned to a low or high experience category. Only the total time taken differed reliably when the two experience groups were compared on the five dependent measures. Thus, computer experience was not a predictor of performance. This study reinforced the earlier results that browsing strategies can be effective but revealed that even simple information-seeking strategies require some introduction and practice before they will be adopted.

A subsequent set of investigations was conducted to determine how access methods influenced information seeking and what designs could lead to adaptable interfaces. In one study, undergraduate subjects conducted fact retrieval searches using a print-based encyclopedia and three different electronic systems – a general electronic encyclopedia, a science and technology electronic encyclopedia, and a hypertext database (Marchionini & Liebscher, 1991). Subjects executed statistically reliably faster searches in the print encyclopedia than in any of the electronic systems, illustrating the additional cognitive load needed to manage the systems that despite minimal training were still novel to them. Those in the electronic conditions examined three to four times as many articles as did those in the print condition. Subjects in the hypertext treatment group outperformed those in all other groups in locating correct answers, and they executed about as many queries as did those in the print condition. Those in the two electronic encyclopedias executed two to three times as many queries as did those in the print and hypertext groups. This study demonstrated that the hypertext environment required users to allocate less cognitive load to the system than did the Boolean-based full-text electronic encyclopedias.

Another study examined access methods in detail. Twelve undergraduate students conducted searches in a hypertext over five 2 hour sessions using different access methods (Liebscher, 1992). The database was an electronic version of a book on the topic of hypertext (Shneiderman & Kearsley, 1989), and five electronic versions were used: a version with only an alphabetical index, a version with only a subject index, a version that allowed only a string search, a version that allowed only hypertextual links, and a version that allowed all four access methods. The subjects conducted individual searches for each of the methods, for a total of 60 searches. They also conducted simulated searches verbally. The results showed an overwhelming preference for string search as an access method. Despite extensive usage, the subjects had relatively poor mental models for the different access methods (e.g., they thought that string search was actually subject search, and that the alphabetical index was less detailed than the conceptual index). These results show that even if adaptable interfaces are provided, the users may select and continue to use simple or default alternatives rather than those that optimize the task and conditions at hand.

Another environment ripe for the study of information seeking is the Perseus hypermedia corpus of materials on the ancient Greek world (Crane, 1992). This system is an aggregation of texts, images, and programs published as a set of HyperCard stacks and data files. Created for humanities scholars and students, the first release of Perseus consists of Greek texts and English translations for 10 authors; a historical overview of ancient Greek culture with explicit links to texts, maps, and images; approximately 7000 eight-bit color images of vases, sculpture, sites, architecture, and coins; textual descriptions of all objects; a Greek–English lexicon and a morphological database for words in Greek texts; an atlas of Greece and the surrounding region that allows users to locate 800 sites; and an encyclopedia of art, archaeology, and architecture. Tools for accessing and navigating these materials include an index of all English definitions for Greek words; a catalog and keyword indexes for all objects; a string search for Greek and English words, a path tool that allows users to save, annotate, and edit tours through the database; and a set of menus that link various components of the database. The system represents a large and complex set of primary materials and tools for access and manipulation of information. While the system was being created, the evaluators were studying a variety of college courses at different sites to determine how Perseus use influenced teaching, learning, and research.[2] These studies used observations, interviews, transaction logging, and document analyses to study how instructors and students used Perseus to teach and learn topics in Greek literature, ancient religion, archaeology, Greek language, and Greek culture and history.

Given its size, design, and the uses to which it was put, information seeking is a primary activity of Perseus users. For any given search task, there are many different ways of locating a target and many targets as well. In our studies we were interested in how users learned to use the system; how the integration of texts, images, and hypertext tools influenced use; and how a complex hypermedia corpus affected teaching and learning (Marchionini & Crane, 1994). The main results of our four years of evaluation follow.

Perseus offered a mechanical advantage to instructors and students. It gave instructors an easily accessible and dynamic alternative to slides and transparencies for augmenting lectures. Furthermore, it provided a construction and delivery platform for instructors to show integrated paths of texts and images that students could study individually or in small groups. From the learners' point of view, it speeded looking up words for language translation, freeing them to spend their time on other tasks such as reviewing previous passages or looking ahead. Perseus also gave learners exhaustive sets of passages containing specific Greek or English words, thus providing more evidence to support their interpretations and arguments. Students using Perseus were found to cite statistically reliably more passages and a wider variety of passages in their essays than did students who did not use Perseus for their essays.

As with the previous studies of high school students using an electronic encyclopedia, flexible and interactive access to large volumes of material did not necessarily lead to better essays. Just as the high school students who used browsing strategies used many irrelevant prepositional phrases in their essays, students who used Perseus rather than paper texts cited more statistically reliable passages in their essays but this did not lead to higher grades. Likewise, although students in a Greek language course could look up words somewhat faster using Perseus than a paper lexicon, this did not lead to superior translations. Although the mechanical advantages Perseus afforded students in finding text passages and translating Greek texts were not alone sufficient to produce superior translations or essays, using Perseus did allow some students to produce superior arguments.

Perseus did enable new kinds of teaching and learning. Instructors and students often noted that the integration of text and graphics materials expanded the scope of course assignments and discussions, and students in literature courses reported using the graphic materials in Perseus to provide context for their textual interpretations. The graphical materials in Perseus were clearly a significant addition to teaching and learning, and the transaction logs showed that much of the students' time was spent locating and viewing images. The path tools in Perseus enabled new representations for students' interpretations of the ancient Greek world, allowing them to present their ideas by weaving textual and graphical primary evidence into their arguments. Students who knew no Greek were able to use the Greek–English lexicon to probe the meanings and contexts of key English words to discover how the ancient Greek authors used these words and thus what the concepts behind the words were 2500 years ago. Thus, students without philological training were able to use the methods of the philologist to get closer to the ancient culture and to appreciate the difficulties and biases of translations. Some students made interesting discoveries while exploring the database in open-ended fashion, and these became the basis for their papers. Students also reported that Perseus encouraged them to use a broader range of materials in their studies.

The design and implementation of the Perseus system itself also affected student performance, as it required concerted effort and time to learn if all its features were to be used.[3] Interface factors were more closely related to performance than were previous computer experience, illustrating the importance of well-designed interfaces for hypermedia systems. The design decision to use implicit rather than explicit links made Perseus somewhat more difficult for novices to use than some hypermedia systems offering explicit instructional paths. These results parallel those in earlier studies of information seeking in electronic encyclopedias and hypertexts, in that browsing and interactive search strategies can be effectively used, but users must apply them judiciously rather than mechanically.

### Lessons learned from novice users of primary search systems

Perhaps the most obvious result of studies of end users of primary search systems is the great diversity of abilities, characteristics, and experiences that the users bring to these systems. A single information system may be used by children or adults, by users with varying amounts of time and patience, in public or private settings, and for a variety of information problems. Clearly, these systems must offer robust interfaces to serve such diverse ranges of users and uses. Nielsen (1989a) conducted a meta-analysis of 30 hypertext usability studies and found that individual differences and task were the two most important usability factors. These requirements have led designers to look for alternative or adaptable interfaces that may allow systems to serve broad user markets. Although user and task factors are most critical to information seeking, the interface is also important. For example, previous computer experience was not a strong predictor of performance, but the learnability of the interface was found to be a performance-related factor in our Perseus studies.

It is evident from these studies that end users apply naive information-seeking strategies and that interactive systems with primary information invite such strategies. These information seekers use browsing strategies and simple string search liberally in all types of electronic environments. Analytical strategies are more difficult to learn, although once they are learned, they typically yield more efficient results. Clearly, there is a need for a better understanding of browsing as an information-seeking strategy and for interfaces that promote and support highly interactive strategies.

Information seeking in primary databases is more directly related to end users' information problems and allows them to make relevance judgments quickly as they interact with potential answers to their questions rather than pointers to possible answers. This situation is more fluid than using secondary sources or a human intermediary. This is a boon for users but changes the meaning of relevance from a system-centered to a user-centered perspective. Relevance becomes totally dependent on sequences of examination and continual assessment by the user rather than on inferences about discrete sets of intermediate results. This makes it even more difficult to assess system performance via traditional recall or precision measures.

The results of studies of end users searching primary systems reveal the importance of feedback. The users' expectations influence what strategies and tactics are used, and the results in turn influence subsequent expectations. The users' expectations are often unreasonable, rooted in cognitive biases or misconceptions about technology in general. Children sometimes posed natural-language questions to an electronic encyclopedia, and adults had difficulty judging the size of a database. The users also tended to rationalize the usefulness of their results by including irrelevant citations or clauses in their essays. Feedback from the system must be carefully considered by designers from the start so that they can match the users' expectations to the system's capabilities and resources, especially in highly interactive environments in which many cycles of feedback take place in single sessions.

Electronic systems have obviously affected the actions that expert and novice users take while seeking information. They have made much more practical such tactics as string search and manipulating intermediate sets of documents with Boolean operators. Analytical search strategies have grown out of expert users' taking advantage of Boolean operators and database structures. Experts can use them effectively; better interface techniques are making them more manageable; and as information seeking in electronic environments becomes more ubiquitous, children will be better trained. Experience with end users has repeatedly shown that analytical strategies are difficult to learn and use and that informal, interactive strategies are preferred. In addition, the emergence of primary search systems that offer interactive interfaces has promoted such strategies. Electronic systems have begun to change users' expectations about what is possible in an information society. Although it is too soon to say how electronic environments have affected general information-seeking patterns, the early indications are that the way we think about and react to information seeking is changing as more of these systems become available to us.

# 6
# Browsing strategies

*Marco Polo had the opportunity of acquiring a knowledge, either by his own observation or what he collected from others, of so many things, until his time unknown.*

The Travels of Marco Polo

*The laws of behavior yield to the energy of the individual.*

Emerson, *Essays, Second Series: Manners*

In contrast with the formal, analytical strategies developed by professional inter-mediaries, information seekers also use a variety of informal, heuristic strategies. These informal, interactive strategies are clustered together under the term *browsing strategies.* In general, *browsing* is an approach to information seeking that is informal and opportunistic and depends heavily on the information environment. Four browsing strategies are distinguished in this chapter: scanning, observing, navigating, and monitoring. The term *browsing* reflects the general behavior that people exhibit as they seek information by using one of these strategies.

Browsing is a natural and effective approach to many types of information-seeking problems. It is natural because it coordinates human physical, emotive, and cognitive resources in the same way that humans monitor the physical world and search for physical objects. It can be effective because the environment and particularly human-created environments are generally organized and highly redundant – especially information environments that are designed according to organizational principles. Browsing is particularly effective for information problems that are ill defined or interdisciplinary and when the goal of information seeking is to gather overview information about a topic or to keep abreast of developments in a field.

The term *browsing* is used in a variety of settings, including forestry, zoology, architectural design, marketing, and information science (Chang & Rice, 1993). The computer and information science literature uses the term *browsing* simply to mean navigating, scanning, and scrolling, and many interfaces include "browsers" that allow users to move across or within screens, windows, records, and databases. In traditional library literature, browsing was most often associated with card catalogs or bookshelves. More recently, Bates (1989) argued for the importance of browsing in conjunction with other online search strategies. We term this *across-document browsing,* because the information seeker browses through records or books to find items to examine more closely. The education and reading literature also have been concerned with perusing a document to extract its gist or to locate a relevant passage, with the terms *skimming, scanning* and *browsing* used to distinguish this activity from reading or studying.[1] We term this type of browsing *within-document browsing* and believe it to be a high-priority research problem for electronic environments. Most types of across-document browsing identify specific documents or objects that may then be browsed or studied according to the information seekers's needs. One exception is across-document browsing in a collection to gain a sense of scope or form. Thus, browsing is a term whose meaning must be taken from its context.

A significant characteristic of browsing in electronic environments is the blurring of boundaries between document collections or databases and discrete documents or records. The implication for design is to provide systems that support seamless browsing across and within documents. A hypertext collection of articles may be considered a single document when linked to other hypertexts or as a collection of documents (nodes) in its own right. In either case, a single node or a collection of nodes is represented on the same display device, and the display is controlled by the same paging, scrolling, and windowing actions. In the current electronic environments, there are no clear delineations for the user in either the physical display device or the physical actions taken to execute browsing activity. This situation is exacerbated in networked environments in which documents from different databases appear in the same window or the same document is represented in different databases.

In regard to the information-seeking framework presented in chapter 3, browsing strategies are more dependent than analytical strategies are on interactions between the information seeker and the system. The system also has more influence on the progress of the search during browsing. Also, during browsing, the information-seeking subprocesses proceed in somewhat more parallel fashion; more time is spent in the examination subprocess; and there are a wider variety of cycles in the overall process.

Browsing offers significant challenges to information seekers and system designers. First, an entry point must be identified. Determining an entry point combines problem definition and query formulation. Entry points can be determined by random selection, by the use of indexes or statistical analyses that return a set of items for browsing, and by opportunistic, iterative examination. The challenge to the information seeker is to relate personal knowledge about the topic to what the system represents and how its representations are organized. The challenge to designers is to make clear the system's scope and organization and to suggest entry points to the searcher.

Second, information must be examined and assessed during browsing. The information seeker's challenge is to make rapid judgments of relevance, and the designer's challenge is to provide flexible display facilities for examination and assessment. These challenges illustrate how browsing blurs the information-seeking subprocesses. Problem definition, query formulation, execution, examination, and iteration are especially intertwined during browsing. This fluidity and integration is caused by the parallel engagement of physical, perceptual, and cognitive processes during browsing; to the close coupling between the information seeker and the organizations and representations provided by the information environment; and to the open-ended information problems that lend themselves to browsing.

This chapter is based on the notion that the natural human inclination to browse and the organizations inherent in information systems are strongly reinforced and harmonized in highly interactive electronic environments that complement and invite browsing. Based on this perspective, we argue for a design philosophy that amplifies human abilities and inclinations rather than one that optimizes organization and task analysis. We consider the variety of reasons that people browse, different types of browsing behavior, limitations of browsing, and the ways that manual and electronic information systems can support browsing.

## Why browse?

Browsing is used for many purposes and is manifested in different ways. Table 6.1 lists the main reasons that people browse. In contrast with analytical strategies, in which goal definition is important to success and efficiency, browsing strategies may be applied to more informal or general goals and depend more heavily on the information encountered during the search.

We browse to gain an overview of a physical or conceptual space. By scanning a scene or a document, we can identify key landmarks and characteristics and use them to form impressions of the scene or document and to make analogies to known scenes or concepts. For example, by scanning the title page, table of contents, section headings, index, and reference list of a book, we gain a sense of the content's scope, depth of coverage, and the author's organizational perspective and thereby can decide quickly whether to invest time reading it. It is important to note that in the case of books, those attributes that we browse first are well-established standards to aid browsing. Hildreth (1982) pointed out that these features of books both encourage and enhance browsing. Electronic environments are only beginning to build in systematic support for browsing. We can browse software applications by spending a few minutes traversing menus, executing generic commands or manipulating system objects, and examining the form and scope of help and instructions. At this point in the development of the science of interface design, it is unclear how a program or a database should "reveal itself" to users to encourage and enhance browsing. Full-text CD-ROM databases allow users to browse through texts by jumping to highlighted query terms, but these systems are limited by the display technology. Browsing Internet news groups or World Wide Web

Table 6.1. *Reasons to browse*

Gain an overview
Monitor a process
Shift/share cognitive load
Clarify an information problem
Develop a formal strategy
Discover/learn
Environmental invitations

nodes gives a sense of breadth to various groups and details of specific postings but few organizational cues to the scope and organization of all the groups.

Another reason that we browse is to monitor a process. When driving, we regularly check how close we are to the road shoulder, look for landmarks and signs, and glance in the rear view mirror to check the status of cars near to us. When systematically examining books on a shelf, we often jump ahead to gain a sense of how much time we will need to complete our browsing. Some electronic search systems provide history or path tools so that users can quickly go back and examine the progress of their search. Readers often scan forward in a book or article to see what remains and to establish an anticipatory frame of reference or scan backward to review what has been read and regain or revise their sense of context. These actions are indicative of the text reinspection–reading strategy used by skilled readers in comprehending text (Garner, 1987). This type of browsing is particularly important for ongoing, accretional information seeking in which the objective is to stay abreast of a field. Many information environments provide aids for monitoring such as sidebars, pull quotes, abstracts, review articles, and book reviews. Developing interfaces that support and amplify browsing through the mass of information created in a domain is a critical problem in information science and human–computer interaction.

We also browse because it requires a smaller cognitive load than analytical search strategies do. Browsing is highly dependent on human perceptual abilities to recognize relevant information. Analytical query formulations require us to apply cognitive resources to recall from memory specific terms that represent the concepts related to our problem. Taken to an extreme, the advantage of a smaller cognitive load may be abused. For example, because of cognitive laziness, information seekers may apply minimal cognitive effort and simply depend on perceptual and motor processes to stumble on relevant information. In general, however, applying recognition allows the information seeker to concentrate more cognitive resources on the problem at hand. For tasks that are ill defined or complex, browsing allows information seekers to devote full cognitive resources to problem definition and system manipulation and to involve the perceptual system in filtering words or images.

Besides bringing additional resources from the perceptual system, there may be symbiotic advantages to applying multiple subsystems that are mutually reinforcing – in effect, the whole result is greater than the sum of its parts. This parallelism effect is perhaps even stronger because browsing requires high levels of direct physical engagement by the information seeker; that is, we must move, scan, scroll, jump, and page more quickly through the shelves, pages, or screens. Thus, browsing may be more of a direct manipulation strategy than the formal methods are because it involves cognitive, perceptual, and motor systems concurrently and continually.

Using both physical and mental subsystems in coordinated activity may reinforce experience and memory for events. Our interviews with and observations of students using the Perseus system suggest that there may be some positive interactions between the physical actions of using a lexicon and the cognitive actions of translating Greek into English. The popularity of video games and simulations that use high degrees of direct manipulation also illustrates the importance of engaging multiple subsystems in complex activity. Our understanding of how the satisfaction associated with direct manipulation affects performance and learning is very poor. There is no definitive evidence whether learners remember more as a result of coordinating their physical and mental subsystems or how intellectual task performance such as information seeking is affected. If performance can be improved by engaging physical and mental subsystems more closely, there must be design efforts to coordinate physical and intellectual actions at workstations. Furthermore, for some specific types of information seeking, such as locating intermediate facts in a chain of processes or repetitive lookups, experience and memory should be minimized and speed and accuracy maximized.

While seeking information, we also browse to clarify the information problem. Because many of our problems are due to anomalous states of knowledge, browsing a space of information in the problem domain can help us clarify and expand our knowledge. We may retrieve a record, article, or book and examine it quickly to look for ideas about entry terms, alternative or related concepts or to learn more about the problem so that we can clarify it and state it in precise language. Likewise, we browse to find something interesting that suggests a more specific or exciting problem that we can then attack more formally. For example, in our study of attorneys and law intermediaries, the subjects noted that one reason to go online rather than use inexpensive printed sources was that the problem was ill defined (Marchionini et al., 1993). The electronic systems allowed these information seekers to quickly locate sets of legal documents that provided feedback to clarify what issues were involved in the problem.

Related to problem clarification, people browse to stimulate or develop a plan or a formal strategy. An information seeker may use a simple query to retrieve a large number of generally related documents and browse through the title words or subject headings to determine technical vocabulary, identify related facets, and generally get to know the intellectual neighborhood before formulating a specific set of formal queries. This strategy is particularly useful if the information seeker is not an expert in the domain or when controlled vocabulary lists or thesauri are unavailable.

We also browse to discover and learn. Regardless of how comprehensive our efforts are to investigate an area, we all experience the pleasure of serendipitous discoveries that are highly relevant to our information problems but found in surprising places and situations. Browsing is an activity that may yield new insights in two ways. On one hand, we may locate a highly relevant item by browsing through resources beyond those systematically coded and assigned as relevant. This has a low probability but a high payoff – like an intellectual lottery. This is the basis of many arguments for serendipity. For example, we may find a highly relevant paper that was not indexed with the terms guiding the search, or we may locate an alternative special-interest group.

On the other hand, we may not locate any specific document that would otherwise have been missed but, rather, gain new insights or interesting associations for our problem by browsing through alternative sources that use different tools, techniques, and data structures. Scholars are highly conscious of such possibilities and support institutional policies to facilitate such serendipity, for example, open stacks in libraries and cross-disciplinary colloquia. By browsing in an unfamiliar field, we may discover methodologies that have not been applied to our own field or gain new perspectives or metaphors to apply to our own work. In interdisciplinary fields like information science, scholars must use results from the many allied fields. In many cases they work at the boundaries of several fields and depend on browsing to span the boundaries to gain synthetic insights and integrate concepts. For example, Auster and Choo (1993) have noted that executives depend on scanning information sources across traditional boundaries to stay abreast of their field.

Finally, we browse because the environment invites browsing – in fact, stores and museums are carefully designed to stimulate browsing. The organizations in nature and created by civilization invite interaction and exploration. The importance of how systems invite and support browsing is considered in a subsequent section.

Browsing has become much more important as more information resources migrate to electronic environments. The interactivity characteristic of these environments affects all the reasons for browsing above but has particularly interesting possibilities for discovery and learning. Humans decide how to use their time and resources for this type of information seeking according to constraints on these resources, probabilities for finding new knowledge, and payoffs for new knowledge. For example, during a brainstorming phase of information seeking or at an impasse in the process, if 20 minutes are available to invest in an environment (e.g., a library), a min–max heuristic may be applied to examine low-probability sources to gain high-payoff information that may suggest directions for beginning or restarting work. Electronic environments provide a good place to lessen time constraints and raise the probabilities of locating high-payoff information. First, electronic environments are more accessible and may invite more frequent explorations. Second, electronic environments can improve the likelihood of a payoff, by providing feedback that the user can control directly or a profile can control automatically.

**Browsing strategies and tactics**

The literature of library and information science contains many attempts to distinguish different types of browsing. Reviews of browsing (Chang & Rice, 1993; Hildreth, 1982) cite a number of typologies developed by different investigators. Although there are differences in how the types are named, there seems to be agreement on three general types of browsing that may be differentiated by the object of search (the information needed) and by the systematicity of tactics used. At one extreme, users perform directed (Herner, 1970) or specific (Apted, 1971) browsing. This form of browsing is systematic and focused and is often driven by a specific object or target. For example, scanning a list for a known item is a highly directed type of browsing because the objective is specific and known by the information seeker. Tasks such as verifying information or retrieving dates or other facts require repetitive and systematic browsing behavior. A second type of browsing is semidirected and predictive (Herner, 1970) or generally purposeful (Apted, 1971). This type of browsing has a less definite target and proceeds less systematically, for example, entering a single, general term into a full-text electronic database and casually examining the retrieved records. This type of browsing allows various degrees of target definition but requires multiple probes of the system and thus is time-consuming. A third type of browsing is undirected (Herner, 1970) or general (Apted, 1971) browsing that is characterized as having no real goal and very little focus – more like recreation than information seeking; for example, repeatedly changing television channels to find something of interest to watch.

In addressing browsing in electronic systems, Cove and Walsh (1988) and others described a similar trio of browsing types based on the not-quite orthogonal dimensions of goal definition and behavioral systematicity. Thus, types of browsing have been characterized coarsely according to the specificity of the object sought, which in turn influences the systematicity of actions the information seeker takes while browsing. These three different degrees of systematicity are from most to least systematic, *systematic, opportunistic,* and *casual* browsing. Systematic browsing exemplifies more linear sequencing and regular iterations of the information-seeking subprocesses; opportunistic browsing jumps from examination to many different subprocesses; and casual browsing exemplifies almost random sequences of information-seeking subprocesses. Such behavioral characterizations are useful for describing browsing as an information-seeking strategy, but a more detailed and cognitively oriented analysis is required to understand browsing, especially in regard to the role of the object of information sought.

One step in this direction is Kwasnik's study (1992) of how people browsed through paper, a command-driven electronic system, and a hypertext to identify the behavioral components of browsing. In preliminary studies of people in a marketplace, she noted that identifying a unit of focus was difficult (e.g., the object of browsing could be an entire menu or a menu item), that people tended to impose structure on the environment regardless of how unstructured it might be, and that even casual browsing quickly became purposeful as people related the activity to their own interests. She identified six actions her subjects used while browsing.

- Orientation – the need to understand the structure and content of the environment; it continues to evolve as browsing continues.
- Place marking – a way to allow users to remember salient objects.
- Identification – decisions about the relevance of specific objects.
- Resolution of anomalies – browsers' attempts to understand objects that were not clearly identified.
- Comparison.
- Transition.

The next to last and last actions, respectively, support orientation and identification and allow browsing to progress. This work provides a more user-centered and cognitive approach to browsing than previous work does.

A user-centered model of browsing based on the general information-seeking framework that distinguishes different browsing strategies follows. In practice, information seekers use multiple strategies and often use default strategies to initiate search, but this model provides a basis for predicting rational initial strategy selections.

Like all information-seeking activity, browsing is dependent on interactions among the information-seeking factors: task, domain, setting, user characteristics and experience, and system content and interface. Although the higher-order interactions of all the factors influence the specific browsing tactics and behaviors that information seekers select and exhibit, five sets of interactions determine the dimensions that are used to characterize browsing strategies. Two of these dimensions relate to the external and mental representations of the object sought, one is specific to the environment, and two relate to the physical and mental activity of the information seeker:

- The domain of the problem and the system mainly determine the external representation of the *object sought.*

- The problem and the seeker's knowledge of the domain and the system mainly determine the mental representation of the *object sought.*

- The system and the setting determine the degree and type of organization of information in the *environment.*

- The system, the setting, and the seeker's mental models for them mainly determine which browsing strategies are available for application and the *degree of interactivity.*

- The setting and the information seeker's past experience and immediate mental and emotional states mainly determine the *cognitive effort,* motivation, and resources used during browsing.

The object sought during browsing must be considered from two perspectives: the characteristics of the object in the world and the representation of the object in the information seeker's mind.[2] The object may be a well-specified, discrete target (e.g., a book) that can be identified by a single attribute (e.g., a call number). Such objects are well managed by database management systems or string-search techniques. If the single attribute is known by the information seeker (i.e., there is high definition in the user's mental representation), such objects may be immediately recognizable on perception (e.g., known item searches that seek to locate a specific fact or item). The object may be more general and complex (e.g., a concept or a document) and identifiable by an aggregation of multiple attributes. These objects are typically represented and managed with value-added techniques such as indexing and abstracting. Browsing for these types of objects requires that the information seeker perceive multiple attributes and execute multiple cognitive comparisons and inferences to ascertain pertinence. Objects may also be highly abstract and active (e.g., threads of argumentation in a longitudinal collection of group discussions) and identifiable by a variety of clusters of overlapping attributes. These types of objects may be saved and displayed by various techniques, but are not easily manageable. Browsing through such objects demands substantial cognitive effort and reflection by the information seeker.

The objects of information seeking must also be represented in the mind of the information seeker. Several factors influence these representations. As discussed in chapter 3, the information problem may be driven by the need to retrieve, to analyze, or to learn and discover; the information seeker has a set amount of domain knowledge, information-seeking experience, personal characteristics, and immediate states of affect; and various setting constraints are active. The object of information seeking may be represented in the seeker's mind as a discrete object with a single attribute (e.g., a date). Such objects allow the browser simply to compare the objects in the world on this attribute – a task with a small cognitive load. In fact, this sort of problem lends itself to more straightforward retrieval, and browsing may demand considerably more effort by the user. Alternatively, the object can be represented in the browser's mind as a complex concept with multiple attributes. This situation will require more systematic comparisons, more rankings of attribute salience, and thus a greater cognitive load. If the objects are represented as anomalous states of knowledge with many possible attributes that are themselves fuzzy, then the browser must not only make many comparisons and inferences, but also make many interpretations about what may serve as attribute values.

The more broadly we decide to browse, the fewer attributes and corresponding objects that we will be willing to admit for careful examination. Furthermore, the attribute values may change as the information seeking progresses, and the information seeker's state of knowledge becomes less fuzzy. Thus, browsing for ill-defined or anomalous objects requires a larger perceptual and cognitive load and more time. It is also possible that information seekers may browse according to a conscious decision to engage in divergent thinking (no object is allowed) or by means of efforts to explore a space to select objects with similar benefits or preferences (choosing one object from many desirable objects). In these cases, as potential objects are perceived during browsing, various levels of cognitive effort may be applied to assess pertinence and determine what action to take next. Thus, browsing proceeds by comparing the mental representation for the object (an image of the object together with a set of attributes believed to be salient to the search) with the system's representation and altering expectations according to the outcome of each pattern-matching event.

The environment is determined by interactions among setting, search system, domain, and task. The environment supports or inhibits browsing according to the level of organization for the objects represented and by the manner in which feedback is provided. A later section is devoted to the important role that systems play in browsing. For the purpose of defining browsing tactics, the degree of organization is used as a key dimension. Electronic environments may be characterized by the degree of feedback provided to users. This is the system's perspective of the amount of interactivity, a dimension considered here from the user's perspective.

The information seeker is central to all information-seeking activity, and because browsing is a specific case of this activity, the information seeker's personal information infrastructure and the immediate situation influence the browsing. The personal information infrastructure determines whether to browse or use an analytical strategy, what entry point to use, and which tactics to apply as the browsing progresses. The user's emotional state, need, and resources such as time, money, and access privilege influence these decisions, determine whether systematic, opportunistic, or casual approaches will be used, and affect persistence and termination. To define browsing strategies, two dimensions are used here: interactivity and cognitive effort. The interactivity dimension is defined by the number and rate of choices and actions the user makes and takes during information seeking. Low interactivity is indicated by few choices for types of actions and infrequent turn taking. Cognitive effort refers to the amount of reflection, analysis, integration, and decision making required during browsing. A small cognitive load is indicated by primarily perceptual processing and simple recognition and matching.

The types of actions that information seekers exhibit when browsing depend on interactions among the information-seeking factors. From a user-centered, cognitive perspective, tactics and moves are mainly determined by the information seeker's internal representations of the sought object and by expectations about how the process of browsing will proceed. Browsers may expect that comparisons will be based on a simple match of a single attribute or on a match of several attributes. In the case of more open-ended browsing, the experienced browser will expect to draw analogies and make inferences about whether information items found in the system are suitable as attributes for the fuzzy objects of interest. The internal representation of the object of browsing and the expectations about the kinds of matching that will be needed influence the tactics and moves that the information seeker makes during browsing. For example, a single, well-defined attribute that a browser expects to find in a section heading of an article will likely invoke a scanning strategy across section headings.

Note that both types of mental representations change as the browsing progresses. The object becomes more defined according to the attribute specification and frequency of occurrence, and expectations about further progress are informed by reflection on the quality and quantity of attributes represented in the system. For example, consider a novice stock market investor who seeks information on how stock options work and has accessed an electronic discussion archive that provides scrollable subject headings posted by contributors to the discussion. Suppose that the terms *stock* and *option* are attributes that the information seeker expects to match while scrolling. As the browsing continues, more terms may be added as attributes if those terms occur frequently with *stock* and *option* (e.g., the term, *contract*) or the investor's understanding may grow based on frequent co-occurrences of other concepts such as *option listing, put, call*. These changes are dependent on feedback from the system and the degree of change is a simple indicator for distinguishing systematic, opportunistic, and casual browsing. An interaction between an information seeker and a system that exhibits occasional large changes in the mental representations for the object and the expectations about the process is more clearly opportunistic or casual than is an interaction in which the object and expectations about how matching takes place vary incrementally as the search progresses.

The behavioral moves exhibited by browsers are manifestations of browsing tactics. The physical actions should be good indicators of cognitive processing because browsing depends on the close coupling of physical, perceptual, and

Table 6.2. *Threshold estimates of browsing strategies*

| | Dimensions | | | | |
| | Object | | Environment | Information seeker | |
| Strategy | External definition | Internal definition | Organization | Interactivity | Cognitive effort |
|---|---|---|---|---|---|
| Scan | high | known | high | low | low |
| Observe | low | fuzzy | low | low | high |
| Navigate | high | fuzzy | high | high | high |
| Monitor | high | known | low | low | low |

cognitive activity. Four types of browsing strategies are defined: scan, observe, navigate, and monitor. Table 6.2 categorizes these strategies by the five primary dimensions critical to browsing. Two dimensions are used for object: degree of external definition (high means very well defined objects, e.g., simple, concrete data) and degree of definition in the information seeker's mind. External definition is mainly determined by interaction between the domain and search system. The degree of environmental organization for object representations is the dimension used for scaling the environment. Environmental organization is mainly determined by interactions among the search system and the setting, with problem and domain to a lesser extent. The degree of interactivity (high means multiple, rapid turn-taking actions) and amount of cognitive effort (high means considerable reflection, decision making, and analysis while examining objects) are used as dimensions for the information seeker element. Interactivity is determined by interactions among all the information-seeking factors, with domain and outcomes contributing the fewest effects. Cognitive effort is primarily determined by the information seeker's characteristics and the problem, with other factors contributing smaller effects. The values given in the figure are considered to be threshold values at which the strategies become useful and typical. Clearly, any strategy can be applied to any browsing situation, but efficiency and effectiveness are determined by appropriate applications. Thus, any of the strategies may be used during systematic, opportunistic, or casual browsing.

*Scanning* is the most basic browsing strategy. It is fundamentally a perceptual recognition activity that compares sets of well-defined objects with an object that is clearly represented in the information seeker's mind. Scanning benefits from highly organized environments that provide clear and concise representations. It can proceed sequentially according to some structural feature of the content, or through some sampling method. Two such tactical approaches are linear and selective scanning.

*Linear scanning* applies perceptual attention continually and sequentially. For example, information seekers may scan title lists to identify potentially relevant documents to examine, or they may fast-forward through television channels to locate an interesting program. Linear scanning is most applicable to sequential arrangements of similar objects with precise attributes that can be recognized in a single glance, and when the collection is reasonably small or the information seeker is confident about being in the general neighborhood that contains the object. Linear scanning is effective because the eye can recognize simple patterns in as little as 50 milliseconds, although eye movement plus recognition times vary from 125 to 500 ms (Potter & Levy, 1969). Simon (1979) reports 250-ms fixations for people scanning squares on a chess board. Latencies are shorter when people know where a target will appear (Rayner, 1978), as is the case in linear scanning or reading.

A special type of linear scanning is monitoring gauges or controls, and there is evidence that linear sequences of stimuli in a stable position (e.g., reading by fixing on a screen position and having the text move through the position) can dramatically decrease response latency. Payne and Lang (1991) termed such techniques *rapid communication visual display* and found response latencies with them to be two to three times faster than with spatial displays. However, these speed increases brought severe penalties in error rates that were twice as high as rates with the spatial displays. How these speed and accuracy trade-offs affect scanning tactics for different tasks and how they may be applied to interface design remain to be determined. For example, there is no evidence for how errors of omission or commission affect browsing for textual information, and increased speed benefits may be worth such error penalties in some types of browsing. Errors of omission, for example, may be acceptable when scanning journals or databases to gain the gist of a text. Linear scanning is fatiguing, but the physiological and psychological bounds of scanning in electronic environments have yet to be determined.

An alternative to linear scanning is *selective scanning*. This tactic applies perceptual attention according to either an inherent or an imposed stratification of the search space. Most search systems offer some inherent partitions that support selective sampling. For example, information seekers may scan the section headings in a book or the reference lists of different journal articles. This tactic is particularly useful for gaining an overview of content or to identify a neighborhood for linear scanning. A variation of this tactic is to scan selectively by sampling the search space according to a partitioning rule. Rather than depending on some features or organizations in the search space, random or purposive samples of the search space are identified and scanned for relevance. For example, information seekers may fast forward a videotape 100 feet at a time to locate a particular sequence, or they may examine every first sentence of each screen of text to get a sense of content. The partitioning rule may take advantage of spatial memory and may be particularly useful in locating objects previously seen in the system (e.g., a statement that we believe appears about two-thirds of the way down a left-facing page about one-third of the way through the second chapter of a book). This tactic could be applied to gain an unbiased overview of database coverage or to determine accuracy or integrity. Sample scanning may also be helpful for discovering promising information neighborhoods in extremely large, unstructured databases.

Scanning tactics are most applicable to organized search spaces of reasonable size. What constitutes "reasonable" is often underestimated, especially in electronic environments; nonetheless one of the most obvious ways that electronic search systems can amplify human information-seeking abilities is by emphasizing and facilitating scanning tactics. Wiberley and Daugherty (1988) summarized the literature on library patrons' across-document scanning behaviors and suggest that users are willing to scan longer lists of citations from online searches than from OPAC searches and longer lists from electronic than manual systems. They report ranges of 7 to 50 items scanned with few above 20 for manual systems, but occasionally up to 200 for electronic systems. They also note that poor interfaces in electronic systems minimize scanning persistence. It seems plausible that if systems are specifically designed to support scanning rather than simply permit it, users will scan substantial lists of references. There is little evidence on how users scan within electronic documents, although simple affordances such as highlighted query terms and indicators of progress through the document clearly assist within document scanning.

Scanning tactics are most useful for tasks for which recognizable and discrete attributes are available. Scanning tactics are most often applied during systematic browsing strategies or for intermediate examinations during opportunistic or casual browsing. One measure of the costs of scanning tactics is attention time, and so research on scanning in electronic environments would be well served by analyzing these costs as influenced by different information-seeking factors.

*Observational strategies* are the most general of all browsing strategies in that they have minimal thresholds for all the browsing dimensions except for cognitive effort. Browsers who use these strategies assume that they are in a promising neighborhood and react to stimuli from that neighborhood. Observational strategies depend on a great deal of parallel input. In busy street scenes, a browser may attend to a variety of sounds, sights, and motions rather than systematically scanning the scene. Advertisements in newspapers and magazines and provocative titles of books on shelves attract our attention as we passively apply observational tactics. Like scanning, observational strategies are rooted in our physiological and psychological survival instincts and thus are naturally and easily applied as defaults. Observation does require interpretation and reflection to make sense of what is observed and to relate it to information-seeking objectives. Observations may lead to interesting discoveries but yield most initiation control to the environment. For this reason, it is most important for the information seeker to be in a relevant neighborhood.

Observations can be executed systematically except for ill-defined objects and fuzzy purposes, for example, regularly reading the morning newspaper or watching a news broadcast. Observation is the primary strategy used in opportunistic and casual browsing because it admits the widest range of objects and unorganized environments. Serendipitous observations are lauded as a benefit of browsing, but they occur as a result of reflection and association rather than simple perception and pattern matching.

Interfaces that support observational strategies should provide alternative views of information. Because observational strategies yield significant control to the environment, information should be clearly represented and demarcated. Alternative representations should be available for the user to transform so that pattern recognition may lead to association and reflection.

The *navigation* strategy balances the influence of the user and the environment. The environment constrains browsing by providing possible routes, and the user exercises some control by selecting which routes to follow. *Navigation* is a term that is used broadly and differently in the literature. In much of the human–computer interaction literature, navigation is considered to be synonymous with browsing rather than one of several specific browsing strategies. One model that does distinguish between browsing and navigation was proposed by Waterworth and Chignell (1991). Their model of information exploration distinguishes querying and browsing, object specification (command interaction styles) and object recognition (menu interaction styles), and navigation from mediation. In their model, navigation is taken to mean a high degree of user control with mediation depending more on system control.

As considered here, navigation is defined by relatively high thresholds for all the browsing dimensions. Objects must be specifable; information seekers must know what they are seeking, actively interact with the environment, and regularly reflect and make decisions about progress; and although navigation may occur in unstructured environments, high levels of organization greatly aid efficiency and effectiveness.

Physical navigation is often used as a metaphor for traversing of a hypertext or a database. The activity that users engage in as they follow links in a hypertext is the navigation that we consider to be a browsing strategy. In this strategy, the process and the information found along the way are what is important. A better metaphor for this strategy may be "grazing" or "berry picking" (Bates, 1989), but the activity is commonly called *navigation* in the human–computer interaction and hypertext literature and so is adopted here. This type of navigation is in contrast with the goal-oriented physical navigation that uses cues from the environment only to check progress toward the goal.

In physical navigation, the object sought is most often a predetermined destination, and the process is adjusting course according to attributes (conditions) provided by the environment. Navigation connotes goal-oriented behavior in which plans and subplans respond to the environment. This dynamic interplay between navigator and environment is what makes navigation a popular metaphor for human–computer interaction. Navigation is a useful name for a browsing strategy in so far as it denotes observations of the environment and adjustments in behavior based on these observations. It is, however, a weak metaphor for browsing through an information space, in two respects: The destination for information seeking is seldom predetermined – intellectual space is highly amorphous, and much of what is called navigation involves problem definition and clarification. Second, information-seeking activity draws information to the information seeker rather than transporting the information seeker to the information. This is especially true of electronic environments, in which we remain physically stationary and gather information to our screen rather than travel to some location and idea. Using navigation as a global metaphor for browsing admits the side effects of becoming lost. In electronic systems this effect has been most often referred to as lost in hyperspace (Nielsen, 1990a). It is useful to distinguish between being lost and confused as a result of the environment (e.g., poor maps or bad road signs in physical space, and poor interfaces in information space) and being lost or confused as a result of the information problem (i.e., being lost in one's own mind). Although it is likely that improved interfaces (e.g., graphic maps, place markers, organizational labels and cues) will minimize disorientation caused by the system, being lost in a collection of thoughts will remain a human problem regardless of system advances.

This point of view, that is, understanding content (mental orientation) is more critical than system orientation, was reinforced by two investigations we conducted to determine the effects of blatant metaphors on learning. Two versions of a hypertext explanation of the information-seeking framework were prepared using the GUIDE system. One version, called the *jump* implementation, reinforced the navigation metaphor. The screen consisted of a single text window, with link anchors immediately followed by the word *jump* in boldface uppercase letters. Clicking on the link anchor replaced the text with the text in the linked node. The other implementation, called the *bring* version, reinforced the metaphor of bringing information to the screen rather than jumping to it. Link anchors were immediately followed by the word *bring* in boldface uppercase letters. Clicking on the link anchor opened a new window that overlapped the active window immediately below the anchor.

Forty-eight library and information science students were randomly assigned to one of the two conditions. They received mouse training and training in their assigned linking mechanism, during which time the metaphor was verbally reinforced. They then were given 30 minutes to study the database. After their study period, the subjects were given a written test to determine their understanding, asked to draw a diagram of the organizational structure of the database, completed a questionnaire, and participated in a focus group discussion. No statistically reliable differences were found between the groups, and there was wide variance on all indicators within the groups. The study was replicated the following semester with a third condition of a linear electronic version of the database added. The results of that study were similar to those of the first study. In both cases, reports of disorientation were not correlated with other results or any of the main treatments. Apparently, the metaphor was not so important to performance as the users' abilities and the complexity of the content.

Navigation as a browsing strategy refers to the ongoing observation of environmental attributes, adjustments to the mental problem representation based on these observations, and the resulting behavioral actions. Navigation is thus information seeking that proceeds incrementally based on feedback from the information system. The ways in which the system provides feedback is a critical factor in navigation.

This strategy is most clearly supported by the structural layouts of museums. Navigation has become an important (but weak) metaphor for electronic systems and is the principal inspiration for static hypertexts. In one navigation variation, users are invited to follow paths through the database by selecting one of possibly many links from a current node to other nodes. Thus, the tactics used are simple selections from the choices active on the path. Navigation strategies can be applied casually or systematically, although they depend on taking advantage of existing links or the user's ability to create new links. Navigation is an attractive compromise between user and system responsibility because the system invites or suggests links to follow but the user is free to choose from among many links or continue in linear fashion. Different systems provide distinct levels of navigational freedom, ranging from highly systematic, mandatory paths to absolutely no guidance whatsoever. Successful systems fall somewhere in between, offering some choice to users but suggesting directions and providing informative cues about progress. Systems that provide explicit hypertextual links support more systematic browsing strategies, and those that provide implicit links support more exploratory or casual browsing.

A *monitor* strategy is often applied in conjunction with systematic browsing or other primary activities such as reading. Monitoring is most similar to scanning except that it tolerates poorly structured environments. For example, while reading text related to a specific topic, a monitor browsing strategy "listens" for concepts related to another topic of interest. Professionals in any field often automatically apply the monitor strategy by spontaneously relating to their own field what they read in an unrelated area. It is this strategy that is perhaps most important to discovery and creative connections among disparate ideas, and it is the reason that scholars revere serendipity. Although this strategy may be partly subconscious, it depends on the user's making associations among concepts in the mind and representations in the information space. Monitoring is enabled by perspectives or views of the database, which in turn are made up of various cues such as words or phrases, movements, or visual characteristics, depending on the information environment.

Monitor strategies focus on attributes of interest to the information seeker and are less dependent on stimuli in the environment than observational and navigation strategies are.

These various strategies are applied by information seekers as part of the information-seeking process. Scanning and simple path following navigation are most often used in systematic browsing in which the objects are well defined in the information seeker's mind and in the environment. These strategies are indicated by typically linear sequences of information-seeking subprocesses. Observation, navigation by cues in the environment, and active monitoring strategies are most often used in opportunistic browsing when exploration, learning, or accretion of knowledge are the goals, when the objects are complex or ill defined, or when the systems are unfamiliar or unstructured. These strategies require a greater cognitive load than systematic scanning or navigation does because they demand reflection and frequent adjustments in objects and their attributes; the information-seeking subprocesses proceed in parallel and with varied branching and looping. In most situations, information seekers apply different strategies at different stages of their information seeking. For example, an information seeker may systematically scan a list of titles but opportunistically scan or navigate documents from the title list.

**Limitations of browsing**

Although browsing is a natural and often effective information-seeking strategy, it does have limitations and costs. These limitations are summarized in Table 6.3 and discussed next. Browsing requires the information seeker to perceive all potentially pertinent information items, and each perception requires time. This "on-the-fly" processing has several consequences. Humans fatigue quickly, especially when doing repetitive tasks. Most studies of information-seeking behavior use subjects in a laboratory setting, in which performance motivation is influenced by study conditions. The Wiberley and Daugherty (1988) work discussed earlier suggests an upper limit of 200 items as the number of citations that users are willing to scan in electronic environments, although these results were based on surveys of the literature and systems designed to discourage examination of long lists of citations. Lee and Whalen (1993) studied an automated "mug shot" system for helping crime witnesses identify suspects. They reviewed consistent results from multiple sources indicating that performance accuracy falls off rapidly between 100 and 200 image examinations. There is no evidence for how persistent users are when browsing through electronic texts and what factors influence persistence and fatigue. In fact, there is a need to determine a variety of physiological–psychological limits for browsing in various environments.

Browsing offers severe temporal penalties when the search task is well defined and a structured search system is available. If indexes or electronic search tools are available and the information problem can be represented in terms of the indexing

Table 6.3. *Limitations of browsing*

| |
| --- |
| High attention demands |
| Inefficient for well-defined retrieval |
| Possible distraction |
| Possible information overloads |
| Influenced by various biases and cognitive inertia |
| Present systems not designed to assist |
| Subject to diminishing returns |

language or parameters of the tool, then a formal query is likely to be more efficient. Furthermore, if the information space is ordered and a known unit is to be located, application of even a simple binary search strategy will be more efficient than scanning the list in order. The value of the information seeker's time and any time-sensitive charges may also discourage browsing. In addition to the efficiency limitations of browsing in large information spaces, browsing may also limit the coverage that is possible. Thus, inefficiencies may lead to less effectiveness. It is mainly for these reasons that professional intermediaries are trained to avoid browsing in order to save connect charges and personal time.

Users who are browsing primary materials have not only these monetary concerns but also the problem of not being distracted by "interesting details" of the context. The nature of opportunistic browsing strategies in particular may decrease the effectiveness of browsing and lead to disorientation or distraction, especially in systems that offer few navigational cues. Observational strategies are particularly prone to distraction, and navigation tactics can lead to both disorientation and distraction.

Garner, Gillingham, and White (1989) described how children and highly skilled adult readers are subject to "seductive details" while reading nonfiction passages. Their work showed that interesting details about the topic of interest distracted both types of reader from recognizing and recalling the main points of the text. Browsing situations and highly interactive environments must certainly exacerbate this effect. As people browse, they may make discoveries, but they also may be distracted, confused, disoriented, or frustrated by peripheral and tangential information. This is especially problematic when browsing is driven by the need for an overview of an area or to get a sense of a text.

In relation to distraction, which wastes time and may mislead information seekers, browsing in rich environments may also lead to information overload. This is especially true in highly interconnected electronic environments in which the richness of relationships leads to confusion and overload rather than a deeper understanding of the concepts represented by the system. Clearly, tools and strategies for minimizing distraction and overload are needed.

In addition to affecting efficiency and effectiveness directly, browsing strategies may have subtle influences on information-seeking performance. Browsing strategies are attention dependent, relying heavily on recognition, and human attention is biased toward what we know and like. Therefore, what we recognize and attend to naturally is biased. Our observations of users of various search systems illustrate the human tendency toward "wishful thinking" as information seekers patch together bits of evidence rooted in availability rather than logical similarity. An artifact of electronic systems is what may be termed *cognitive laziness,* a malady invited by systems that allow mindless search or browsing. Users flounder under the illusion of productivity as they enter queries or scan items without reflection or inference.

A related bias may be termed *cognitive inertia,* a tendency to continue following paths or lines of evidence rather than examining contrary or alternative directions. Linear text reinforces such thinking, and this may be one of the best information transfer qualities from author to reader. However, nonlinear environments offered by electronics discourage such information flow and may lead to breakdowns in information transfer.

Because technology usually has not been specifically designed to support browsing, there are hardware and software limitations on electronic browsing. The requirement of using a display device has so far limited how users can take advantage of the designers' physical and spatial creativity in regard to retrieval. Intellectual space must be broken across screens or windows that are temporal rather than static – all the pages of a book may look alike, but each page is a distinct physical entity. Because all the information objects used on a display are confined by the same static area and position, users are unable to use physical characteristics such as size, shape, thickness, or paper quality as access points for locating those objects. Because there is good evidence that human memory is episodic (e.g., Walker & Kintsch, 1985), the absence of physical cues to distinguish different intellectual experiences makes people even more dependent on symbolic retrieval mechanisms that cannot be manipulated directly.

Browsing strategies, like many other problem-solving methods, are subject to a law of diminishing returns. The limitations of browsing parallel the limits of full-text searching. Although there is evidence that adding additional terms to a query statement will improve recall in full-text systems (Gomez, Lochbaum, & Landauer, 1990), such improvements must have limits because the salience of the additional words must eventually decrease as various facets of the concept are exhausted; that is, eventually, all documents will be retrieved. Likewise, total reliance on browsing will yield a superficial perspective on a limited portion of an information space. Analytical search, browsing, and careful reading or study all have roles to play in most information-seeking problems.

The key to using browsing strategies is selectively using them for appropriate problems and with those search systems that best support it. Users who simply wish to retrieve information in primary systems rather than learn about the context of the information may choose to use intermediaries to minimize costs or avoid the limits of the strategy.

## How systems support browsing

Support for browsing across objects is built into many environments. Streets and buildings are organized to direct physical movement, and museums and stores invite users to explore personal interests while providing overall organizational constraints. As Zoellick (1987) stated, "Browsing presumes a document collection is structured in some way" (p. 74). Although browsing can be used (and perhaps is the only approach to use) in random collections, organized environments make most browsing strategies much easier. Product catalogs group together like items for easy perusal and comparison and place related groups nearby to suggest other products that customers may purchase. Video controllers and automobile radios provide scanning mechanisms to quickly browse through their respective information spectra. Libraries that provide open stacks to patrons shelve books according to a classification system that groups related books together, thus mapping conceptual similarities onto physical proximity on the shelves. A major limitation of this arrangement is that each book can exist in only one shelf location but may be related to many topics. Electronic libraries can overcome this limitation because the electronic document can be instantiated at many places in the classification system; that is, electronic systems are able to manage many-to-many relationships. Although this potential has yet to be tapped, the probability of locating a specific item by browsing through an electronic catalog that assigns items to many main topics is likely to be greater than the probability of locating the specific item by browsing through only physical shelves.

Objects such as books also provide structural support for browsing. Tables of contents, chapter and section headings, and indexes are provided to make the organization of a book explicit and to allow users to examine contents in a non-linear fashion. Journal articles offer abstracts and organizational structures such as headings and tables that support browsing and nonlinear reading. Some journals require specific organizational structures and promote browsing in various ways. Medical journals often provide augmentations such as sidebars, use typographic techniques like placing methodology sections in type font sizes that are smaller than those of other sections, and require authors to write structured abstracts (Huth, 1987). Electronic documents can provide the same types of support for browsing and offer additional elements such as hypertextual links that invite browsing.

Most browsing is highly interactive and blurs distinctions among the information-seeking subprocesses. Determining an entry point combines search system selection and query formulation; examination, extraction, iteration, and problem definition progress concurrently as the browsing continues. A primary challenge for electronic systems is to support this close coupling of the information-seeking subprocesses. Closely linking input and output mechanisms is one way to parallel and reinforce highly dynamic browsing behavior. Users initiate queries or probes in the database, and the system displays results that the user in turn rapidly manipulates. Thus, input mechanisms for query formulation and display control must be provided by the system seamlessly and rapidly so that user control and system display are synchronized. Various types of electronic information systems support browsing (e.g., bibliographic, full-text, hypertext, image databases, hypermedia), and different techniques have been demonstrated (e.g., text processing, image processing, visual browsers, and information retrieval techniques) that support browsing. However, today's systems provide only one or two features or techniques added on to support browsing as a secondary strategy to analytical search (e.g., allowing users to page or scroll through document sets of titles returned by a query).

Electronic environments offer significant possibilities to support browsing as well as analytical search strategies. In fact, electronic systems that support combinations of browsing and analytical strategies are the most helpful to users choosing the most appropriate strategy for the problem. Many systems claim to support browsing, thereby demonstrating the widespread recognition of the need for such systems and for specific techniques and mechanisms. There is a dearth of evidence, however, related to how browsing in these environments affects information-seeking performance, which techniques and mechanisms are most applicable to different search tasks and with what user populations, and how these techniques and mechanisms may best be combined and integrated into general-purpose search systems. Table 6.4 provides a framework for various features and techniques that may be useful in supporting browsing. Examples of systems that illustrate one or more of these techniques and features follow. The examples are organized by generic type of database represented (bibliographic, full text, and graphical) and by types of mechanisms (visual queries and browsers, information retrieval techniques). These examples are not meant to be exhaustive but just to show some of the ways that browsing is supported in current systems.

### *Bibliographic and online search systems*

Early OPAC systems did very little to support subject searching at all, let alone support browsing (Hildreth, 1982). Second-generation OPACs provided for subject access by allowing queries to be posed according to controlled subject headings (e.g., Library of Congress Subject Headings) and, in many cases, through keywords in the title. Several of these systems refer to one of these access methods as browsing, leading to more confusion about what browsing means. Beheshti (1992) noted that current OPACs lack display characteristics to allow browsing and proposed a graphic interface that represents MARC records visually rather than simply

Table 6.4. *Features and techniques to support electronic browsing*

**Representations**
  *Conceptual display*
    Document structure (e.g., outline, SGML codes)
    Alternative levels of detail (e.g., citation/abstract/extract/overview)
    Alternative views (e.g., indexes, filters)
    Maps, webs
    Paths/tours/links
    Neighborhoods/clusters
  *Physical display*
    Text features (e.g., highlights, fonts)
    Color/shape/positional cues
    Multiple, coordinated windows
    Link anchors (e.g., hot words, buttons)
    Icons, graphical objects (e.g., iconized windows)
    Fisheye views
    Thumbnails/miniatures
    3D perspective
    Compressed images/feature extracts
    Animations

**Mechanisms**
  *User control*
    Display manipulation (e.g., scroll, jump)
    Zooms/pans
    Usage monitoring (e.g., histories, bookmarks)
  *Query styles*
    Text queries (e.g., string search, guess and go)
    Selection (e.g., hierarchical menus)
    Graphical queries/pattern matching
    Relevance feedback
  *Manipulation*
    Cut and paste
    Add value (e.g., concordance, link plot)
  *System help*
    Entry point
    Profiles
    Suggestions
    Statistical analyses (e.g., term densities)

**System features**
  Rapid response
  High resolution, large display
  Advanced retrieval algorithms (e.g., vector processing, clustering)
  Advanced data structures (e.g., indexes, vectors, document spaces)
  Alternative input devices (e.g., gesture monitors)

textually. Other OPACs have also used graphic interfaces to aid users in browsing through either the bibliographic records or the book surrogates (e.g., The Science Library Catalog of Borgman et al., 1990; Pejtersen's 1989 Book House system) and provide alternative strategies for search, including hypertext-like browsing capabilities. Figure 6.1 illustrates the graphical display used in the Science Library Catalog. Studies of children showed that they used picture browsing (various icons) almost as much as they did analytical search strategies and that they were highly satisfied with the interface and their results. OPAC designers have begun to consider browsing as a legitimate search strategy, but this is not generally the case for online systems because connect charges encourage off-line planning and analytical strategies. Because bibliographic databases on CD-ROM are not constrained by connect charges, some systems provide browsing support in the form of highlighted query terms, scrollable indexes, and jumps between query terms in text.

Allen (1992) found that perceptual speed and cognitive abilities such as logical reasoning and verbal comprehension influenced information seeking in a CD-ROM bibliographic database. This free-text searching was named *browse* and it was the option most often selected. Based on these results, Allen recommended that the display of linear lists of hits be modified for users who lack perceptual speed, perhaps using a hierarchical display of document lists. His results are related to those of Vicente, Hayes, and Williges (1987) who reported the importance of spatial ability to users of hierarchical file systems. These results are interesting because they remind designers to consider browsers' perceptual and spatial abilities.

### Full-text search systems

Given the quantity of text that professionals must deal with, techniques for browsing through full-text systems are important. Tenopir (1985) noted that full-text searching allows users to make immediate judgments about relevance and recommended that careful consideration be given to how text is displayed. She also found that documents containing more than 10 occurrences of a query word or the word occurring in four or more paragraphs had an average precision three times higher than the overall precision. These results demonstrate that statistical analyses of terms and documents should be useful in helping information seekers select entry points for within-document browsing and in locating promising sets of documents when browsing across documents. Tenopir and Ro (1990) noted that users frequently browsed through articles for background information on topics and required good scrolling capabilities as well as multiple windows to allow several documents to be used at the same time.

Three techniques have provided clear advantages for browsing: string-search capability, highlighted terms in the text, and hypertext links. First, string search is

Figure 6.1. Science library catalog screen display. Subject headings are customized for children, and bookshelves are used as visual cues to support selection and browsing. (Courtesy of Prof. Christine Borgman, UCLA)

available in most hypertext and other full-text search systems, serving as the principal way to query and probe the database for promising entry points. Liebscher's 1992 work demonstrated users' preferences for string search even over hypertext links. Second, highlighting query terms in a text is a simple but effective way of supporting browsing and information seeking in general. Much of our work at the University of Maryland showed that users make good use of highlighted query terms in electronic encyclopedias, computer science articles, and legal literature. Many users jumped from highlighted term to highlighted term rather than paging or scrolling. Egan and colleagues (1989) also found that highlighting query terms was a powerful tool for subjects using a SuperBook version of a statistics book. Third, the essence of hypertext is browsing by following links, and the development of hypertext systems has led to an interest in browsing techniques from both physical and conceptual interface perspectives. Hypertext systems support both explicit links among text fragments by means of highlighted terms or phrases (embedded menus; Shneiderman, 1992) and implicit links by means of string search or pull-down menus. Figure 6.2 illustrates how multiple representations are used together with string search and highlighted query terms in the SuperBook system. Figure 6.3 illustrates the embedded menus approach to hypertext link anchors in the Hyperties system.

Other developments have improved the browsability of electronic text. Larger screens, better type font and size control, and better screen layouts have somewhat reduced the penalties of reading text on a screen rather than on paper (e.g., Hansen & Haas, 1989), although reading text on electronic displays takes longer than reading paper documents does (Gould et al., 1987). Many full-text systems provide simple ways to scroll, page, jump to the next highlighted term, and jump to the next document in a list, and skilled users may be able to use such features to mitigate reading-speed penalties. More important, these mechanisms for moving rapidly within texts should facilitate browsing and it remains to be determined how browsing speeds differ in paper and electronic settings.

A variety of techniques to structure and display hypertext links have been proposed and tested. Furuta and Stotts (Furuta & Stotts, 1989; Stotts & Furuta, 1989) defined a browsing semantics based on a Petri net model to limit how users navigate hyperdocuments. Their Trellis system (see Figure 6.4) can determine whether or not a link should be active, depending on previous traversal events. It helps users make browsing decisions by displaying the current state of the network and four text windows related to nodes in the net. Thus, browsing can be supported by making links available according to context and by allowing users to see links and the overall organization.

### Graphics search systems

Improved computing systems have led to the development of image databases. Slide collections, clip art, images of magazines or journals, and video sequences have been made accessible in a variety of ways. Most image collections can be searched only through words or phrases assigned to each image. Some systems provide close linkages between words found in texts and images. For example, the city Olynthus described in a textual passage in Perseus can be used to bring up a site plan and an image of a coin minted there (see Figure 6.5). These linkages can be found through a word search that locates all occurrences in texts as well as occurrences in catalog cards that use the target word somewhere in the description of the object (all objects are attached to catalog cards, which may contain multi-paragraph textual descriptions in addition to basic identification and provenance information). Although these systems provide good access to either analog or digital images, browsing is often tedious, owing to the time it takes to retrieve and display images. These approaches also depend on access through textual descriptions rather than graphic properties.

A technique that directly supports browsing through images should provide what are called *thumbnails* or miniatures (Nielsen, 1990b) of the images. Erickson and

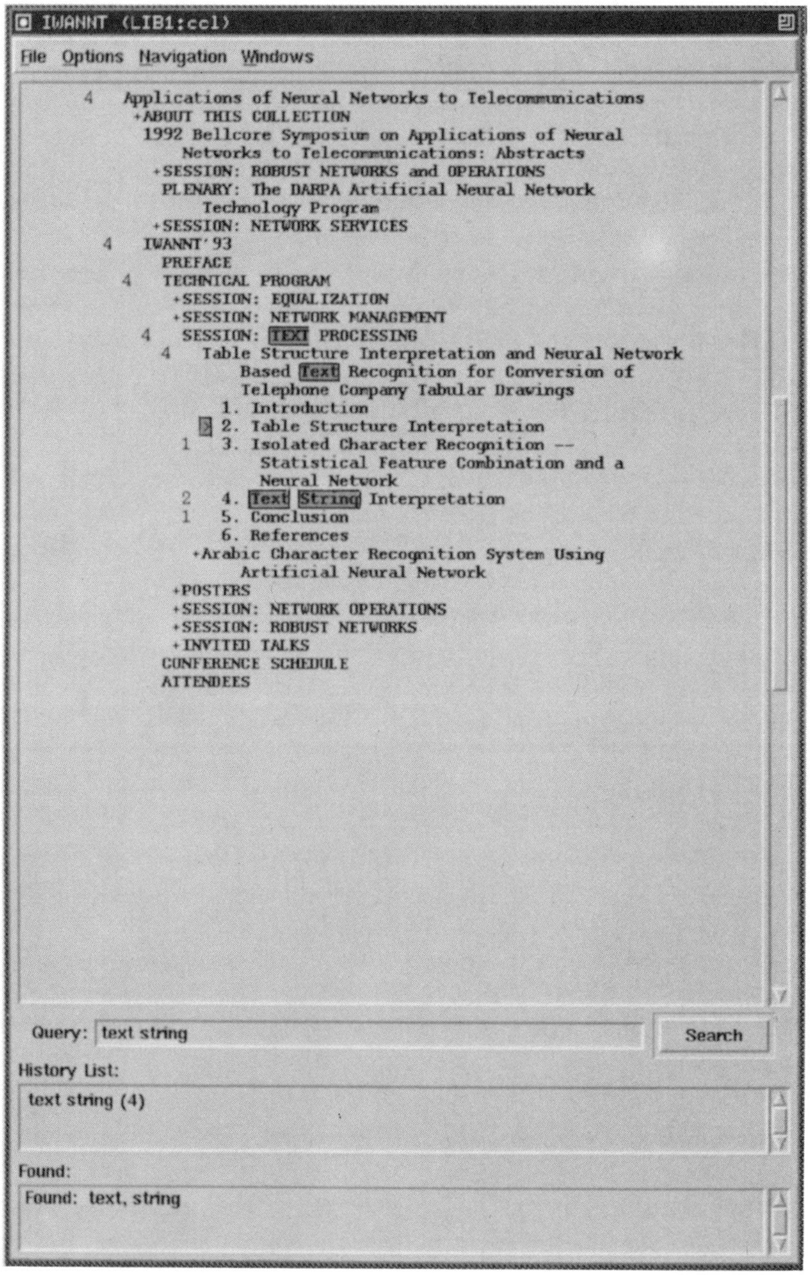
IWANNT (LIB1:ccl)
File Options Navigation Windows
4 Applications of Neural Networks to Telecommunications
+ABOUT THIS COLLECTION
1992 Bellcore Symposium on Applications of Neural Networks to Telecommunications: Abstracts
+SESSION: ROBUST NETWORKS and OPERATIONS
PLENARY: The DARPA Artificial Neural Network Technology Program
+SESSION: NETWORK SERVICES
4 IWANNT'93
PREFACE
4 TECHNICAL PROGRAM
+SESSION: EQUALIZATION
+SESSION: NETWORK MANAGEMENT
4 SESSION: TEXT PROCESSING
4 Table Structure Interpretation and Neural Network Based Text Recognition for Conversion of Telephone Company Tabular Drawings
1. Introduction
2. Table Structure Interpretation
1 3. Isolated Character Recognition -- Statistical Feature Combination and a Neural Network
2 4. Text String Interpretation
1 5. Conclusion
6. References
+Arabic Character Recognition System Using Artificial Neural Network
+POSTERS
+SESSION: NETWORK OPERATIONS
+SESSION: ROBUST NETWORKS
+INVITED TALKS
CONFERENCE SCHEDULE
ATTENDEES
Query: text string
Search
History List:
text string (4)
Found:
Found: text, string

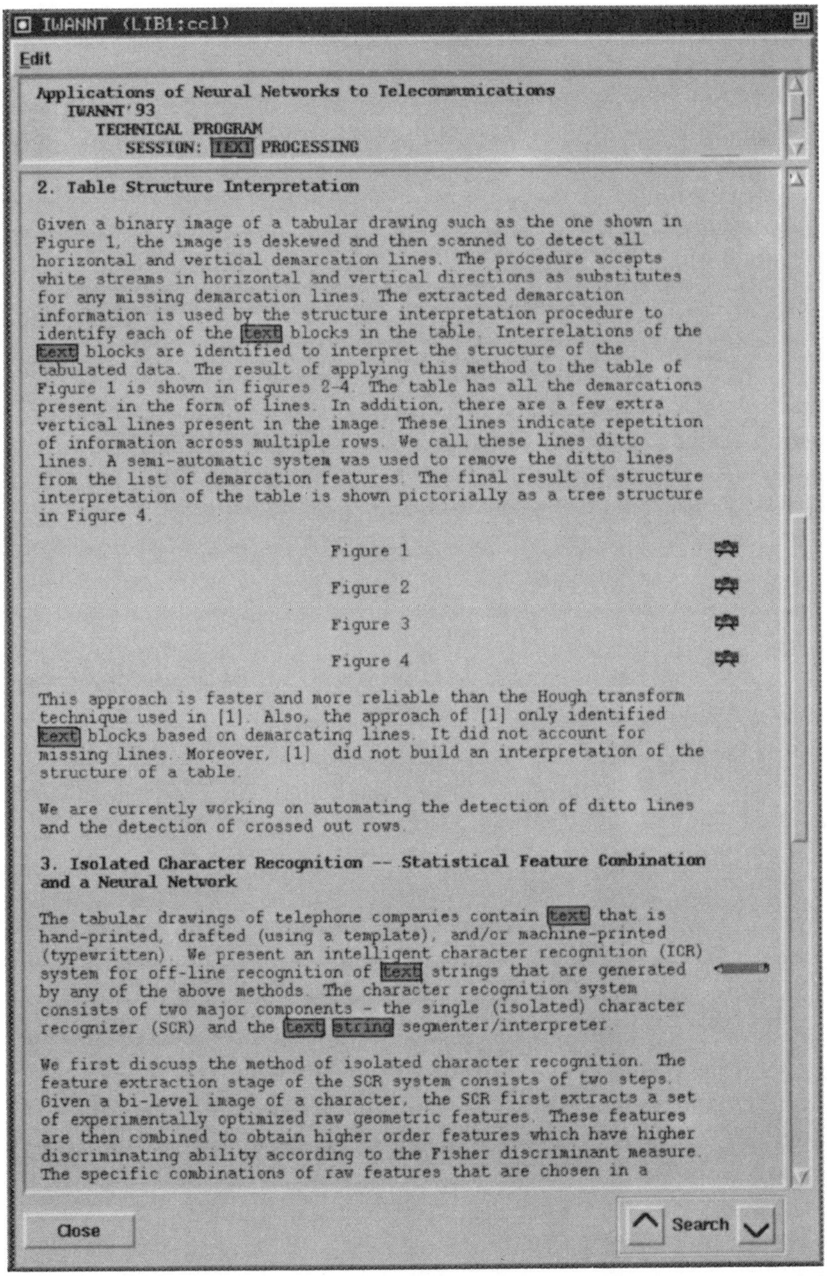

Figure 6.2. SuperBook screen display. Query terms are highlighted (boxed) in table of contents (left window) and text (right window). Images and notes are available by clicking on the icons to the right of the text. (Courtesy of Dr. Dennis Egan, Bellcore)

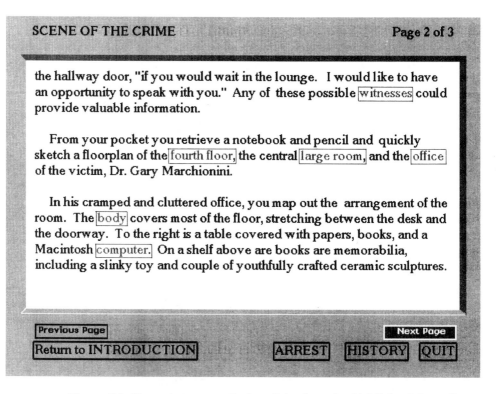

Figure 6.3. Hyperties screen display. Selection of a highlighted (boxed) text term displays an "article" on that topic. (From a group project in one of my classes at the University of Maryland)

Salomon (1991) described an interface to a large-scale news story database that includes browsing support through what they term "bird's eye views" of the database. These views are miniature displays of articles that show surrounding articles and graphics. Information seekers can scroll through these views and use visual cues to select and display the text or images in a large window. The Perseus Project has a thumbnail browser that displays up to nine miniature views of graphics objects in the corpus. Users can rapidly scan through these miniatures before selecting and displaying detailed views to study. In Figure 6.6, the nine thumbnail views for a vase that has several different images allow users to quickly select a view for detailed study or to display the next nine images.

Another approach to supporting graphical search is to let users pose a graphical query. A system developed by Garber and Grunes (1992) permits art directors to search an image database by either providing an example image to act as a template or selecting criteria from menus. This interface was designed according to a careful study of how art directors actually search for images and demonstrates how impor-

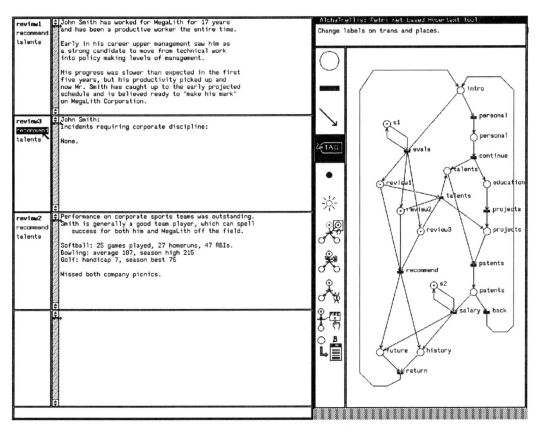

Figure 6.4. Trellis screen display. Three different text nodes are displayed in the left window panes, and a Petri graph of the network displayed in the right window shows all the hypertext links that are possible from the current state. In the figure, circles represent nodes; bars represent possible transitions; and labeled nodes with dots correspond to the displayed text. (Stotts & Furuta, 1989; used with permission of the Association for Computing Machinery)

tant this task analysis and these customized interfaces are to different problem areas. This approach is an analog of word queries, and progress in pattern-matching research may make such systems more viable.

A combined graphic and textual approach to chromosome mapping is the Image-Query interface at the Lawrence Berkeley Laboratory (U.S. Department of Energy, 1992). As part of the Chromosome Information System, this interface allows researchers to specify queries or browse through miniature icons of the images. Buttons for zooming in to different magnifications of the image and displaying textual descriptions and parameters are provided in a multiple-window environment.

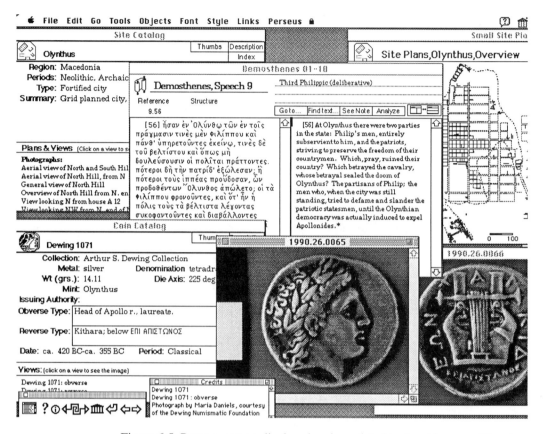

Figure 6.5. Perseus screen display showing related text and images. (Courtesy of Prof. Gregory Crane, Tufts University)

A different approach to accessing image collections is to compress image collections by displaying only the most significant elements or scenes. This is particularly useful for film or video. Rorvig (1993) described a method for "abstracting" video, that is, for selecting frames from video sequences that results in 700:1 compression for scanning visual documents. Frames are selected according to a set of visual characteristics (e.g., hue, line frequency, angle frequency) and a statistical analysis that focuses on large deviations in characteristics. Elliot and Davenport (1994) have developed a technique that displays each frame of video as a line in a composite image (block) that represents about 30 seconds of play. Thus a single glance can easily identify scene changes. The block can be viewed in real time as the video plays, which allows viewers to monitor specific patterns. Although users must become familiar with decoding the graphical patterns, this system illustrates another way to compress video by using only specific components of each video frame.

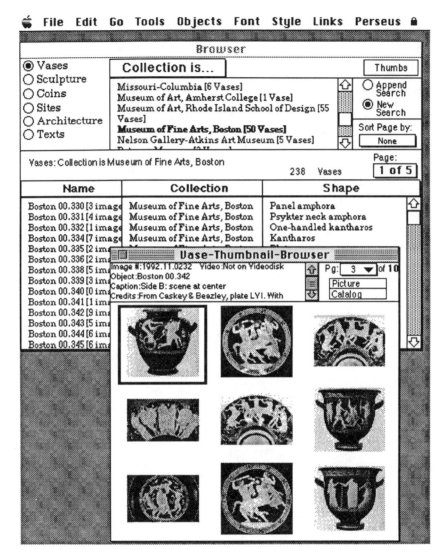

Figure 6.6. Perseus screen display showing thumbnail images. (Courtesy of Prof. Gregory Crane, Tufts University)

These examples demonstrate that the current state of work on browsing graphics databases is concentrating on finding workable representations and mechanisms, that is, technical developments. As more technical alternatives are developed, they will advance our understanding of how users work in graphics databases and what principles should guide interface design. Such progress is crucial as video and other moving images are included in digital libraries and video-on-demand services.

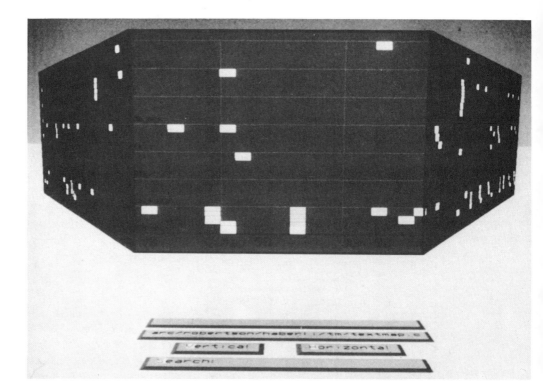

Figure 6.7. Perspective Wall screen display. (Courtesy of Dr. Stuart Card, Xerox Corporation)

### *Visual queries and browsers*

Representing information graphically has long been recognized as a powerful way to aid understanding and dissemination (Tufte, 1990; Tukey, 1977), and there is substantial interface work under way to develop visualization tools for scientific phenomena. Graphical approaches to information retrieval have also been proposed and developed, especially for database management systems (e.g., Fogg, 1984; Herot, 1980). Larson (1986) described a visual approach to browsing through well-structured databases. His system supports four types of browsing operations: structuring objects for examination, filtering objects, panning to nearby objects, and zooming in to different levels of detail. Users perform these operations by manipulating a graphical scheme that shows database objects and relationships. Travers (1989) developed a hypertext interface for the CYC database that uses boxes to represent hierarchical relationships among nodes. Color saturation is also used to reinforce semantic distances among outer and embedded boxes. A technique proposed by Furnas (1986) gives users ways to focus on objects of interest

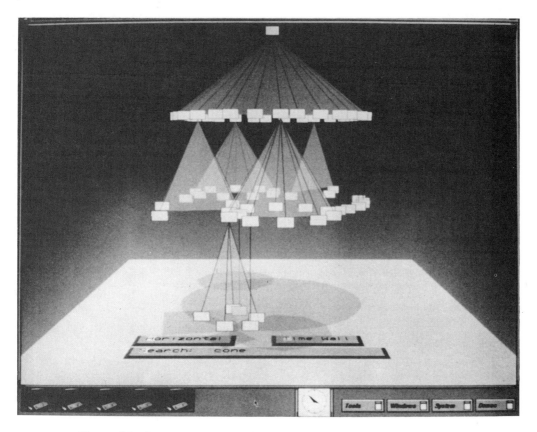

Figure 6.8. Cone Trees screen display. (Courtesy of Dr. Stuart Card, Xerox Corporation)

while maintaining a sense of context through peripheral views of the database. An intuitively appealing approach to viewing an information space, his "fisheye" views have been implemented in several systems, including SuperBook (Egan et al., 1989).

Perhaps the most extensive collection of graphical techniques was that implemented by Card, Mackinlay, and Robertson at Xerox. Based on a general cognitive model of human performance and using three-dimensional graphical techniques, their systems allow users to view and manipulate significantly more information per screen than other interfaces do. Their perspective wall (see Figure 6.7) displays three sides of a rectangular solid in perspective so that the "front" wall shows a large rectangular array of cells and the two "side" walls angle back in perspective with diminishing arrays of cells (Mackinlay, Robertson, & Card, 1991). Users can easily slide walls to bring arrays of interest into front view. Another technique (see Figure 6.8) uses "cone trees" to represent large hierarchical structures that users

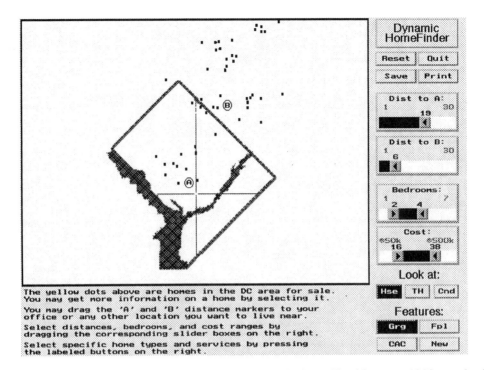

Figure 6.9. Dynamic query screen display. (Shneiderman, 1993, used with permission)

can rotate and manipulate to find information (Robertson, Mackinlay, & Card, 1991). In one example, 600 directories comprising 10,000 files were represented on a single display. These techniques offer promising directions for systems that support browsing through high-performance displays, although they require sophisticated workstations.

Another collaborative effort that involved many researchers is the work of Shneiderman and his colleagues at the University of Maryland Human–Computer Interaction Laboratory. This work applies direct manipulation techniques to information seeking under the name of *dynamic queries*. Systems that support dynamic queries provide sliders for setting interval data values and hierarchical menus to select categorical data values and immediately display the results of settings. A museum system allowed users to select types of archaeological sites, historical periods, dates of visit, and participation costs (Plaisant, 1993). Another implementation (see Figure 6.9) permits users to manipulate sliders for cost, location, number of bedrooms, and other house features, to visualize what homes were on the market (Williamson & Shneiderman, 1992). Each change of slider immediately resulted in an updated map with the available homes plotted on it. This approach is intuitive and pleasing to use, and the users in their study consistently conducted faster searches with this system than with paper or natural language interfaces. This type of system may be best for problems that lend themselves to graphical representation and have ordinal criterion values. Another representation called *tree maps* uses horizontal and vertical slices and color to display large hierarchical structures such as directories of files (Shneiderman, 1990). Using this technique, directories of over 1000 files can be browsed through according to various parameters such as size and file type.

### Information retrieval techniques and mechanisms to support browsing

Although traditional information retrieval research is aimed at optimizing analytical search, often omitting informal browsing strategies, many of the fruits of information retrieval work may be applied to systems that invite and support browsing across documents. The most obvious information retrieval advance to support browsing is relevance feedback. As described in chapter 2, relevance feedback adjusts users' queries based on assessments of retrieved documents. In a review of relevance feedback, Harmon (1992) reported that variations of relevance feedback doubled the performance of the systems she tested. The best techniques were those that expanded queries rather than simply reweighting terms in the original query. She found that expanding with only 20 selected terms was superior to expanding with all terms. This seems to be another example of a law of diminishing returns in specifying terms in queries – more terms are generally better but after a point, too many terms either lead to intolerably low precision or do not yield any additional recall. Systems with relevance feedback interfaces include Salton's SMART system (Salton & McGill, 1983), Frisse's Dynamic Medical Handbook (Frisse & Cousins, 1989), Williams's RABBIT system (Williams, 1984), Walker's OKAPI (Walker, 1987), and Erickson and Salomon's Desktop Information System (Erickson & Salomon, 1991). The Wide Area Information Server (WAIS) interface has become popular for searching Internet sources and uses relevance feedback (Kahle & Medlar, 1991). Relevance feedback is like browsing in that it depends on feedback as the user explores and probes the system interactively. The underlying mechanisms of relevance feedback depend on statistical or probabilistic techniques, but these may be hidden from the end users. However, future systems could permit sophisticated browsers to manipulate the underlying relevance feedback parameters (e.g., how terms are reweighted for query modification, what terms are used for query expansion).

Another collection of information retrieval techniques connected with browsing interfaces are clustering algorithms. Salton (1989) noted that browsing is promoted by the proximity of similar documents that results from clustering (see Rasmussen, 1992, for a discussion of different approaches to clustering). Cutting, Karger, Pedersen, and Tukey (1992) reported a technique that applies clustering to allow

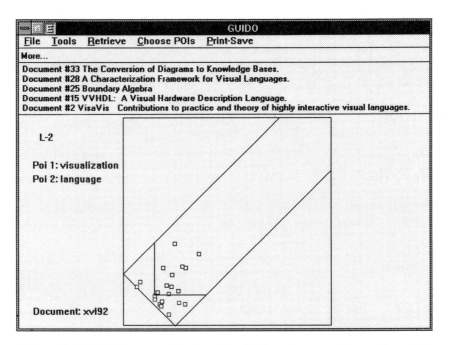

Figure 6.10. GUIDO screen display. The display plots one of several possible clusterings (this one is based on Euclidean distance similarity metric) for documents, using "visualization" as a point of interest for the horizontal axis and "language" as a point of interest for the vertical axis. The user can select cutoff bounds (the right angle bounds disjunctively; at least one distance is within the bound). Clicking on a square displays specific documents. (Courtesy of Prof. Robert Korfhage and Assadaporn Nuchprayoon, University of Pittsburgh)

browsing of large databases. Their "scatter and gather" technique is specifically designed to assist users in exploring open-ended or ill-defined problems and to work in conjunction with analytical approaches as needed. They contrast searching an index in a book that requires a term or query with examining a table of contents that offers a sense of what types of questions the book may answer, and they base the browsing part of their scatter and gather approach on the latter. The basic approach is to use a clustering algorithm to scatter the collection into document clusters and to report the cluster summaries to the user. Based on which clusters the user chooses for further study, the system gathers these clusters and reclusters them to produce a smaller scattering. The process continues until there is a small number of documents that can be examined individually.

The increasing computational power of computers has prompted some researchers to combine sophisticated information retrieval techniques with graphics

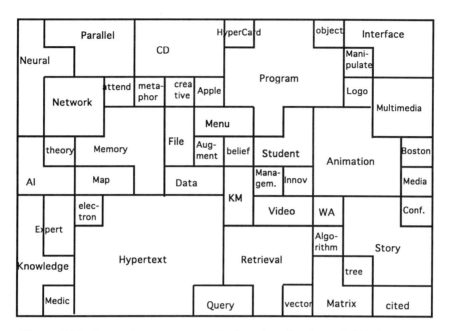

Figure 6.11. Semantic map screen display. A collection of 660 documents generated this map, which reveals major research interests. Area sizes indicate relative frequency of occurrence of concepts and juxtapositions of regions indicate co-occurrence associations. (Courtesy of Prof. Xia Lin, University of Kentucky)

display techniques to support browsing. Korfhage (1991) created a technique for reducing the high dimensionality of a document space to display graphically the space according to the users' queries and profiles. The queries and profiles are reference points from which all other documents are distanced according to similarity metrics. High-resolution display of the distance space allows users to view clusters of documents according to their own queries and profiles rather than some absolute clustering based on frequencies and co-occurrences alone. Korfhage's GUIDO system illustrates a pioneering approach to personalized graphical views of semistructured document collections (see Figure 6.10).

Lin (1993) proposed a framework for presenting two-dimensional displays of document collections that is based on a neural network clustering of documents. He used Kohonen's feature map algorithm to cluster documents and prepare a graphical map that represents topic importance by area size and topic similarity by proximity. Instead of ranking documents in linear fashion based on some similarity measure, the algorithm maps the collection's high-dimensional vector representation of titles to a two-dimensional map that preserves similarity through geometric distance. The resulting map defines areas for topical clusters that are juxtaposed with semantically similar clusters and whose areas are proportional to the frequency of occurrence in the corpus (see Figure 6.11). Lin compared his computer-generated maps with maps produced by humans and found that the subjects could use the different maps equally effectively to locate titles. Both the computer-generated maps and those produced by humans were superior to a random map. Although generating such maps is computationally expensive at this time, such maps offer good possibilities for supporting the informal information-seeking strategies collated under the term *browsing*.

In this chapter we defined browsing strategies and contrasted them with analytical strategies. Four different browsing strategies were defined according to how the various information-seeking factors interact during information seeking. Limitations of browsing were discussed, and the importance of the environment was illustrated with examples of systems that support various aspects of browsing. Clearly, browsing strategies and analytical strategies complement each other, and systems should support the preferences and abilities of diverse users. In the next chapter we examine how such systems can be developed.

# 7

## Designing support for browsing: A research and development perspective

*Many things difficult to design provide easy performance.*
                              Samuel Johnson, *Rasselas*

*Imagination is more important than knowledge.*
                              Albert Einstein, *On Science*

Many specific system features have been shown to invite and support browsing as an information-seeking strategy. We are beginning to acquire a set of techniques that define what is possible in designing such features. Determining what is optimal for different users, tasks, and settings requires systematically testing techniques across the range of information-seeking factors. Because browsing requires users to coordinate physical and mental activities, systems that support browsing must solve both technical and conceptual problems. Technical challenges such as the computational power needed to manipulate huge vector spaces on-the-fly and display problems such as resolution limitations, refresh and scroll rates, window sizes, and juxtapositions are difficult enough in isolation but must be coordinated with other technical problems such as mechanisms for selection and control of information and conceptual problems such as what the best representations of meaning are for specific information items and what should be displayed at what time, in what form, and at what level of granularity. Programs of research are needed that address the technical problems of designing interaction styles for browsing, that determine the physiological and psychological boundaries of browsing activities, and that test various representations for browsable information. These are technical, user, and organizational areas, respectively. Although different researchers and groups typically specialize in one of these problem areas, ultimately the support for browsing will depend on integrating results from all three.

Developments in physical interfaces, especially in integrating multiple devices (e.g., Jacob et al., 1993) and progress in designing screen displays, metaphors, and dialogues will be informed by answers to questions about human capabilities and needs. Consider the following questions: What are the perceptual and cognitive limits of recognition for symbols and images? What are the trade-offs between time and accuracy? What are the implications of these trade-offs for the immediate use of information versus its retention? How many windows can be concurrently scanned for different types of targets? What are the temporal and spatial limits on concurrent scanning and monitoring? Answers to these and similar questions about physiological–psychological interactions will help designers develop or select

139

better physical and conceptual interfaces. Although we have good measures of perceptual abilities in reading (e.g., Rayner, 1978), text editing (e.g., Card et al., 1983), and other cognitive tasks, our understanding of how perception is used in different browsing strategies is quite limited. In addition, the results are mixed regarding the ways that humans can rapidly recognize and understand information and research on cognitive processing for all types of information activity remains a long-term problem.

Of particular interest here are conceptual interfaces in general and the ways that information is represented and managed by browsers in particular. Because browsing is more data driven and less goal driven than analytical search is, it is critical that data be well represented and easily managed. By *well represented,* we mean that appropriate data types are provided; information is given at appropriate levels of granularity; and information is displayed succinctly and aesthetically using organizational structures that are appropriate to the task and user. Also, because the same information can be useful for different types of problems and for different users, these representations should be flexible and adaptable. By *easily managed,* we mean that usable and effective mechanisms are provided for access (specifying representations), display (organizing representations), and manipulation (linking, filtering, aggregating, and analyzing information representations). In addition, it is essential that systems offer an instant response as users apply these mechanisms and that tools for cutting, pasting, saving, and tracing search history be available.

The representation problem is fundamental to information science and addresses how information is organized and articulated mentally and in the world. In particular, we are concerned with providing a closer mapping between information seekers' mental representations of an information problem and representations of information objects in a search system. Because cognitive science offers a variety of theories about how humans represent knowledge, it is prudent to take a design approach that provides alternative representations and allows users to select from them according to their personal style, experience, and the problem at hand. Thus, the first challenge of design is to identify and create useful alternative representations for information. The cost of such an approach is that users must remain active and make choices as the information seeking progresses. This trade-off leads immediately to the second design challenge – supporting the user in understanding and manipulating the alternative representations. This chapter considers the problems of representation and mechanisms in systems that support browsing strategies and then calls for interfaces that support highly interactive browsing strategies as well as analytical strategies.

## Representations

Ideas find many forms of expression, and the problems associated with the representation of knowledge are central to research in information science. Whereas artificial intelligence is concerned with creating machine-manipulable structures and mapping concepts onto those structures, information seeking is most often concerned with locating and interpreting existing representations that can be manipulated by humans. Information seeking includes asking people for information, because seeking information from an expert requires locating the expert and interpreting representations generated through conversation. These representations include objects such as books, articles, photographs, discrete utterances, and films. These human-manipulable representations vary greatly in scope, time required for human processing, and physical space required for storage. To support the information-seeking process, information systems are challenged to

- Provide mechanisms for the access, display, and manipulation of information.
- Display these representations to facilitate interpretation.
- Support the extraction and manipulation of information from them.

Systems that allow information seekers to use browsing strategies provide tightly coupled representations and mechanisms so that the information subprocesses proceed in parallel and problem definition is maintained as a continuously active subprocess.

Simple systems store representations in their entirety, arranged in some specific order. For example, a file of incoming correspondence arranged chronologically in a file cabinet provides access by date, displays the entire document a page at a time, and depends fully on the information seeker for extraction and manipulation. Some systems store only surrogates, abbreviations, or summaries instead of full representations. For example, a computerized transcript file for grades summarizes many tangible representations of performance. Such a system may support access by some key (e.g., last name or identification number), may display one student's records at a time, and may support standard printing formats and possibly some computational functions across parts of the file.

More sophisticated systems separate the full representation from surrogates for these representations. For example, a card catalog provides access to books through author, title, and a few subject headings; displays a full bibliographic record on one or more cards (screens in the case of OPACs); and offers little extraction or manipulation help beyond screen dumps. Current archival practice has at least three main levels of representation, ranging from directories (e.g., the Directory of Archives and Manuscript Repositories in the United States), holdings for a specific archive (e.g., record groups, series and subseries in an archive), and specific record groups (e.g., boxes, folders, and items). Still other systems store representations in their entirety, provide access through multiple indexes, and store pointers or entire representations that are related. For example, consider a system that stores the full text of a book together with reviews of the book and a citation file for other works that cite the book. Access may be provided at many levels;

display may be simply scrollable or highly controllable by the user; and extraction may go beyond cut and paste to grammatical analysis.

These examples illustrate the range of possibilities for representation, and designers of systems that support browsing strategies must consider both the type of collection and the types of surrogates in meeting the challenges of access, display, extraction, and manipulation. Collections may contain full representations (primary information), only surrogate information (secondary information), or various levels of each. Electronic systems have increased the likelihood of including both secondary and primary information, but designers have yet to grapple with the distinctions of across-document and within-document browsing. Surrogates may be descriptive or semantic, and either type may be extracted automatically or crafted by hand.

A system may represent an item in full or in part. A book may be represented simply by its title or in its entirety depending on the users' needs and resources. Clearly, some levels of representation are useful for locating a specific item and others for studying or browsing within that item. A system may also present alternative representations of the same item. For example, software comes in different versions for different platforms; textual documents may be represented as simple ASCII files or as formatted text with different fonts and styles; and data sets may be displayed in different tabular or graphical forms. Similarly, a text may be represented by its words or by SGML codes or page layout pictures, depending on what is to be done with the document. Information objects may also be represented with added value – with extensions and links to objects beyond themselves. A fundamental difference between paper and electronic systems is how electronic systems blur the distinctions among these different types of representations. Because it was earlier argued that browsing blurs the distinctions among information-seeking subprocesses, the combination of electronic environments and browsing makes for highly fluid and amorphous information seeking.

Systems aid browsing across documents primarily by providing partial representations or surrogates. In across-document browsing, salient surrogates for documents help the user decide whether or not to examine the document more closely. There are many such representations used in manual libraries and databases, and electronic systems offer new classes of surrogates to aid users in browsing collections. These representations can be classified as *descriptive* or *semantic*.

Descriptive surrogates identify the attributes of items. Consider the following attributes: Creator attributes such as author, translator, producer, director, animator, editor, conductor, performer, programmer, designer, or artist can be useful in assessing the relevance of items. Creator attributes are subsets of information objects; they can be extracted directly. Attributes associated with creators, such as institution, cultural background, historical environment, philosophical perspective, or methodological approach also may be useful in judging whether to examine objects more carefully. Notes on creators are especially useful when the information seeker is not an expert in the domain and does not know the people active in the field. These attributes may be part of the object or an added value for the purposes of retrieval. Metainformation such as the medium of representation (e.g., text, video, computer graphic, sound, multimedia) may be a useful attribute for quickly identifying or eliminating large portions of a collection. Physical attributes such as size, number of images, running time, and provenance may also indicate potential relevance and so are especially useful in retrieving physical objects. Other descriptive attributes are copyright date, version or edition, and vendor or publisher.

Semantic attributes represent the meaning of objects in a collection. For text collections, titles and subject headings are perhaps the most valuable indicators of possible relevance, and many systems list documents by title as a default key. For image collections, thumbnail miniatures, low-resolution surrogates, or video abstracts may serve as browsable surrogates for objects in the collection. The main problem with semantic representations is capturing the "aboutness" of an information object (Saracevic, 1976). A major area of information science research is devoted to discovering methods for representing the meanings of objects in a collection and to determining to what extent these representations may be automatically extracted. It seems clear that for complex objects such as books, articles, and films, the best descriptors are tied to the information problem rather than to some generic classification (Soergel, 1985). This is why systems that invite browsing must represent information according to individual users' needs. An ongoing research problem is how much preprocessing can be done and how much must be done on-the-fly during the interaction between the user and the system. Systems that support analytical search strategies will be able to use more preprocessing, and those that support browsing strategies will require more on-the-fly processing.

Descriptive and semantic representations provide important cues to information seekers as they browse across document collections. Both types of representation can also be useful for within-document browsing, but current systems do little beyond paging or scrolling to support within-document browsing. Systems that support descriptive and semantic indexing should allow users to select from many documents and to move into, around, and back out of those documents in seamless ways. The current systems require users to execute a discrete set of actions using different input–output mechanisms at each step. Queries are typically specified according to a query language or from screen, and a list of titles or other surrogates is then displayed on a different screen or window. Different menus or commands are then used for browsing through the retrieved list and selecting an item for display. This results in yet another screen or window with possibly another set of commands or menus to browse through the item and return to a previous step. In electronic environments, representations for collections and specific objects should be represented and controlled in common and compatible ways.

Representations are, by definition, structured to support processing, and these structures can be used to support within-document browsing. Some of these structures are provided by the creator, and some are added by publishers or editors to produce a final, "published" document. Textual databases such as books or articles may contain abstracts, tables of contents, section headings, paragraphs, sentences, quotations, footnotes, indexes, sidebars, tables and figures, appendices, and reference lists that browsers may find useful for extracting gist or focusing on specific details. Electronic environments permit users to display any or all of these structural components in a variety of orders and juxtapositions. Users, should be able, for example, to display and scan only footnotes or tables according to their needs.

Software also provides many structural elements that could be useful to those seeking information in the code. Global and local variable declarations, functions, procedures, run-time ranges, print ranges, and comments all help users understand the program. Likewise, documentation, tutorials, and user support services help end users understand and use programs. Modular programming techniques and the integration of tutorials and online help have complicated the examination of software codes, making a single application program more like a collection of documents and thus blurring within- and across-document searching.

Artifacts of the electronic format may also offer structural enhancements to aide users even more. Standard general markup language codes (SGML) used for typesetting purposes may be useful representations in electronic texts and hypertexts, allowing users to search or scan according to code (Raymond, 1992). For example, searching for all quoted passages or for boldface text may help users locate specific types of information according to their particular needs. The visual layout of documents may also aid users in identifying parts of documents for browsing. One prototype document image analysis system uses page layout formats for specific journals to segment text for recognition and browsing (Nagy, Seth, & Viswanathan, 1992). The system lets users select documents based on pictures of page structures. Thus, information seekers can use their visual memory for journal layouts to aid in browsing. Although the prototype requires handcrafted descriptions for hundreds of production rules for each journal layout grammar, the system demonstrates how spatial structure cues can be added to electronic search systems to help information seekers identify and select potentially relevant documents during across-document browsing and then to move to particular sections of the text itself. These examples show how structural aspects of documents can enhance within-document browsing and may be extended to across-document browsing as well. In addition, they illustrate how electronic technology not only allows new levels of representation for authors and their collaborators but also lets compilers and individual users manipulate those representations and add new ones.

Besides taking advantage of structures in paper or electronic documents, representations may be enhanced; alternatives may be provided; and new representations may be added to support browsing. One type of enhancement is to offer new representations that augment abstracts and other compressed expressions. Florance

(1992) proposed extracts for the medical literature to help physicians use the medical research literature in the clinic. Her extracts are frame-based representations of epidemiologic, diagnostic, treatment, and learning information in articles and permit a large community of information seekers to examine the literature from any of these specific perspectives, depending on their immediate needs. These extracts are similar to the concept of database views, as they provide a problem-oriented and personalized entry to a database.

Value may be added to documents or databases in a number of ways. Reviews, apparatus criticuses, commentaries, forewords or prefaces, movie outtakes or montages, demo modes, and sample chords give information seekers additional information for decision making. In traditional environments, these added values are carefully crafted as part of the production and marketing process or as part of the growth of a scholarly field. Other forms of added value include notes on allusions or metaphors, bibliometric features such as documents that cite the document of interest or sets of documents that are cocited with it. Hypertext links and network gateways serve as obvious electronic connections to related materials that add value to specific information objects. In fact, the links or network nodes themselves provide useful interpretive value because they make relationships explicit. Special-interest group lists provide structures for extended conversations among various participants, and specific argument threads may be isolated and linked together according to the users' needs. Consider a video collection. Descriptive representations that are part of the entire representation include title, scenes, visual effects, and credits. A form of video translation is illustrated if the scenes are shown as compressed (e.g., Quicktime) displays. Value may be added in many ways, including descriptions, reviews, awards, promotional "rushes," and specially constructed montage abstracts. Although electronic representations are not necessary for most of these attributes, the benefits of electronic technology accrue by making it easy or automatic to create additional and alternative representations.

Electronic environments offer end users possibilities for easily adding value. For example, in textual databases, users can form concordances, run grammar analyses, compute readability indexes, or run clustering analyses to examine documents according to their specific needs. Spatial management systems (geographic information systems) permit users to produce their own thematic maps rather than simply accessing and viewing existing maps (Laurini & Thompson, 1992). In hypermedia databases, users can produce simple node-link ratios, link plots that represent the degree of connectivity across all nodes (Bernstein, Bolter, Joyce, & Mylonas, 1991), or in–out indices that indicate which nodes serve more as indexes and which more as references (Botafogo & Shneiderman, 1991). Nielsen (1990a) suggested combining word frequencies within nodes (intrinsic weights) and nodes directly linked to those nodes (extrinsic links) as indicators of relevance to guide hypertext navigation. These added values could be provided by the creators, but electronic systems could give end users tools to add these values themselves.

The possibilities for added values grow in shared environments. For example, in a library, borrowers could be asked to provide subject headings, abstracts, or commentaries for items, and these could be made part of the total document. Books that borrowers underline or highlight offer benefits to some users but may distract and annoy others. Defacing books is moot in an electronic environment because comments and highlights can be saved separately and linked as desired by the user. However, the usefulness of other users' commentaries or markings still depends on who those users are and what their information problems and goals were when they entered their commentary. For this reason, user contributions to a document must be accompanied by profiles or contextual information about those users and their goals in using the materials, leading to privacy concerns. Electronic environments make these types of added values in shared environments much more feasible technically. If social and economic issues are solved, users can choose to display or hide other users' contributions or select them according to various sorting and filtering criteria.

This discussion illustrates the many levels, alternatives, and added types of representations that designers and users must consider. A book can be examined at a coarse level (e.g., the title alone) or a fine level (e.g., the full text,) depending on whether an information seeker is browsing across documents or within the document. Document structure (e.g., table of contents, headings) may be used for examination, and additional related information (e.g., a book review) may be sought. These various representations may be useful to information seekers locating a book in a large collection, determining whether to examine it more closely, and examining it for relevant information. In general, manual environments offer basic support for access, good display characteristics, and little support for extraction and manipulation. Electronic environments complicate this situation in several ways. Electronic environments support across-document browsing by providing multiple descriptive and semantic surrogates. They are presently quite weak in supporting within-document browsing, but as more ways to take advantage of document structures are discovered, this may improve. Because the same physical display device is used to view the database, the text, and any related items, electronic environments tend to blur the physical distinctions of across- and within-document browsing. Although it is advantageous to click a mouse and immediately display the full text or a cited article, the interface must clearly demarcate these representations and provide the selection mechanisms themselves. The trend toward interconnected systems offers opportunities and challenges for linking representations according to a variety of relational conditions and managing the representations themselves in addition to the content of interest. Most important, electronic systems can provide alternative representations and access mechanisms that enable users to manipulate, analyze, and re-represent information according to their particular needs. Because electronic systems also may allow the users to change the documents, entirely new classes of problems, especially for representations that depend on preprocessing, are created. Currently, users find themselves in roles ranging from overwhelmed kids in a candy store to mystical information alchemists. Controlling the richness of representations requires interface mechanisms, and at present, we have little guidance as to how to best design such mechanisms.

### Mechanisms for managing representations

Electronic environments offer alternative representations that can be controlled by users. Users can choose what levels of detail to display and what types of added value to include during information seeking. All these structural elements are useful for specific types of information-seeking conditions but having them all available at once may actually lead to overload and confusion. Consider, for example, a hymn book that provides a dozen indexes for various types of users and purposes and an electronic version in which these preprocessed indexes are available and users can create their own on-the-fly. The possibilities increase for spending all one's time in pointer information rather than ever getting to the primary information. Clearly, a major problem is how best to organize and control these representations. Electronic environments, on the one hand, exacerbate the problem by providing detailed sets of options and, on the other hand, offering new mechanisms for managing the representations.

In addition to other mechanisms for storage, transmission, and help, systems must provide a range of mechanisms for managing representations. From the end users' point of view, mechanisms include widgets and tools for

- Specifying constraints on the universe of information available (e.g., queries) in order to access relevant information.
- Managing screen and window displays.
- Linking, filtering, aggregating, and analyzing information representations.

The following discussion is meant to provoke questions and raise research issues as much as to guide designers. We assume a graphical user interface workstation connected to Internet resources over a high-speed channel. The universe of available information includes large, well-structured databases, data directories, semi-structured files, and specific objects such as programs and electronic mail messages. Three general classes of mechanisms allow users to search and browse in such an environment. These classes are based on visual metaphors for different problem-solving tactics that people use in the information-seeking process. The three classes of mechanisms are not mutually exclusive and may be used together during information, but each offers specific advantages to the information seeker. Probing mechanisms for quickly locating specific items such as words or records have advantages in well-defined information-seeking situations and for identifying general neighborhoods for browsing. Mechanisms for zooming and panning in, out, and across levels of detail enable users to go across and within documents to meet their information needs and manage displays. Mechanisms for filtering and restricting information allow users to limit levels of detail or types of documents and manipulate information.

### Probes

*Probes* are specific investigations launched by information seekers, ranging from simple queries in a database to multiple-step examinations of segments of the information space. Probing is a form of hypothesis testing – hypotheses are formed, posed to the system, and results reflected on. In the simplest case, hypotheses take the form of questions rather than predictions, for example, asking the system whether a word matches words in the database. String search has repeatedly proved its usefulness in information seeking and represents the first significant advantage of searching in electronic environments. String search allows users to probe a database or document for highly specific units – word fragments, words, or phrases. Full-text word search mechanisms are similarly useful for testing matches in textual databases. Full-text search allows users to launch highly focused, complex analytical queries or highly interactive *guess-and-go* probes. Analytical probing of a database is the basis for most online systems today, and highly focused, complex queries allow extremely precise predictions to be tested in huge databases. The guess-and-go approach was observed repeatedly in our studies of children and adults using different full-text environments. Information seekers use a word or phrase to find matches in document collections and then use browsing strategies to examine the context of those matches for relevance. This simple approach has proved remarkably effective in small and medium-size collections and should certainly be supported in text-oriented systems.

We can imagine, however, more sophisticated types of probes for large collections and more complex problems. Systematic queries to a bibliographic database and the subsequent merging of result lists are a common way of probing databases to determine coverage or of discovering neighborhoods or research fronts. Furthermore, relevance feedback may be used. For example, words or phrases from existing objects can be "picked up" using a pointing device and launched into a database. Queries may also be restricted to specific types of sources for similar purposes. For example, the MEDLINE system allows queries to be limited to review articles. This function is considered more fully in the section on filtering and illustrates how the different mechanisms overlap and work together in practice.

Because Boolean queries cause users so much difficulty, another direct manipulation approach may be used for established systems based on inverted indexes and exact-match retrieval; for example, to allow users to specify single-term queries that return separate windows of document sets. These windows can then be dragged to merge or overlap. In the case of merging, one window can be dragged to the start or end of another and the records combined and sorted. In the case of overlap, one window can be placed on top of the other with only the overlapping records displayed. In both cases, easy undo features must be provided so that users feel comfortable quickly and directly merging (OR) and overlapping (AND) document sets in exploratory ways.

Instead of focusing a probe on a single database, it can be broadcast. A single query can be sent to multiple databases; for example, the WAIS interface (Kahle & Medlar, 1991) allows queries to be sent to any number of databases. It may be informative to study both redundancies and unique results from the different databases. Queries posted to listservs are good examples of probes that use technology to broadcast to a specific community of people who may be able to help the information seeker solve the information problem.

More sophisticated probes may take the form of agents or "knowbots." Agents have simple inference capabilities and can be given more than a word or phrase by the information seeker. An agent launched for a specific purpose may carry a form filled out by the information seeker which serves as a profile of the information need. When matches are found, inference rules are applied to the weights and conditions in the form to determine whether to add the matching object to the report of results. More complex agents can be imagined that remain active and regularly report results. These types of probes may be considered to be *selective-dissemination-of-information agents* that keep people apprised of developments in specific areas of interest. Further speculation leads to anthropomorphic icons that engage the information seeker in dialogues to determine rule-setting parameters, conceptual clusters of words and phrases identified and weighted as a kind of dynamic thesaurus, specific constraints or value assessments for information sources, and highly relevant "pearls" that act as exemplars. As is always the case with imagination and speculation, the engineering problems are significant. (See the July 1994 issue of *Communications of the Association for Computing Machinery* for a series of articles on agents.) Building user models for such agents is a huge challenge because the efforts to date have been stymied by defining what the essential components of generic models are, when they should be applied, what level of granularity should be included, how they should be evaluated, and human adaptability to situations in general (Allen, 1990; Daniels, 1986). Furthermore, management of agents will itself require time and effort by users. In addition, many of the serendipitous fruits of information seeking may be lost if information seekers limit their time to profile-specific documents.

Probes may be supported by many different interaction styles. Command languages are most obvious and exemplify the well-known trade-offs between difficulty in learning and efficiency in use. Natural-language processing seems obvious for asking questions but may promote imprecision and sloppiness in stating hypotheses. It is unlikely that query articulation will benefit much from verbal or typed language capabilities, but verbal dialogues that clarify and define the problem seem promising. Form fill-in and query-by-example interfaces offer a rich context for designing probes and will continue to find wide application for well-defined problems. Menu systems severely limit expression but offer information seekers explicit categories or vocabulary for shaping a probe. These are particularly helpful if domain-dependent hierarchical sets are provided, such as the object-search menus described in the Perseus system in the previous chapter. The advantages of direct manipulation for maps and other physical/spatial domains are obvious. Direct manipulation interfaces may also allow users to directly construct probes by "picking up" words or objects, placing the probe into sources, and possibly watching the activity, but it is unclear what benefits it offers other than physical ease of selection and placement. It is even less clear how useful the virtual reality mechanisms will be that allow users to launch themselves as probes into the information space.

Probes seem most suitable for across-document searching and finding neighborhoods or entry points for browsing tactics, although some subjects in our studies of full-text searching said they would like to do string searches in a retrieved document. Probes are the main mechanism used in today's retrieval systems because in the simplest case, they are queries. They also lend themselves to the full range of interface styles. Probes are most useful in query formulation and execution processes and must be augmented with display mechanisms and manipulation mechanisms.

### Zooms and pans

A natural metaphor for displaying different levels of representation is a camera that allows users to zoom in and out of levels of detail and to pan across a scene. If representations of information objects are strictly nested, it makes sense to move up and down the levels of representation by mapping the screen to a lens that may be zoomed in and out at different levels of detail. A *zoom* is a mechanism for changing display by moving up and down levels of representation (e.g., from document list to a specific document). A *pan* is a complementary mechanism for changing the display by moving within a level of representation (e.g., from one part of a text to another).

The zoom metaphor may map the lens onto physical levels of detail or onto an alterative hand-crafted or computed representation. Zooming within physical levels is illustrated by the RightPages system, which displays journal covers and allows users to zoom in to tables of contents and then to full text (Story, O'Gorman, Fox, Schaper, & Jagadish, 1992). In their system, a "zoom in" and a "zoom out" button are provided to permit moving among the three levels of representation. Many other application packages have zoom mechanisms for moving in and out of physical levels of detail (e.g., *Virtual Museum,* Apple, 1992). Zooming has also been used as a metaphor for moving across alternative representations or views of a specific level. For example, the European Space Agency's Information Retrieval Service offers a zoom command that allows users to examine subsets of retrieved sets ordered according to frequency of occurrences for various attributes such as subject heading or date (Ingwersen, 1984). Many other systems (e.g., Microsoft Bookshelf) use zoom to move from hit list to specific entry and back out.

For representations that are not hierarchical but, rather, alternative or added value, the pan may be appropriate. Just as a camera can zoom in or out, it may be made to move laterally rather than in and out. Panning facilities would admit paging within a document or moving to a related document. Zooming and panning provide a powerful visual metaphor for many browsing activities. Systematic observation is a powerful problem-solving strategy and underlies this set of control mechanisms that permit information seekers to examine a field of view and move across different fields of view.

A particularly interesting interface that uses zooming as an interaction metaphor is the PAD system (Perlin, 1991) and the PAD++ descendant (Bederson, 1994). This system treats the screen as an infinitely scalable surface. Notes and addendums can be squeezed between any other objects in recursive fashion by zooming the screen in and out. This is especially useful for nested data such as document citations, outlines, texts, and notes. The continuously zoomable interface allows the user to select different views easily. It also illustrates an amplification of human eye–hand coordination by enabling graphical tools to be applied at any level of magnification. Common paint programs allow two or a few levels of drawing detail (e.g., moving from full size, to 50% size, to "fat bits" scales), but PAD supports a continuous and potentially infinite set of levels.

Zooming and panning lend themselves to direct manipulation interaction styles. Users apply perceptual feedback to determine where to focus and thus have direct control over the environment. This control is costly, however, in very large databases because so much information must be perceived, if only briefly. Zooming and panning may thus be best used in small- or medium-scale environments or after analytical or guess-and-go strategies have identified a promising neighborhood. Several interface design problems related to how zooms and pans are implemented must be solved. For example, should a zoom button work like a fast-forward button and provide continuous movement through different levels, or should it move in a stepwise fashion through the levels? The stepwise implementation is technically easier, but what would be the costs to the user? Similarly, how much of a level should be shown, and how long should it be displayed for users to make decisions about zooming further?

Panning is particularly good for within-document browsing, and zooming provides natural opportunities for users to move easily across reasonable numbers of documents as well. As boundaries among specific documents, ancillary materials, and document collections continue to dissolve, effects on users must be studied to determine whether interfaces that support zooming and panning should provide clear distinctions as objects are displayed.

### Filters and templates

Probes are particularly good mechanisms for accessing representations, and zooming/panning are particularly good at managing the display of representations. *Templates* are mechanisms that limit what is probed or displayed and are particularly useful for filtering information. Since both filters and templates are used as metaphors for the function of filtering information, both will be considered here.

Information seeking for the purpose of learning or acquiring knowledge or for open-ended tasks is not so much a problem of finding information as it is of filtering out irrelevant information. Even rather narrow fields of interest generate huge volumes of information that may be relevant only to the needs of experts in those fields. The challenge is to use one's knowledge of the field to ignore most of the information available and focus on what is most pertinent to one's needs. Much of the work on information filters (e.g., Fischer & Stevens, 1991; Lai, Malone, & Yu, 1988; Malone, Grant, & Turbak, 1986) has focused on ways to manage incoming streams of information such as electronic mail or Internet broadcast news postings. Belkin and Croft (1992) argued that information filtering is conceptually congruent to information retrieval and that techniques for retrieval should be useful for filtering. They contended that principles for information retrieval apply to incoming streams of information as well as to the usual purpose of searching out information in different locations. According to this view, the user profile is synonymous with the query in information retrieval.

It is natural to use filtering metaphors such as light and sound filters or chemical solution filters to represent the filtering process and the interface icons that initiate them. For example, Young and Shneiderman (1993) implemented a filter-flow interface for database queries that proved superior to a SQL query language for novice users. Users controlled the flow of water through a system by selecting attribute values as filters and arranging them in linear (Boolean AND) or parallel (Boolean OR) arrangements. The visual effects and attribute selection presumably combined to improve the users' understanding and performance. This system demonstrates the visual use of the filter concept to augment probing mechanisms.

We can imagine other metaphors for filtering, for example, a recycling metaphor. Consider a toolbox organized around tools for sorting and organizing objects. The toolbox might contain sieves for separating coarse and fine objects; shaker boxes used to order items according to some weight (e.g., frequency of term occurrence, length of document, cost); a set of specialized magnets used to grab all items with a specific property (e.g., a Boolean query, all photos taken before 1936); catalysts that interact with items to eliminate unwanted objects, highlight those with specific characteristics, or change representation (e.g., dissolve all items from a specific journal, change all tabular data to bar graphs); and conveyor belts to support hand sorting of various objects (e.g., rapid visual browsing of documents).

Just as simple inference capabilities can be added to probes, they can also be added to filters. These filters may be more readily compared with sentinels instead of active agents. Sentinels can "listen" for specific classes of information, reject most, and classify other information units according to its rule base. Although sentinels are preferred to more active and "intelligent" agents, the same problems of specifying profiles and managing one's sentinels become an issue. Clearly, intelligent probes and the sentinels used as filters differ only metaphorically; functionally they are identical and exemplify the similarities of selective dissemination of information and information filtering.

An alternative metaphor to filters is the notion of templates. A template for drawing guides the pencil by restricting where the instrument may go. From another perspective, a template allows only viable objects or relationships to show through. For example, a spreadsheet template limits the worksheet by assigning labels, values, and relationships to each cell. We can imagine information seekers selecting or designing templates for specific databases and types of information problems and placing them over incoming streams of information or on databases intentionally accessed. For example, a medical specialist could design a template that allowed only new MEDLINE records added since the previous day to pass through. Thus, templates can be user profiles that users can directly manipulate according to their personal needs. For well-defined databases such as MEDLINE, templates are easily designed according to the database fields and are simply stored queries for automatic execution. Each template "cell" could contain verbose sets of items acceptable for that particular field. For example, dozens of medical subject headings and free-text terms could be included in a subject cell, and when that template was applied to the database alone or in combination with other templates, large numbers of records would be blocked out. The resulting set of records may be large but could be simply scanned or further restricted with other templates. In addition, computational tools could be applied to specific cells or collections of cells, for example, links to previously located documents, aggregations with related documents, and statistical or lexical analyses. The template mechanism developed with such capabilities represents what Kay (1984) described as the next generation of spreadsheets.

Another implementation of the template metaphor is exemplified by the Perseus system. Juxtaposed pull-down menus contain scrolling lists of descriptors for various object classes. These object classes were handcrafted to the classical Greek world and the resources in Perseus. For example, to locate a vase image of domestic animals, a user might pull down the object menu and select vases and then pull down the classes menu and pick animals. Menu selections restrict what parts of the database shows through in the results window. Other menus can be used in combination to restrict what remains, for example, another object menu could be used to restrict objects to the Munich and Tampa museums.

A different implementation might allow users to directly manipulate, drag, and place templates over the universe of information and immediately see what remains. The templates manipulated in this manner would need identifiers and control panels for setting or defining constraints. Using menus for categorical attributes and sliders for interval attributes seems a reasonable way to aid users in setting template constraints. Once one or more templates were in place, the settings could be adjusted and the residual information immediately perceived. Thus, placing and setting templates serve as an implementation option for what Shneiderman (1992) calls *dynamic queries.* The part of the database that is displayed depends on the parameter settings. Changing a setting with sliders or menu selections instantly redisplays the data elements that "show through" the newly configured template.

It is unlikely that any of these classes of mechanisms would be, by themselves, robust enough to support all types of browsing. Probes, filters, and templates are similar in that they require the user to specify some hypotheses or constraints to begin, whereas zooms and pans permit immediate direct manipulation. Just as information seekers apply different browsing strategies according to the task, setting, information system, and personal experience, they will want to apply different mechanisms in different situations. Balancing rich sets of alternatives against learnability costs remains a design challenge. The pros and cons of each mechanism are summarized next.

Easily manageable mechanisms are desired that let users access representations, control display, and manipulate information. Probes give good access capabilities; they allow users to specify what is wanted. Probes give generally poor display control; users either have to specify the display format as part of the probe or accept default displays. Manipulations of information such as aggregations or analyses are possible through highly qualified queries or systematic queries that produce combined sets. Filtering manipulations are possible by adding field limitations to the query. Mechanisms for probing are the most common tools that information seekers have in today's systems.

Zooms and pans provide excellent display capabilities, as they enable users to display information at various levels of granularity and in juxtapositions that meet their needs. Zooms and pans are generally poor for access in large systems because they rely on perception and the user's viewing, if only briefly, information in order to accept or reject it. Manipulations such as links may be effectively controlled with zooms and pans, but filtering, aggregation, and analysis cannot be supported with these mechanisms.

Templates provide excellent filtering capabilities, and if template cells are properly instrumented, new ranges of linking, aggregation, and analysis are possible. When used alone, access is coarse, letting all information in the database pass through, except that explicitly filtered out. Thus, templates may be unacceptable in very large databases. Filters and templates give good display control if users can instantly see the results of parameter changes, as in the case of dynamic queries.

From the information seeker's point of view, browsing in electronic environments is a problem of determining what representations to use for objects in the information universe and then examining these representations to identify relevant information or to change their choice of representation. From the system's point of view, supporting browsing is a problem of giving the user alternative representations and mechanisms for controlling them. Distinctions have been made among representations according to granularity (e.g., whole/part), form and context (e.g., different formats for the same data), and value added (e.g., addition of new representations, links to others). Generic metaphors that may be useful for organizing classes of control mechanisms have also been discussed. What is needed is a unifying metaphor for representations and mechanisms that admits both the user's and the system's points of view.

### *A geometric metaphor*

Our present conceptions of browsing are constrained by manual and paper-based systems, and it will take some time before browsing mechanisms are modeled on standard electronic system features. One way to press the search for new thinking is to start with a generic and robust mathematical model and ask how a specific problem maps onto the objects and operations of the model. Such an approach focuses the search for new discoveries and has proved useful in various scientific fields (e.g., chemical elements, new planets). A first step in this process is to choose a model and apply it as a metaphor for information seeking.

One mathematical model that has been proposed is to consider algebraic mappings from one form of information to another. Heilprin (1985) suggested that compression of information from one form to another is a fundamental phenomenon in information science. Rather than well-defined isomorphic or homomorphic mappings, he argued that a flexible similarity relation is necessary and calls such mappings *paramorphisms*. Although this model is powerful for capturing compression and decompression, a geometric model is proposed here that may be more familiar and concrete. Because one reason to present such a model is to provoke thought, familiarity should admit thought by larger segments of the community.

Geometry provides a framework for defining specific types of objects and the operations on those objects. In geometry, operations vary according to how they preserve attributes such as angle, distance, and shape. Isometries such as reflections, rotations, and translations preserve all these attributes but change the context (e.g., orientation in a plane) of objects. Projections preserve shape attributes such as the number of edges but permit attributes such as angles and distance to vary. Dilations, a special type of projection, preserve angles but not distance and yield similar figures. These represent the most obvious and numerous information compressions. Topological transformations preserve neighborhoods but not shape, distance, or angles. Mathematical systems are appealing because they offer a framework to test new ideas and to determine where components of the framework are missing. Using such a model, we may be able to define information objects and operations that behave predictably and to determine what types of objects and operations deserve the most attention for development.

Consider transformational operations defined on information objects. The most obvious operation, similar to a geometric dilation, is to represent a document at different levels of granularity. For example, moving from a bibliographic record to a table of contents, to a list of section headings, to a list of first and last sentences for all paragraphs, and finally to the full text illustrates applying four negative dilations to the document. Of course, what is preserved is not angles and shapes but concept classes and the essence of the document. Document dilations try to preserve the primary meaning or "aboutness" of a document. The greater the dilation is, the less defined the intrastructural relationships and details of the document will be, but we gain overview perspective for comparing documents (e.g., screen display real estate) and minimize the time to scan the entire representation. Abstracts, thumbnail images, and most of our examples of alternative representations and added values listed above are types of document dilations. Radiation readings from different altitudes or area resolution of photographs taken by satellites define scales that also lend themselves to dilations.

Isometries for document operation are less obvious. What is required is to keep the same representation but to change its orientation. Displaying the same document in different intermediate sets of retrieved documents or from different databases may help users view the many contexts of a document. Translations of a text by different translators or different editions of a work also illustrate such transforms. Changing images from PICT to TIFF formats or a word-processing file from one platform to another also are translations. Isometric operations may be good for images because backgrounds, colors, or brightness may be varied for good effect. Three-dimensional renderings of organs based on CAT scans are examples of rotational transforms. Different maps of the same region for different criteria such as geography, political unit, topography, vegetation type, or population density also are possible isometric transforms.

A large void exists with respect to topological transformations, which seem to be information alchemy. By posing the question, we may stimulate novel rerepresentations and mechanisms for manipulating them. Displaying tables of data as graphs is one example of such a rerepresentation. Simple reformatting is an isometry, but reformatting that provides new access may be more significant. For example, reformatting text for learners has proved effective for readers with visual perception disabilities (Stueben & Vockell, 1993). Besides varying the font sizes and adding more space between words, underlining the first words of each line helped readers with such disabilities track text more easily while reading. Another example of topological transformations is morphological variations for words. Synonymic transformations may also be considered as preserving meaning but not word form. Perhaps if this book were in electronic form, the reader could apply a customized thesaurus to systematically augment (or replace?) words.

Just as geometric objects can be combined under various composition functions, information objects can also be combined. For example, documents can be merged, integrated, or linked. Although literal merging may not be promising for text, graphic overlays have been demonstrated by using a transparency film metaphor to aid information seeking and analysis (Belge, Lokuge, & Rivers, 1993). For textual databases, composition functions may use morphological comparisons or a simple match of concordances.

## Browsing and human–computer interaction

Because browsing is both highly interactive and parallel, the interactions among the various components of the information-seeking framework are more fluid and concurrent than they are during a more formal analytical search. The nature of browsing demands interfaces that support easy and flexible control, high-quality display, and rapid response time. The close coupling of user, domain, setting, task, and system is reflected in the information-seeking process. The phases of the information-seeking process are more integrated during browsing, especially when the browsing is driven by learning, exploring, and accretion of knowledge goals.

Problem acceptance and definition are especially well integrated during browsing. Casual browsing may be initiated by recognizing and accepting the opportunity for browsing rather than some information problem or need, although as Kwasnik (1992) pointed out, goals emerge as browsing progresses. While browsing, the information problem is continually redefined, and in many cases it is the user's desire for redefinition that initiates and drives the browsing. The human–computer interface most affects these subprocesses by means of the quality of display and the system response speed. These are necessary so that the flow of interaction is not interrupted as browsers continue to get a better view of the information problem.

Search system selection during browsing may be a matter of availability or situation (e.g., whatever environmental stimuli are at hand) but typically involves information seekers making inferences about the probabilities of success of specific systems or accepting default systems based on experience. Because the environment plays a significant role in browsing strategies, information seekers must develop strategies for monitoring the degree to which they are "pulled" by the environment rather than controlling it. Hypertext linking can lead to distraction, and trivial details in "edutainment" environments can easily distract those who have a propensity for casual browsing and observational tactics. Search system selection and query formulation blur in networked environments because they both entail selection of entry points for browsing. The development of standard query languages and generic network interfaces are a first step in disassociating the interface from specific databases, but it remains doubtful whether any single, generic "window" on the universe of information will be sufficient to support the views required for all purposes and users.

As environments become larger and more complex, determining entry points becomes more crucial to finding promising conceptual neighborhoods for browsing. This is especially true in online and networked environments in which many databases may be available. One approach is to create intelligent guides to database selection. Wang (1990) designed an algorithm for a database guide to bibliographic databases in the field of business and management. His algorithm depended on characterizing the databases according to factors such as scope, coverage, and indexing. Another approach is to create mechanisms for browsing the various neighborhoods. Zoom and pan mechanisms are promising for this purpose. This approach requires high-level views of systems and reinforces the need for multiple levels of representation within and across search systems.

Query formulation, a subprocess that requires significant cognitive resources in analytical search, is manifested during browsing as identifying a neighborhood. This is a particularly crucial activity when browsing large search systems. In electronic environments, this means choosing a representation to examine. In libraries, the catalog is typically used to identify relevant items, and those items are located as an entry point for browsing. This works when books are shelved according to a classification system and the stacks are open. When using an analytical strategy, a query is carefully formulated and isolated from other steps in the process. Much of the interaction with the search system and significant amounts of time revolve around this step. When browsing, the information-seeking process is more fluid. The query formulation step identifies an entry point for extensive execution and examination that is guided by problem definition and reflection/iteration. The interface is critical here with respect to presenting representations and control mechanisms that allow easy selection, rapid feedback, and alternatives based on feedback. Whereas an interface designed to support analytical search may offer suggestions and help, an interface designed to maximize browsing offers direct manipulation of the information space and usually leaves interpretation and decision making to the user.

Whereas execution of a query and examination of results are discrete activities in analytical search, execution and examination are inextricably linked during browsing. In fact, the concurrent and mutually reinforcing physiological and cognitive activities are an important characteristic of browsing. Actions such as scanning, jumping, and navigating are much more common during the execution and examination subprocesses and likewise distinguish analytical and browsing searches. Because the display of information is critical to examination, interfaces should provide organized representations and window arrangements, high resolutions, rapid responses, and flexible tools for changing representations and marking traversal points. Because execution and examination require extensive selection actions, natural-language styles may not be as useful as point and select styles.

Information extraction similarly aids problem definition and reflection, iteration, and termination whether information seekers are searching formally or informally, but in both cases, search systems can provide better tools for helping users integrate extractions into their internal and external knowledge bases. Interface designers should try to develop new tools beyond cut and paste and bookmarks to improve this subprocess. Because the extraction of gists and ideas is usually the real aim of browsing, contextual information may be useful. For example, showing where in a list or array a record appears or displaying the data dictionary as well as the record may be especially helpful when customized views or indexes are used.

Reflection is an ongoing metaprocess necessary for any type of search to continue and eventually terminate. The speed and quality of feedback from the system are essential to the monitoring process. Too much delay or too little interpretable feedback causes frustration and early termination. Good display characteristics and the ability to change the representation level easily lead to more perseverance. The information-seeking framework and results from human factors research provide some guidance for system design to support browsing by informing the types of representations that may assist browsing and how mechanisms for manipulating those representations should be implemented.

Research on eye movements during reading, picture scanning, and visual search illustrate the importance of task and user expectations in predicting processing efficiency. Evidence that saccade latencies are significantly shorter when people know where the next target will appear (Rayner, 1978) would point to linear or systematic screen layouts and task–action grammars. Basic physiological–psychological research such as this and results from studies of motor control latencies (e.g., Fitts's law that predicts time to completion based on distance to target) provide the basis for interface design metrics such as layout appropriateness that minimize mouse movements and ensure predictable and consistent placement of objects such as menu items or icons (Sears, 1992). Because browsing is dependent on physical–psychological interaction, such considerations are even more critical to interfaces designed to support browsing. Representations must be not only rapidly displayed and easily interpretable but also predictably and consistently placed and organized to promote rapid eye-and-hand coordination. Likewise, selection and control mechanisms must be optimally placed and sequenced. These obvious transfers of results to browsing must be tested and extended by human factors researchers. For example, since left-to-right eye movements are expected by readers of English (and consequently lead to faster left–right saccades than to right–left saccades during reading), do similar expectations hold for menus and icons? Likewise, because parafoveal vision is thought to be important during reading to prepare the eye for the next saccade and subsequent fixation, what similar value do adjacent screen objects offer during browsing?

Models for HCI, such as the GOMS model of Card, Moran, and Newell, have been useful for predicting behavior and informing design for text editors. This model does not include metacognitive aspects of cognition and ignores learning effects, but Peck and John (1992) extended the model to a well-structured information-seeking domain. Their intensive study of a user of a help system suggested that GOMS may be extended to this particular type of browsing. Carmel, Crawford, and Chen (1992) also applied the GOMS framework to explain browsers' cognitive processing. The information-seeking framework presented here is more global (considers setting and domain as well as user, task, and system) and less precise than a GOMS model of information seeking, but it does reflect similar primitives. The GOMS goal relates to the information problem manifested as an information-seeking task; operators relate to the system tools such as probes, zooms, and filters for representing information; methods are the strategies and tactics known to users and possible to apply in a system; and selection rules are based on the information seeker's personal information infrastructure and how the system invites and supports various methods.

## Design perspective for supporting information-seeking strategies

The many techniques that have been proposed and implemented in prototype systems must be tested, compared, and integrated into full-scale production-level systems used on a daily basis. It is unlikely that any information environment will be complete without supporting both analytical and browsing strategies. General-purpose systems must provide a variety of access methods and tools to accommodate different communities of users, and successful systems must allow users to customize different analytical and browsing strategies. At present, there are two approaches to bringing about this integration.

One approach is to create integrated systems that offer a broad range of retrieval functions and mechanisms for controlling those functions. One such system that uses expert system techniques to help users apply powerful statistical retrieval techniques and browsable displays is Thompson and Croft's I$^3$R System (1989). They report good performance with the system, even though it requires significant computational resources. It provides a glimpse of the top–down approach to integration and depends on central intelligence built into the system to enhance the users' local intelligence. Another example is the prototype multimedia browsing system of Gecsei and Martin (1989), which uses a fisheye display and weighted vectors to support browsing in a multimedia database.

A different approach to integration provides a variety of tools and depends on users using their local intelligence to choose the proper tools for complex information problems. The desktop metaphor illustrates this approach to integration, in that rather than using large, integrated packages that handle many classes of problem, independent packages (e.g., word processor, painting program, file manager, communications program) are able to share data objects on the desktop. A similar bottom–up approach to information retrieval would provide a collection of analytical and browsing tools and allow users to select them according to their particular needs. In either case, users must understand the distinctions between browsing across documents and within documents, what different levels of representation are available, and how to manipulate and control these different representations.

Clearly, humans do not employ strictly analytical or strictly browsing strategies for exploring complex information but, rather, various patterns, strategies, tactics, and moves associated with both. Search strategies are defined on a continuum with analytical and browsing extremes. The distinctions among search strategies are largely indicated by how parallel and tightly integrated the information-seeking subprocesses are. The most carefully planned analytical search shows the sequential steps through the subprocesses, and the most casual, observational browse illustrates the examination of the environment, which stimulates acceptance, definition, and reflection in parallel. Design practice was driven first by simple performance parameters such as returning sets of objects in an acceptable time and more recently by returning sets of objects that are useful for the task at hand. Task-oriented design improved the usefulness of information retrieval systems for professional intermediaries, and user-centered designs have begun to emerge. Designs that support browsing are well advised to build on human capabilities and propensities first.

# 8

# The continuing evolution of information seeking

*Life is change; how it differs from the rocks.*

Jefferson Airplane, *Crown of Creation*

*Knowledge comes, but wisdom lingers.*

Tennyson, *Locksley Hall*

As more information becomes available in electronic form, more systems are developed to support electronic information seeking, and more people gain experience using such systems, our overall expectations change and evolve about the value of information and the roles it plays in our lives. In the previous chapters we considered how technical developments have led to complex and rapidly changing electronic environments. These developments include

- Hardware advances in storage, processing, display, and networking.
- Integration of application software such as text management, database management, communications, and hypermedia.
- Retrieval algorithms and techniques such as inverted indexes, vector representations, and clustering.
- Human–computer interface developments such as user-centered design, direct manipulation, and graphical user interfaces.

These electronic environments have influenced information-seeking by amplifying what is possible in manual environments and requiring new information-seeking strategies. In this chapter, we summarize how electronic environments have already changed information seeking and examine some of the constraining conditions that moderate these continuing changes.

## Effects of electronic environments

To examine how information seeking is affected by electronic environments, we should distinguish between the physical and intellectual consequences of information in electronic form. This distinction must be qualified as one of convenience, because physical and intellectual changes are interrelated. Physical changes include greater volumes of information, remote access (allows users to transcend space), transfer speed (allows users to minimize time requirements), multiple formats and flexible management of those formats, behavioral actions of users, and capital investments. Intellectual changes include alternative organizations, representations and access points; special tools and interfaces to support information seeking; interactivity (help and feedback); more focus on the information-seeking process itself; and new tactics and strategies.

### Physical consequences of information in electronic form

Electronic systems most obviously affect the physical attributes of information such as quantity, time, location, and format.

*Changes in volume.* Paper-based information systems are more common than electronic systems today, but the volume of information in electronic form may soon exceed that in manual systems. The predictions about paperless information systems made by technologists decades ago (e.g., Lancaster, 1978) were premature and overly optimistic but were prescient nonetheless. It is clear that manual and electronic systems will continue to grow and complement each other, although electronic information will eventually far exceed paper-based information in quantity. The volume of textual information in a large research library is in the neighborhood of a few terabytes.[1] One Geostationary Operational Environmental Satellite (GOES) today generates 7.8 gigabytes on "nonevent" days and over twice as much on days when hurricanes or storms are tracked more intensively – well over 3 terabytes per year. Furthermore, the Earth Observation System (EOS) will bring down about 1 terabyte per day! When we consider the volume of data that the broadcast media transmit and maintain as well as the scientific data generated by huge international efforts such as EOS and the Human Genome Project, it is clear that electronic systems are essential to generating, collecting, and managing huge volumes of data in a variety of forms. Electronic technology allows the volume of information to increase dramatically by facilitating its creation and collection as well as by providing possibilities for managing larger collections.[2]

*Changes in time and effort.* Electronic environments can support enormous savings in time and effort. Although document delivery systems are still in their infancy, using tools such as an online catalog or full-text database from one's home or office can save trips to libraries or information centers. Several document delivery services are available through OPACs and online services to permit information seekers to search journal literature and order fax or paper copies of articles by simply entering a credit card number. Even in today's rather primitive electronic networks, it is possible for users to access enormous data sets, bibliographic databases, and primary literature anywhere there is a network connection. Immediate access from any site makes possible virtual libraries that "exist" wherever and whenever an information seeker with the proper authority and resources needs it. Access, however, is necessary but not sufficient for successful information seeking. Access time and effort are dramatically improved by electronic environments, but access does not ensure the extraction of relevant information. Although it may be argued that these changes in volume and accessibility are simply quantitative rather than qualitative, Kay's (1984) example of the qualitative difference between many individual static images and those images at 20 frames per second is illustrative. Quantitative changes can be the basis for qualitative change.

*Changes in format and management.* More subtle than the changes in volume, speed of access, and remote access is the flexibility in format provided by electronic environments. Multimedia computing is a strong growth area for the computing and information industries because electronic systems are better able to support text, sound, and static or moving images (Fox, 1991; Koegel-Buford, 1994). Although most information environments support multiple formats, the capability of electronic environments exceeds such capabilities in paper-based or broadcast systems, in two important respects.

First, electronic environments shift some control of manipulation from the producer/distributor to the end user – they make information products malleable. Authors, broadcasters, and other disseminators traditionally provide stable information packages that consumers use as is. Users may mark or highlight their copy, extract quotations for use in another work, or even make a complete copy, but digital representations of these packages clearly simplify extraction (e.g., cut and paste) and copying and also permit more radical possibilities for users to edit according to their needs. There is currently no way to tell whether a digital product has been edited; moreover, digital products can easily be copied and transmitted to many other potential users. Paper-based information is static; films, videos, and sound recordings offer linear dynamics, but users typically cannot edit them. Digital representation allows reordering and editing. Some schemes to represent a variety of information formats in digital forms for computer-based systems provide full dynamic possibilities for end users. Nelson's Xanadu (Nelson, 1987), for example, promises full access and manipulation to the universal corpus and permits derivations to be easily added with credit and appropriate payments managed automatically, although the practicality of his approach was questioned by Samuelson and Glushko (1991).

The technological possibilities obviously lead quickly to intellectual implications. Consider, for example, the differences between downloading a film and substituting characters or changing character attributes to satisfy personal tastes, and changing the actual date of the Battle of Hastings in an electronic encyclopedia to a date that fits the needs of a term paper's argument. As multimedia workstations become the norm rather than the exception, users will be able to integrate more easily text, sound, and graphics. Some producers will ultimately develop malleable products that take advantage of such integration. Although electronic environments provide the potential for local control over information, the economic realities of the marketplace lead to the creation of products aimed at a lowest common denominator of technology. Thus, although many users may have excellent display devices, products may not take advantage of those capabilities because they must operate in a broad installed base of equipment. In addition, control over the intellectual rights of information discourages rapid developments in fully manipulable, digital products. One of the dilemmas of government and the publishing industry is how to ensure fairness in protecting intellectual property rights in an environment in which every user is empowered to create and easily transmit derivative works.

Second, multimedia information extends intraobject and interobject connection and integration. Figures and tables are closely connected to text in paper-based systems, and textual graphics are carefully integrated with visual/verbal information in television broadcasts. Electronic environments support these types of connections but provide possibilities for alternative connections dependent on the users' choices or computed conditions. Books or films refer to other works through citation and allusion, but electronic environments broaden proximity and invite hypertextual links across information objects and formats. Each line of a play by Sophocles requires the reader to make mental connections with his or her past experience and knowledge. If a mouse click offers 20 images of vases, sculpture, maps, and related ideas expressed in other texts, then the experience of each line may be enriched enormously. Realizing these riches comes at the cost of time to examine the related objects, and the possibilities of endless discursions.

A problem of reading in such an environment becomes curtailing connections rather than suffering from lack of details – instead of starving for the explanatory information sometimes found in footnotes, the reader may gorge on detail and miss the total experience of the feast. There also may be learning benefits associated with having to puzzle out some connections – discovering connections is surely one of the most intellectually stimulating activities. The degree of connectedness of information in electronic form has, in fact, changed the concept of what a document is. Bolter (1991) believes that the multiple windows and hypertextual connections of electronic environments make even scholarly documents more like newspapers or magazines that pull readers back and forth among the various blocks of text, ads, headlines, and images. Users must parse windows and icons as well as textual structures while browsing, reading, and studying electronic information. At present, we have no guidelines for managing such richly connected intellectual worlds.

*Changes in users' actions.* Information in electronic form changes our physical actions while seeking information. First, we sit at workstations using primarily our eyes and hands to locate, examine, and extract information. Such access is physically passive, saving time and effort related to physical actions such as travel, reaching, and turning pages. Loss of the physical exercise entailed by information seeking may be doubly disadvantageous to intellectual workers who already get little physical exercise as part of their work day. The effects of eye and muscle fatigue and repetitive movement injuries are becoming more apparent, and concerns about radiation surface periodically in the human factors literature. Although video display terminals provide the advantage of dynamically displaying multiple formats, people read electronic text more slowly than paper-based text; few people can now afford broadcast-quality video on their workstations; and few argue that reading on a screen is more comfortable than reading on paper. Thus, electronic environments bring trade-offs related to the physical actions of information seeking.

Second, we must learn to work in these environments. Substantial investments in time are required for users to become computer and information literate and to learn to use specific applications. Billions of dollars are spent training workers to use systems and specific application packages. In addition, computer anxiety has been estimated to influence about one-third of all new users (Torkzadeh & Angulo, 1992), and policies and programs are needed to deal with this general problem as we approach full saturation of the workplace with computers. Third, working in electronic environments may lead to physiological and psychological changes. Huge volumes of information require substantial amounts of time and effort and may overload users and lead to physical reactions to such stress. On the other hand, the potential to provide information in multiple formats allows users to personalize their information display according to their individual styles, abilities, and preferences.

*Changes in resource allocation.* In addition to the substantial costs associated with adding electronic environments to our personal information infrastructures, the capital costs of technology for public information infrastructures is a significant concern. For example, millions of dollars have been spent on library automation in the past decade but we have no clear evidence of how this has improved access, let alone productivity. When we consider the materials (e.g., books and serials) that were not acquired and services not provided (e.g., reference) because funds were used to acquire and install OPACs, CD-ROM workstations, and library networks, the changes that electronic technology have already brought begin to come into qualitative focus. Data collected by the Association of Research Libraries (Cummings, Witte, Bowen, Lazarus, & Ekman, 1992) show that operating expenses (the component of library budgets that typically include automation costs) steadily grew as a proportion of the overall budget from 1963 to 1991, whereas salaries and binding portions generally fell, and materials acquisitions remained more or less fixed. Dreams of amortizing capital costs for technology over time to enable more and better access are surely mitigated by ongoing maintenance and upgrades, and the effects of shifting resources from people and information is difficult to assess. What we know for certain is that electronic environments have changed the resource mix.

Similar changes have occurred in business, government, and educational settings. Other costs, such as security, reliability, and dependency on electronic systems for basic public services, are beyond the scope of this book but must also be taken into account (see the Risks Column of *Communications of the ACM* for examples of costs and risks related to computing applications).

## Intellectual consequences of information in electronic form

We have been primarily concerned in this book with the intellectual changes that electronic environments bring to information seeking. These changes are related mainly to how information is organized and represented in information systems and how information seekers interact with these systems to access and use information.

*Changes in organization and representation.* Electronic storage capacities support large databases at multiple levels of granularities, and computational power allows system designers to use a variety of preprocessing techniques to support multiple access points (e.g., indexes), and to apply decision rules that depend on conditions at run time to provide alternative representations for information (e.g., user-sensitive interfaces). Ultimately, all levels of representation will be integrated, but during this transitional period, two gross levels of representation are supported in distinct secondary (e.g., bibliographic) and primary systems. For each of these types of systems, electronic technology has brought significant changes.

Electronic bibliographic systems offer more access points and yield larger sets of potentially relevant documents than manual systems do. For example, although OPACs have been slow to move beyond simply automating the card catalog, most provide more than author, title, and a few subject headings as access points. Keyword indexes and automatically expanded controlled subject heading assignments have been made possible by computational power. We are only beginning to explore richer indexing, including personalized indexes for OPACs and database directories. Furthermore, the availability of OPACs through networks provide worldwide access.

Online databases allow users to focus queries on specific database fields. Some offer dozens of access points; for example, business databases enable users to search specialized indexes for geographic region, members of boards of directors, and various financial parameters. Indexing a broader collection of attributes (i.e., creating more indexes) provides more links to documents. More access points per document complicates the types of queries that users can generate and therefore changes the probability of retrieval with respect to these queries. Taking advantage of indexing on a broader range of attributes thus requires information seekers to have and use more knowledge about how information is organized and also tends to increase the number of documents returned.

Technology has changed indexing practice by altering the number of subject terms assigned to each document. Without changing the controlled vocabulary used to assign subject terms, more terms can be assigned to each document because additional physical cards or additional lines of text are not needed. Indexes can apply as many terms as appropriate without the constraints imposed by physical objects for each entry point. Alternatively, the controlled vocabulary itself can become larger. Retaining all content-bearing words in titles is a common extension to the assignment of controlled terms (keywords). These additional access points yield more items for a query than more parsimonious indexing does. The large sets of results can, of course, burden the information seeker, and so better tools for examining these results are needed. This is a major motivation for developing interfaces that support efficient browsing of document sets.

Some online systems provide multiple indexes and links to related objects. Citation databases have benefitted immensely from computers, growing from simple citation compilations to systems that allow cocitation analysis and bibliographic coupling (Garfield, 1955; Paisley, 1990). The earliest electronic systems represented well-defined, bibliographic pointer information modeled on database designs, and these models shaped the expectations and strategies of information seekers. Users already use bibliographic databases to explore rather than retrieve, and as these systems move beyond simple exact matches on well-defined fields, new expectations and strategies will emerge. First of all, users will expect to gain immediate access to the primary material and to use the same interface tools and techniques to work in both types of materials.

Primary information is increasingly available in electronic form, which is leading to new levels and forms of representation as well as new types of human–computer interactions. The availability of primary information in electronic form is a significant trend and creates new demands for intermediate representations between terse surrogates and full documents. Full-text and other primary information sources also demand new information-seeking approaches and strategies. Reference materials such as encyclopedias, atlases, and almanacs; technical publications such as newsletters and research updates; and communication forums such as electronic mail, news groups, and listservs have led to new layers of representation across and within individual items.

Electronic systems have begun to blur the distinctions between secondary and primary materials and the respective search strategies for across- and within-document searching. This melding is due to several factors. First, the same physical device is used to conduct both types of search – the same computer and display are used for searching for a document as for reading it. Second, each information item can be represented at differing levels of detail, from a terse bibliographic record, through various intermediate abbreviations, condensations, or extracts, to a full explication of the entire item. Information seekers can work at any of these levels and may use the same control mechanisms or tools to search, browse, and study across multiple documents or within specific ones. Third, the increased connectivity within and between information allows users to move across documents and levels easily – whether or not they actually want to.

Manual systems clearly distinguish between secondary and primary information sources. Printed indexes provide citations (very coarse representations such as a title) for books or journals (distinct objects containing primary information) that may or may not be physically proximate. A similar situation exists in the bulk of electronic systems today. OPACs and online bibliographic databases point to articles, books, and reports that may be inaccessible to the information seeker.[3] As designs move beyond replicating print-based organizations, we will see these distinctions blur. Document delivery services are increasingly available from online systems, and large primary corpuses often provide sophisticated within-document search tools as well as links to related primary materials. In addition, primary documents have multiple levels of representation, for example, tables of contents, chapters, sections, and paragraphs. At the present, interfaces are emerging that allow information seekers to take advantage of these levels almost as easily and naturally as they do in paper-based sources. In time, these interfaces will exceed what is possible for searching and browsing paper-based sources.

As full-text and multimedia databases become more common and we develop standards for designing interfaces for them, distinctions between secondary and primary databases will disappear. Secondary and tertiary information will simply be viewed as two of many levels of representation in an integrated information space. Ultimately, a major structural change will emerge that views information as a continuous space rather than as a collection of discrete sets of documents and pointers. One dimension of this space is composed of a series of representations for an intellectual work (e.g., a book, a film), and other dimensions consist of connections to other intellectual works at various levels of representation. For example, a collection of titles are connected according to some dimensional parameter such as publisher, date, or concept cluster; and a specific book chapter is connected to several other chapters or articles or film segments according to subject, style, or other attributes. In sum, electronic environments have already provided richer and more varied representations in a single location than manual environments can and this trend will continue to accelerate in the future.

*Changes in intellectual tools.* A significant difference between manual and electronic environments is in what software tools and interfaces are provided. Much of the previous two chapters was devoted to such interfaces. In general, electronic environments offer a range of computational tools and dynamic feedback that fundamentally changes the information-seeking process. These include

- Data dictionaries for different databases, term dictionaries and thesauri, and menus or query completion forms may be used to assist in source selection and query formulation

- String search, highlighted query terms, multiple windows, hypertextual links, and graphical displays may be used to examine results
- Cut-and-paste tools and annotations may be used to support information extraction
- Search history tools, grammar or statistical tools, and online assistance may be helpful in reflecting, iterating, and terminating search and in refining the information problem.

Electronic environments offer basic search functions that are difficult or impossible in manual environments. Combining concepts according to Boolean or proximity limits is extremely tedious in manual environments but is made simple by careful preprocessing in electronic environments. Limiting search to specific ranges or fields is likewise simple in electronic environments. This function provides great power for formulating precise and complex queries that match well-specified attributes of tasks and documents. A consequence of this power, however, is that users and designers often neglect the restriction on specifications and assume that information seeking is strictly a matching process. As I have argued throughout this book, information seeking is a dynamic problem-solving process, and matching is only one aspect of it.

*Changes in interactivity.* Electronic environments change the way that we seek information by offering high levels of interactivity. Rapid feedback provides a sense of interaction, and carefully planned programs suggest "intelligence" by acknowledging input, offering "suggestions" or critiques, and giving help on request. Although we have much to learn about online help and documentation (see Brockmann, 1990, for an excellent overview of electronic documentation, and Carroll & Aaronson, 1988, for a framework for online help), electronic environments offer users much greater flexibility in learning and using the system than is possible in static, manual environments. Context-sensitive help provides focused assistance, and transaction logs provide historical contexts for specific sessions or across many sessions. Electronic critics (Fischer & Girgensohn, 1990) provide advice triggered by chains of events rather than single instances. Online reference materials, by virtue of their electronic format, offer users the same type of search and display properties that make electronic documents more flexible than paper documents (e.g., searchable on multiple keys, customizable display, highlighted terms, visual juxtapositions of disparate items).

All these specific attributes combine to give information seekers a highly interactive environment that offers more finely grained steps and more iterations of activity than manual environments do. More access points, more tools, and more immediate feedback all lead to a process that is highly specifiable. This result is significant and leads to secondary changes such as inviting broader communities of users, changing the expectations of users and the strategies they use to seek information, and ultimately changing the way that information is organized and how systems are designed to make that information accessible.

One consequence of having primary and secondary information in a highly interactive, electronic form is that more end users are attracted to it. Although we can assign bibliographic searches to intermediaries, we must do our own browsing through and studying primary materials. If more people are using electronic systems to work with the primary information, they may as well use the system to locate that information in the information space in the first place. End-user searching is a double-edged sword. Electronic environments have empowered end users to broaden and improve their personal information-seeking infrastructures. Presumably, this has also led to better and more efficient solutions to information problems. However, these benefits are not without costs. In addition to the physical costs discussed earlier, information overload, confusion, and disorientation are increasingly problematic. These contraindications are of two types: those that stem from the system itself and those that emanate from the information accessed. In the first case, the disorientation of menus systems, hypertext, and other access mechanisms are well documented in the literature. These problems are mainly technical and will likely become less troublesome as computing becomes more ubiquitous and user interfaces improve. The second case is more problematic because it is a result of human mental capabilities. We can hold only so much information in our heads at one time, and there is no technical solution to information overload. The best we can hope for is to use the technology to augment our limited memory capacity. In essence, electronic environments broaden access to a larger community of people and widen the resources available for people to solve information problems, but they also demand new skills and do not diminish the need for people to think.

*Changes in our view of the information-seeking process.* Electronic environments have begun to change the way that we think about information seeking as well as the strategies we use to do it. The impatience that users demonstrate while waiting a few seconds for the Perseus system to locate and load graphic images or conduct morphological analyses of Greek words is an example of the fundamental change in expectations that computers bring with respect to temporal matters. No one would expect a person to take less than 10 seconds to go to a library, locate a book containing a photograph of a vase, and find the right page, but everyone becomes impatient waiting for the computer to do this. Just as our expectations about time have changed, developments in computational and display capabilities lead us to expect high-quality displays of text, images, and sound augmented by comprehensive annotations. Likewise, users are beginning to expect document delivery rather than bibliographic pointers. In an age of fast food, jet travel, and global telecommunications, our expectations about the time needed to seek information and the quality and breadth of information available have evolved beyond the physical limitations of manual systems. Electronic environments heighten our expectations about information access; however, as always, the ultimate bottleneck is our physiology and psychology – we still must perceive, process, and comprehend information if we are to achieve our goals.

Changes in our expectations about time have led information seekers to focus more attention on the information-seeking process – large changes in time to accomplish tasks make us more conscious and reflective about what has changed. This shift in attention and effort has implications for those who use information and those who work at finding it. Many strategic and tactical alternatives, and multiple access points, imply decision making; high levels of interaction imply active participation; and the power and volume of electronic information systems require more evaluation of results. Because our cognitive capacities are limited, the effects of channeling significant amounts of cognitive resources to the search process rather than on the problem and content at hand needs careful examination. This may be good in the long run because problem definition is constantly engaged, but it may also lead to missed opportunities for study and careful concentration.

Professionals allocate relatively fixed amounts of time to seeking and reading information on the job (Griffiths & King, 1991). Although the proportion of seeking and reading may change, the total time available will not. Thus, time devoted to finding comes at the expense of time for reading. These results are used as one of the rationales for providing information retrieval services, thus allowing the engineer or scientist to maximize his or her reading and studying time. It is too soon to know whether increasingly more integrated electronic environments will make it counterproductive to disassociate seeking and reading information. If seeking and reading are inextricably interlinked, then people may spend less time reading and studying, and information specialists will spend less time finding information for clients and more time collecting, organizing, and evaluating it.

*Changes in tactics and strategies.* In the previous chapters we explored how electronic environments first led to powerful analytical search strategies and are beginning to support highly interactive browsing strategies. Information seekers expect to use more guess-and-go strategies that allow them to isolate materials to browse through for possible answers, leads, and ideas. Browsing strategies that take advantage of alternative representations and highly dynamic mechanisms have become practical, and these expectations about information seeking lead to more dependence on such strategies and to the need for interfaces that support them. New strategies for systems that support relevance feedback and that search multiple databases in parallel also will develop as users gain experience.

It is important that in our efforts to accommodate these changes we do not neglect to develop and revise analytical strategies that allow precise query specifications. String search and Boolean search dramatically change what is feasible. Although theoretically possible in manual environments, these strategies have become standard features in electronic environments. Systems that provide ranked retrieval will spawn new analytical strategies as users learn to control term weights and automatic query expansion parameters. Our wants are infinitely beyond our needs, and our expectations about the world almost always err on the side of optimism.

Subject access is the grand challenge of information science, and the most grandiose claims for electronic environments have concentrated on this problem. There are two distinct approaches to the challenge of subject access. By far the most common approach is to assume that the "aboutness" of a document can be ascertained and represented. This belief obtains matching information problem representations to document representations as the fundamental operation of information systems. This view is rooted in scientific philosophy that assumes that information and human behavior can be studied and understood from an external, objective vantage. Indexing and various knowledge-based representation schemes adopt this approach to the challenge of subject access. It is attractive because it allows people not directly involved in the production or use of information to play a role – either by adding value to support matching operations or as intermediaries working to find matches. This approach is clearly viable because it is partially successful and supports an entire industry. Computation is useful to this approach in several ways. First, computers can be used to aid in the indexing process or possibly to replace human indexers (e.g., Milstead, 1992). Second, computers can provide alternative views of information to end users, for example, different indexes or different levels of record detail. Third, computers can support complex matching mechanisms such as Boolean combinations and rapid string matching. Alternatively, computers can be used to determine approximate matches and rank results according to any number of computational schemes (e.g., statistical or probabilistic approaches).

An alternative approach assumes that all information may ultimately be related in some way to all information problems – the creative problem solver applies the available information to the problem at hand. This belief views subject access as situation dependent, and the function of the system is to provide source material. This view is rooted in humanistic philosophy that assumes that information and human behavior are personal and contextual and can be studied and understood only from an interpretive, subjective vantage point. Computation is also useful to this approach in several ways. First, computers may help in accessing and representing information rapidly, efficiently, and according to the individual needs of the information seeker. This access can be based on the individual user's experience and knowledge rather than on some standardized scheme. Second, computers may be used by individual persons to manipulate information according to their own information needs. Personalized indexes or ontologies (Wiederhold, Wegner, & Ceri, 1992) may be defined and used. Third, computers can support alternative or customizable interfaces and tools for representation and manipulation. Although it appears a bit ironic that logic-based tools such as computers should be so applicable to a human-centered view of information seeking, it is the development of highly flexible electronic environments that has rekindled the possibilities for this approach. The connectivity, virtuality, and malleability of electronic environments can lead to decentralization and personal freedom and enable natural, human-centered approaches to information seeking. Imagine the discoveries and connections that children will make as they explore the worldwide networks. Such images sharply contrast with the efficient and targeted inquiries that busy professionals demand from highly organized electronic environments. Both views are necessary. Just as electronic environments have spawned new analytical and browsing strategies, they also have created new expectations and ultimately new behavior and thought.

## Constraints and challenges for continued evolution

There is a lively literature related to the relationship of technology and society. Points of view range from "gee whiz" prognostications about the future to Luddite-like trepidation. Some people view technology as value free, and others as the means for despots or governments to control society. Some see it as a "chicken or egg" problem of whether society creates technology or vice versa (see Teich, 1990, for a collection of diverse views). Technology influences culture and is shaped by the culture in which it exists. To some extent, technology is shaped by the needs of society; more important, society does not undergo all the changes that technology may make possible. Taviss (1972) discusses the social and cultural adjustment that must be made with the introduction of technology. Andriole (1984) argues that technology has already changed the nature of risk in our world and examines various security issues related to large information systems. Forester and Morrison (1990) provide a good collection of examples of how computers have affected individuals and institutions. Mesthene (1968) argues that technology causes intellectual, social, and political changes and that the ways that knowledge is sought and created will change as knowledge gains in social importance. Information technology is subject to these strong interactions. There are many social and political factors affecting the evolution of information seeking. We discuss next a few of these factors.

### *Physical, economic, and technical constraints and challenges*

Ideas and their representations are limitless in number, but their physical manifestations consume resources and occupy space. Manual information systems pose obvious constraints on growth and access. Offices can support only so many filing cabinets, and libraries regularly struggle with a lack of adequate shelf space. Electronic technology appears to overcome this constraint by improving storage densities many orders of magnitude over paper- or film-based systems. Electronic technology will continue to improve, but matter and energy will eventually be consumed and physical limits to what can realistically be made accessible will influence acquisition and access. More important, access severely constrains the "save everything" mentality because without proper indexing, finding information becomes impossible. There is a critical need for a life-cycle view of information so that dispensation decisions are considered at the times of creation and storage. Archivists may offer some guidance in developing such strategies (Burke, 1981). Although the current antidote to the "save everything" mentality is the difficulty of intellectual access, physical limitations are also at issue.

A central theme of this book is that technological developments have already influenced the evolution of information seeking. There are many technical challenges that limit as well as cause change. Hardware and software developments will surely continue to drive many of the changes, but interface design and implementation offer severe challenges to progress. Multiple, portable, unobtrusive, physical devices that allow transparent control and high-fidelity feedback must be developed. As information seeking becomes more like thinking – wondering, free-associating, remembering – our physical links to the external world of information may become less distinct as input or output devices and more like multidirectional channels among our local and remote information resources. For example, Bolt (1984) offered novel examples for using eyes as output devices to control as well as perceive the world. Beyond such engineering challenges are the conceptual interface challenges to organize, represent, and make manipulable the world's information resources. Discovering different representation forms and levels, creating meaningful connections among the various representations and related corpuses, and presenting mechanisms that support easy interpretation and control are huge design challenges. Creating systems that can be personalized according to the special physical, intellectual, and emotional needs of different information seekers will continue to determine how information seeking evolves.

Many of the constraints of information processing are economic. Most obviously, there are enormous capital costs in the hardware and software components of electronic environments. Although immense technological investments have been made by all economic sectors, there is no clear evidence that productivity, quality, or satisfaction gains commensurate with these investments have followed. In fact, it may not matter from a global perspective, as the new products, jobs, and markets that electronic technology entail have caused overall economic growth. Individual people and corporate entities must, of course, consider these capital expenses in light of their local economic parameters. Many economic constraints are more subtle and interact with the psychological, social, and political factors considered next.

### Intellectual property, authority, and copyright

Governments provide legal protection for intellectual property rights to ensure the continuation of innovation and progress. Fair returns on intellectual effort reward creators and distributors and provide continued access to the community. As technology changes how information is created, organized, shared, and used, legal and economic factors must also evolve. One aspect of electronic information is the ease with which it may be copied. Photocopy machines assaulted copyright laws, but mass copying of printed material still requires significant investments of time and material resources. Furthermore, photocopies degrade in quality over generations. An electronic document can be as easily copied to a hundred network addresses as to one floppy disk, and if these recipients choose to copy to others, each subsequent copy is an exact replication.

Even more problematic is the malleability of electronic documents. Photocopies cannot be changed, but electronic documents can be edited without leaving any traces. Creative authority is separate from the issues of property because reputations and beliefs are foremost – an author may not care about monetary royalties but may care a great deal about the accuracy of reproduction and receiving intellectual credit for ideas. Electronic documents can be easily altered without the author's permission or knowledge, and so authoritative warranty schemes (electronic versions of tamper-proof packaging or shrink wrap) are required. Bit-mapped images (pictures of text or graphics such as those provided by fax machines) may be easily copied, but they cannot be easily edited and thus provide some level of editorial integrity. This is only a temporary delay in the transformation from paper to electronic publishing, and we will eventually need new rules and techniques to ensure fair use and editorial authority for electronic information. Certainly, video-editing software packages have already destroyed the authority of any digitally stored video. Eventually, authority will be verified through encryption or digital signatures, but the malleability of electronic documents will make users even more dependent on technological aids to their senses.

Electronic technology raises new intellectual property issues. Electronic networks facilitate collaboration among people, and pinpointing ownership or crediting contributions in such environments is difficult. Text fragments from listservs and discussion groups, algorithms and code fragments from software libraries, graphics from clip art libraries, and databases or knowledge bases from governmental systems are commonly aggregated and modified to create new intellectual works. Digital slide libraries and video archives complicate this issue. Reusability is an ecologically positive trend, but it is unclear what property rights accrue to the various creators. A similar problem has emerged with respect to the "look and feel" of interfaces, with some contending that "look and feel" is a definable intellectual property (e.g., Shneiderman, 1993) and others that it is not (e.g., Samuelson, 1992). Much of the debate centers on whether the interface is functional (and therefore cannot be copyrighted) or expressive (and therefore can be copyrighted). One side argues that because good design is informed by research and theory, the products cannot be copyrighted, but another view is that the sum combination of well-designed displays and mechanisms is a creative expression and therefore can be copyrighted.

Another issue is related to the notions of added value and derivative works. Significant components of the information industry profit from packaging and selling information produced or collected by government agencies. Likewise, publishers create books of readings from existing publications. Aggregating, organizing, packaging, and distributing all add value to information, and for many years it was enough simply to transfer paper-based documents to electronic form to justify reselling public information. As more government information originates in electronic form and as industries (e.g., security and exchange reports) and individual people (e.g., tax returns) actually provide information in electronic form, information brokers must find new ways to add value. Governments are beginning to take advantage of technology to aggregate, index, and distribute information as part of their service mission. As information brokers develop new forms of displaying and linking information, new clarifications will be needed to decide when enough value has been added to justify a copyright claim. Three different vendors' CD-ROM versions of the same database can provide different levels of performance and satisfaction. Clearly, customized indexing, links to other information sources, and interfaces for locating and using information are added values that will continue to define markets for derivative works.

A classic form of derivative work is an edited volume of previously published papers. An editor provides a valuable service by selecting papers that represent interesting themes, may provide an introductory framework for the selection, coordinates copyright acquisition, and assists the publisher in the marketing and distribution. For paper books, the property issues and copyright arrangements are well established. It is less clear what policies should be followed when a collection of printed papers are aggregated and linked as a hypertext. The intellectual effort of forming links requires substantial editorial interpretation and effort. In addition to editorial rights and responsibilities, authors' rights become more complex.

One issue relates to situations in which hypertext navigation may juxtapose one segment of an author's work to segments of other works. Because links may be made at fairly finely grained levels, this is quite different from having one's article included in a book with another article that expresses a differing view. In the case of hypertext, specific passages may be linked without benefit of the surrounding context in which they occur. In essence, parts of one author's work may be embedded in another author's work, or the two or more works may be intermingled in a variety of ways. Another issue is related to ownership of links. Links are editorial acts and thus may be considered the intellectual property of the editor. Authors of nodes, however, may claim ownership of links coming in or going out of their works (Samuelson & Glushko, 1991, provide a good discussion of these issues). If the highway system is used as a metaphor, the problem becomes one of determining exactly where public streets become private drives and how private drives are demarcated and connected.

As discussed in the previous section, electronic environments blur such distinctions and the roles for those who use them. In electronic publishing, the roles of authors, publishers, and consumers also become less distinct. The fluidity of electronic environments break down customary distinctions and create new challenges for governments to provide legal guidance, for libraries to provide access, and for business to ensure a fair return on investment.

### Social and political constraints and challenges

The notion of ownership of information ignites a lively debate between those who view information as a commodity and those who view it as a right. Devotees of free enterprise point to the progress engendered by competition in the marketplace. They argue that all people should be able to profit from their intellectual effort and that the market should determine how much people should pay for access to such information. This position is applicable to privatized information networks and the metered use of information services. Devotees of social management point to the progress made by cooperation and community programs such as public safety and education, and other government services. They contend that information is a birthright and should be made freely available to anyone who needs it. This position is applicable to public libraries and information networks that provide equal and unlimited access to all. Because governments are leading producers of information, policies for making information available to the public will greatly influence how information seeking evolves. Policies may make freely available all, some, or none of the information that governments generate. Policies range from mounting all government databases on the Internet for free access to subsidizing the information industry by releasing all government databases to vendors who provide dissemination and value-added services commercially. Different governments will determine different levels of basic information rights for its citizens, thus determining equity of access for fundamental corpuses such as legal and medical databases.

Providing free access to information is only part of the equity problem. People must be aware of the availability of information and possess the skills to access and use it. Public libraries in the United States have served as the "poor people's universities" because those who learned the basics of reading could gain access to the main elements of the world's knowledge. Just as reading skills are necessary to take advantage of libraries, reading skills, computer skills, and information-seeking skills are increasingly necessary to take advantage of the virtual library and worldwide information networks. Those who are privileged to acquire such skills as part of their education have a great advantage over those who do not. Clearly, not all people will become equally skilled, but all should be assured of some basic competence. The degree to which all the world's people acquire such basic skills will influence the continued development of electronic information seeking. This is so because the provision of minimal, standardized, and culturally diverse interfaces will lead to rapid changes as more users acquire habits and preferences. Consider the following argument from a mass/inertia perspective.

Information technology has created new industries and is beginning to influence the social and cultural milieu. The early stages of any innovation are chaotic and revolutionary, characterized by rapid changes, lack of standards, missionary zeal on the part of developers and early adopters, and high-risk decision making. Eventually, entropy begins to build; different levels of stability are created; and an installed base of objects, procedures, and thinking becomes important. As the installed base grows, the energy needed to influence its inertia becomes greater, and the probability of change decreases. Electronic technologies have certainly been among the foremost innovations of the second half of the twentieth century, but the pace of change in electronic environments cannot be maintained. The installed base of equipment, software, user knowledge, and institutional policies has grown beyond the early adopters to the general population at large. The policies, skills, and biases related to it will continue to evolve, but the rate of change must diminish because so many people participate. Stabilization will allow basic skills to be learned more globally.

Another cultural constraint that influences how electronic information seeking will evolve is related to the nature of ownership. Many people take pleasure in possessing things, and some people enjoy possessing information artifacts such as books, videotapes, or video games. Just as libraries have not put bookstores out of business, video rental centers also sell videotapes and games. This will likely continue in the future, but much more focus is being placed on access to information rather than ownership of it. This is clearly the case for libraries struggling to maintain large research collections, and it is reflected in the number of resource-sharing consortia in business and industry. The shift from ownership to access is a fundamental change in perspective that is also reflected in the economic movement from manufacturing to service. What are the information complements of this trend? A statement that most teachers hear sooner or later from their students is "I really do not have to know this; I just have to know where to find it when I need it." According to this reasoning, learning is the development of a mass of indexes to knowledge. This is a highly positivistic view of the mind as an organized system of pointers and knowledge. A holistic perspective is that the mind is a fabric of experiences and reflections. Associations and organizational structures are imposed after the fact. The ultimate augmentation of the intellect by computers may be to fulfill the indexing function, thereby allowing humans more time and effort to acquire primary experience and knowledge.

## Subject access and information problems

Technology may have changed the things we choose to think about, the strategies we use for directing our thinking, and the behaviors we exhibit when thinking, but thus far it has not changed our fundamental physiological processes associated with thinking. Likewise, technology has changed the way that we represent and share expressions of thought but has not thus far changed the fundamental forms and rules of language and communication. The basic problem of conceptualizing an information problem and translating information from the external world to solve that problem has not been much affected by technology. Consider how hard the problem really is! Concepts are manifested through some finite expression of tokens from a language – eventually the book or painting is finished, and enormous varieties of tokens are left unexpressed that could also have been used to convey the creator's ideas – only one instantiation of a creator's noumenal clouds has been expressed. Any expression is but one possible form for the concepts, ideas, and feelings of the creator. The problem of understanding such expressions is likewise imperfect because the receiver may associate many ideas with the specific tokens perceived. Communication is a creative process, and it is redundancy and shared experience that permit usable levels of effectiveness. The process is even more problematic when one is seeking information rather than trying to understand what is being communicated. This is so because we have to imagine the tokens that may have been used to represent ideas relevant to our information problem. This is doubly difficult because our lack of understanding (the information problem) means there are few likely tokens for the problem. That is, we have difficulty expressing what we do not understand, let alone imagining the tokens used by those that do understand. The novice cannot guess whether the brush strokes, color combinations, or shapes are the tokens of greatest interest in an abstract painting. This is essentially the problem of subject access – imagining how creators expressed their ideas.

Indexing and classification were created as bridges between the information seeker and the creator. The flexibility of electronic environments can broaden and extend the bridge.[4] A thesaurus or controlled vocabulary serves to standardize some set of tokens where information items and information seekers can meet. This is a fundamental problem of representation and communication, and electronic environments offer some possibilities for addressing part of the problem. Solving the problem fully means eliminating creativity and interpretation – whether we can do it pales by comparison with the question of whether we should do it perfectly.

One of the ways that technology has begun to influence subject access is to enable automatic indexing that affects the costs of producing indexes, and as a result, the potential for additional or alternative indexes for individual works. Although it seems apparent that a carefully handcrafted index may be superior to an automatically generated index, the time and effort trade-offs are substantial. In addition, there may be some global advantage as more indexes are generated automatically, for example, off-the-shelf clothing has improved the variety and quality of clothes for humans in general. Automatic indexing may ultimately provide multiple indexes for most purposes, and handcrafted indexes may be reserved for only the most important or unusual documents. Furthermore, it is possible that end users themselves may use these tools to create their own indexes.

The availability of full-text searching has so far been the most prominent change resulting from computers. Indexing items for every word that appears greatly increases the number of tokens that information seekers may use to identify those items. Although this change can dramatically improve the retrieval of specific items, it has three important limitations. First, even though all words are available as potential tokens for information seekers to use, unless supplemental indexing is provided, tokens not used in the work may nonetheless be useful expressions for the ideas in the work, and information seekers may actually use them as entry points while seeking information (i.e., a writer does not use a particular word or phrase, although it could just as easily have been used). Second, because items may contain large numbers of tokens and specific tokens may have multiple meanings, items containing tokens that are present in queries are not necessarily appropriate in degree or kind – many peripherally useful items will be retrieved. These two problems are a direct result of the richness and imprecision of language. Third, because searches are usually initiated in collections of items, the number of items that may contain specified tokens may be quite large. If each word, with the exception of some stop words, serves as a retrieval cue, then each document will have hundreds or thousands of tokens. The number of items with common tokens grows as a function of the size of the collection if all unique terms are indexed. Term weighting based on inverse document frequency or other normalizations can minimize this problem but simple queries posed to large databases will still return large numbers of highly ranked documents. In collections in which controlled vocabularies are used for indexing, the number of overlapping items will also grow monotonically with the size of the collection, but at a rate constrained by the size of the controlled vocabulary and the indexing policy. For systems not based on exact-match retrieval engines, it seems reasonable to expand the notion of query to include extensive descriptive text, as the inclusion of words in a query need not exclude documents.

Thus, more access points lead to greater recall, which in turn requires more filtering. This is not necessarily bad if good tools for browsing and filtering are available once a first pass through the database has been made with word-matching probes. Given the nature of human language and the problems of subject access, a general strategy seems prudent: Use general (gross) queries and probes to identify a neighborhood of interest, and then browse and filter. This strategy implies that system design and development support both parts of this approach.

### Human nature

Human beings revel in diversity. We appreciate alternative expressions for ideas and vary our behaviors to gain new experience. It may be argued that this is so because so much of our life is filled with redundancy, but nonetheless, variety is the spice of life. Thus, the most efficient action is not always the most satisfying, and easier is not always better. Cooking from scratch, growing our own vegetables, and repairing our own products may in some cases yield superior results, but these actions are usually motivated by the satisfaction gained from the process itself. One result of this characteristic is that we sometimes purposely choose less efficient and less effective means to accomplish tasks. This very human characteristic is in direct opposition to the principles of science and management. Although we tend to aim at optimal processes most of the time, human nature nevertheless admits suboptimal or counterproductive exceptions.

Human–computer interaction design often aims at optimality. It assumes that people always want to be more efficient in their work and that logical procedures are either superior to or coincident with natural procedures. In subtle ways, these assumptions underlie much of our work. We try to develop organizational schemes that will minimize storage requirements and access time and that will maximize fidelity of representation. Likewise, we try to develop interface mechanisms that will minimize physical effort and will maximize productive outputs. Optimal design may, however, be neither functional nor successful for human activity. Although many of the behaviors aim at reducing monotony, seeking alternative sources of information and reconstructing procedures rather than retrieving them (e.g., seldom-used mathematical formulas or recipes) reiterates our basic understanding of principles and reaffirms our self-confidence.

Consider the metric system, which is obviously superior to the English system of measurement with respect to logical organization, extensional power, memory load, and learnability. The degree Celsius is carefully mapped to two critical physical points (transition states of water) as well as to the decimal numeration system. However, this system seems inferior to the Fahrenheit system, for two reasons. First, in many parts of the earth, temperatures for large portions of the year are below freezing, thus requiring negative values to be written and spoken. Second, the Celsius unit is almost twice as large (1.8 times as large) as the Fahrenheit unit, which is a discernible amount of heat for the human system. Thus, although the system is optimized according to logic, it is somewhat disassociated from human needs and conditions. Metric units of length are even more obviously removed from human-centeredness than are inches and feet derived directly from the human condition.

When we examine interface theory and design, it is easy to see the influence of optimization assumptions. Designs that minimize movement may in fact short-circuit mutually reinforcing or pleasurable interactions between physical and mental activities. Designs that emphasize regularity and repetition may make tasks boring and performance sloppy. Airline pilots may override automatic landing systems to keep their jobs interesting and their skills sharp; clerks may vary sequences of actions to minimize monotony; and drivers may take alternative routes to see new areas. If people do not always want to work optimally and some of our physiological and psychological characteristics do not map directly onto logical data structures and procedures, what can designers do to accommodate them? Let me make clear that I do not advocate abandoning systematic design based on task analyses. In fact, humanism provides a basis for user-selectable and adaptable interfaces. What may permit information seeking in electronic environments to evolve according to human needs and characteristics is to consider design an art that admits variation and even playfulness. Certainly, we should strive to create systems that users can alter at will in order to accommodate those times when they wish to abandon efficiency and work for fun.

## Evolution and mutation

The changes in information seeking that have occurred as a result of electronic environments are a part of a larger evolutionary process. These changes will be refined and extended, and new developments will emerge subject to the constraints discussed earlier. Information seekers must acquire new skills for using technology and extend their personal information infrastructures with new mental models for specific systems. More important, electronic environments change our expectations about information seeking – changes that range from the optimism of users who blithely enter natural-language queries because they expect machine intelligence, to the reactionary pessimism of those who refuse to use systems on grounds of losing personal service and human interaction. Thus, the central factor in the information-seeking framework, the *information seeker,* changes and adapts to new environments. The other factors are affected as well. Information *tasks* are influenced insofar as users consciously take advantage of better system vocabularies and interfaces when mapping their mental articulations of the problem onto queries and probes. Tasks may also be changed as a result of users' considering amounts, types, or availabilities of information accessible in electronic form. Information-seeking tasks that have been avoided or executed at minimal levels using manual systems are more readily expected and accepted and more broadly executed in electronic environments. The *search system* is the most obviously changed because the representations and mechanisms are dynamic, typically broader, and always physically distinct from manual environments. *Domains* may also change because of electronic environments, for example, fields that progress through scientific visualizations that yield new theory (e.g., astrophysics, molecular chemistry, meteorology). It is possible that medical research will change dramatically as a result of the development of databases of the human genome. Clinical research may, for example, yield to searches through genetic databases (Mathison, personal communication, October 8, 1992). In the humanities, the creators of Perseus argue that the availability of the textual and graphic corpus may lead to more integration among literature, art, archaeology, and philosophy. The *information setting* is also changed by technology, because information seekers can work from home or office and work with machines rather than paper. Finally, *outcomes* are changed by electronic environments because there often are more results to examine and better tools to extract information, and electronic environments often lead to more iterations during information seeking.

# 9

# Future directions and conclusion

*The open society, the unrestricted access to knowledge, the unplanned and uninhibited association of men for its furtherance – these are what make a vast, complex, ever growing, ever changing, ever more specialized and expert technological world, nevertheless a world of community.*

J. Robert Oppenheimer, *Science and the Common Understanding*

Evolution proceeds in many waves, some brief by human temporal sensibilities and some lasting for centuries. Some changes in information seeking take place before technological investments are fully amortized (e.g., the latest CPU or software upgrade brings with it access to new information resources), and some take place over careers as strategies and patterns of use learned in school evolve based on new sources and tools. This final chapter examines one long-term change that computing technology brings to cognition in general and to information seeking in particular, considers how different domains interact to influence the evolution of information seeking, and concludes with some ideas about what types of systems we should strive to build.

## Amplification and augmentation

Applying computational power to information problems has been a research and design goal from the first days of computing. The dreams of language translation and cybernetic assistants have given way to dreams of artificial realities and intelligent agents, but our fascination with the manipulation of symbolic data and with interactivity remains a driving force behind much of the research in artificial intelligence and engineering. One way to consider how computation may be applied to information problems is to examine how it may be applied to amplify and augment intellect. Engelbart (1963) provided an early explication of how computing could be applied to amplify and augment the intellect and many of the developments he envisioned over 30 years ago have been fulfilled.

*Amplification* refers to an increase in an existing value or capability, and *augmentation* refers to the addition of a new value or capability. Electronic technology allows us to reach more people while seeking information and to scan or search more sources. Technology amplifies information seeking when it provides mechanical advantages for some of the information-seeking subprocesses, which in turn allows reallocations of time and cognitive load. As the mechanical advantage grows, it begins to change what is possible – a form of augmentation. Determining when there is enough amplification to enable new capabilities is a central problem in many fields (e.g., when velocity overcomes the force of gravity, when sufficient political dissatisfaction accumulates to force a parliamentary election, when multiple images become motion pictures). For information science, determining when speed and quantity of access enable new types of questions to be addressed is an important issue. One indicator that amplification has led to augmentation is in how our expectations change, such as when we come to expect as commonplace those things that were impossible or difficult beforehand. In turn, our expectations determine our actions, and the manual actions we amplified with technology eventually lead to entirely new actions. This chain of changes is one form of progress and is repeated for different technologies and different generations as part of the evolutionary process.

Lest this argument be overgeneralized, an important distinction must be made between changes in behavior and changes in thought. There is little evidence that basic cognitive and affective activity have changed because of any of the technological changes of the centuries, although many argue that television and video games have fundamentally altered attention spans. What has changed are the objects of thought and external tools for representing and transmitting the products of thought. Technological amplification leads to time savings that may lead to more thought and creativity (augmentation), or these savings may simply be filled with other, similar work – a menial productivity gain. One version of Parkinson's law tells us that jobs expand to fill the time available, and most of the productivity gains that technology provides suggest amplifications of behavior rather than augmentations of thought. An often-debated example of this distinction is the question of whether word-processing tools have improved the quality of writing or have simply created additional time for writers to perform clerical tasks and write more.

From an information-seeking perspective, an augmentation is indicated when the types of questions change. If factual access is less behaviorally demanding, then teachers, researchers, and workers can change assignments, problem focus, and tasks. A key decision is whether the diminished demands lead to more fact retrieval (amplification) or to interpretive information seeking. Some instructors who used Perseus in their teaching changed the types of assignments they gave to students so that the students explored primary materials and thought critically about them rather than studying textbook explications of what scholars wrote about those materials. This was an augmentation of the course, because it enabled new types of activity. Some students blossomed with the freedom to discover and invent their own theories; some floundered about without much effect; and still others complained that they missed the safety of scholarly interpretations. Clearly, these assignments took the place of traditional assignments and in many ways used time less efficiently.

Another way to address the distinction between behavior and thought is to consider specific tasks, the larger activity or job in which those tasks are embedded, and the general intellectual activity required for the job. When technology is used to amplify a specific task (e.g., get results faster, reach more people), the result is a gain in available time or a saving of effort. The time saved by the amplification can be used in different ways: for leisure activity, to perform more similar tasks, or to enable new types of tasks to be undertaken. When more similar tasks are performed, a simple gain in productivity results may be considered an amplification of the job but have no effect on general intellectual activity. When new tasks are undertaken as a result of saving time, the job is augmented and intellectual activity may also be affected. For example, automating serials ordering in a library can save the time usually required to manually fill out and mail order forms. Time savings in this case may permit more attention to evaluation and selection and require different levels and amounts of intellectual activity. When amplification saves effort rather than time, productivity gains may not reflect more throughput but yield higher-quality products. For example, if an electronic search yields many more documents, more time may be required to examine them, but the overall quality of the solutions may be better. These examples illustrate a plausible chain of inferences regarding how amplification of tasks may lead to augmentation of the larger activity and possibly to augmentation of intellectual activity. Whether these inferences obtain is dependent on individual wills and institutional policies.

Interfaces are amplifications because they enable people to easily and effectively map tasks onto information resources. This book has argued that design should amplify human behavior rather than augment it directly. In regard to human performance, augmentation flows from amplification rather than from some external intervention. If we ever learn to be telepathic, it will come from learning about human physiology rather than from the invention of some device. Amplification evolves into augmentation only over a long time, largely because of the constraints of the physical and cultural environment. Humans evolve rather than transform, and the systems that support intellectual activity should amplify intellectual activity rather than directly transform it.

## Communities of perspective and interdisciplinarity

Because information seeking is a generic cognitive activity, different communities develop views and strategies that are most useful for the knowledge and problems specific to their fields of interest. Although there has always been commonality of fields such as psychology, education, and library and information science, the advent of electronic information systems has broadened the overlap, extended the commonality to other fields, and led to increased collaboration and interdisciplinarity. This book is aimed at communities interested in human–computer interaction and information science. These communities, in turn, draw theoretical principles and active participants from the fields of computer science and engineering, education, communications, psychology, philosophy, sociology, and library and information science. Each of these disciplines is concerned with seeking information and has developed particular views, languages, and techniques. Rather than a Tower of Babel, there is strength in this diversity of views, but researchers and practitioners must extend their reach beyond the comfortable confines of their discipline to cognate fields and perspectives.

Research results have demonstrated that information seeking depends on many interacting factors and is evolving in conjunction with developments in electronic technologies. Although much of the research on information seeking has focused on cognitive processes in the information seeker, much more remains to be discovered about how people formulate information problems, plan strategies, express those formulations, reflect on the results, extract and use information, and monitor the entire process. Little work has been done on the affective factors that influence information seeking, and so this seems to be a promising area for research. Although there has been considerable research on the physiological processes related to information seeking in manual environments, we need basic evidence on the physiological limits of human capabilities for scanning, recognizing, and browsing in electronic environments. Thus, there is a need for research on the cognitive, affective, and physiological aspects of information seeking. These problems invite multidisciplinary teams of psychologists, information scientists, and sociologists.

Another research area focuses on the search system. Many engineering problems related to computational speed to process huge amounts of data on-the-fly, high-quality display, and novel input and output devices remain to be solved. More central to the concerns of this book, interface design and development have many challenges, including customizable interfaces for diverse user communities, new mechanisms for browsing and managing multiple views, the integration of analytical and browsing strategies into a common interface, rich and smoothly integrated representations for information objects at different levels of granularity, and a balance of user control with system help and documentation. These challenges invite interdisciplinary teams of engineers, computer scientists, and information scientists. Because information-seeking performance is also determined by the underlying information structures of search systems, computer scientists and information scientists must develop more powerful and more flexible data structures and indexes. Organizations that provide alternative, preprocessed views must be augmented by structures that allow on-the-fly views to be extracted according to information seekers' immediate and evolving needs.

The results of research thus far and the directions for the future have implications for practitioners. Designers of electronic search systems have a huge marketplace for their work and can best succeed by adopting a user-centered design philosophy and attending to the possible interactions among the information-seeking factors. In addition to task analysis, designers must know their user population and conduct formative evaluations. Just as most programming is maintenance rather than original work, interface work must increasingly aim at improving existing interfaces that have large installed bases. Thus, software engineering principles of reusability and incremental improvement should be adopted. Designers and developers should consider ways that browsing strategies can be supported while not losing the power and precision that analytical strategies provide.

Information specialists are perhaps most challenged by the evolution of information seeking because their roles are shifting to training and assisting end users who conduct their own searches, rather than conducting searches for them. Librarians and information specialists are more often collaborating with end users rather than serving as modular consultants on projects. These professionals have always been concerned with organizing and presenting information, and these skills and experiences will be adapted to electronic environments. They have valuable contributions to make to interface design, especially in regard to conceptual interfaces. In addition, information specialists are increasingly active as information entrepreneurs, creating new information products and services that take advantage of electronic technology. Most important, information specialists should be engaged in the evaluation process. Information in many forms and in huge quantities must not only be organized for access but also judged for accuracy and value. Information specialists can coordinate the domain specialists who make such judgments and make sure that evaluative information is included at all levels of representation, starting with the bibliographic record. In addition, information specialists in the publishing industry should organize and disseminate digital multimedia representations in ways that provide a fair return to the creators yet ensure equitable access for all.

## What kinds of information environments do we want?

Given that electronic technology will play a role in most cases of information seeking in the future but has not yet reached levels of maturity that bring stabilization and predictable growth, it is worth speculating on how we envision information seeking in the future. Several technological trends are candidates for improving the state of affairs.

Natural-language processing has developed through several stages, from early machine translation approaches based on brute-force algorithms to knowledge-based approaches depending on huge amounts of organized information and sets of inferencing rules (e.g., Lenat's CYC Project; Lenat, Guha, Pittman, Pratt, & Shepherd, 1990). Another promising stream of development uses common syntactic structures in different languages to create an interlingua that is used as the basis for machine translation (Dorr, 1992–93). Whether computers can "understand" human language is an issue for philosophers, but what is clear is that computers can recognize speech or typed text that adheres to regular patterns and has as their object the execution of some well-defined task. As the work on natural-language processing progresses, the ranges of patterns and tasks will certainly grow, and interfaces that apply human language will be more common. As is the case with all systems that support information seeking, people must still be able to articulate their information problem, make decisions about progress, and interpret results.

Intelligent agents have generated considerable interest, possibly because of the naive notion that we all can use personal secretaries or assistants in our professional and personal lives. Agents are reminiscent of batch processing, in which tasks are defined and the user goes on to another problem while the system executes the task. Two problems with agents for information seeking are apparent. First, the information seeker must articulate the task to the agent. This entails specifying where, what, and how the agent should search. It also requires that information seekers manage their agents – a requirement that itself could become time-consuming. Second, we have argued in this book that information seeking is a process, and so simply being involved with the input and output robs the information seeker of significant parts of the process. It is easy to imagine sending off agents to perform simple retrieval tasks, but it makes no more sense to believe that people will give up the experience of complex information seeking and learning to agents than it does to believe they would send their dog to the theater to see a play.

Another technology that generates considerable interest is virtual reality (telepresence). Visions of gliding through the bookshelves of virtual libraries and picking up animated volumes of information make for good conversation, but what real advantages can virtual reality offer? Information seeking is most often associated with nonfiction, with representations for abstractions related to reality. For virtual reality to be useful, it is necessary for designers to represent ideas and concepts as objects that can be observed and manipulated. This may be possible for spreadsheet values or database entries, but moving in and out of spaces of concepts and ideas requires that such spaces be defined and filled with appropriate information sources. This is the essential problem of classification systems (e.g., the Dewey Decimal System, the Colon Classification System). The problems of categorization that such systems encounter are intellectual and interpretive, and any virtual representation is only as good as the underlying categorizations. Virtual reality seems promising for managing things, but it is unclear how it can help people manage words and ideas. Virtual reality seems most appropriate to entertainment based on fictional contexts or to training simulations for complex systems (from which it developed).

Another technological trend that offers some interesting possibilities for information seeking is ubiquitous computing, in effect the aggregate advantages of having interconnected computers everywhere. Computers on the person (ranging from "Dick Tracy" communication watches to wearable robots) unite with computers in the home and workplace to provide constant access and control capabilities. Beyond the obvious possibilities of using commuting time to access and use remote information, having computational devices in the world around us offers new levels of control. If we consider putting computers into books and other information sources rather than simply putting books on computers, we may be able to invite information to come to us rather than having to go find it.

In addition to looking at specific technological trends, it may be instructive to consider global functionality. Do we want uniform information systems? Should everyone in the world be given a standardized device that enables uniform training and supports equitable usage? Although the final results from competitiveness in the telephone industries of the world are not yet in, there clearly seem to be some advantages to diversifying systems and services. A more idealized functionality is what might be called *information alchemy*. Given a potentially relevant information item, systems should be able to rerepresent it in a different form that better suits the needs of the information seeker. In the simplest case, a data set should be displayable in tabular or graphical forms. In the extreme, a text should be representable as a video. Rerepresentation is made possible by electronic environments, and many information-seeking innovations will come as we move from the simple rerepresentations toward the impossible extremes.

One way to encourage divergent thinking about possibilities is to consider some scenarios that use various technologies in problem contexts. The following three scenarios are meant to provoke thought about possible directions for future systems.

### Scenario one: Multimedia knowledge bases

Deanna is a first-year engineering student assigned to a team that must design and build a windmill as a semester project. Cost constraints are provided; the model must be built and tested using reliable metrics; and a comprehensive written report that defends the procedure with literature and practice must be delivered. As part of the first group discussion, each member agrees to spend 2 weeks learning as much about windmills as possible before assigning specific tasks to individual members. Deanna accesses the Net from her dorm room and verbally describes her information needs to the system, at times reading phrases and sentences from the assignment provided by the instructor. A series of video descriptions appears. She does not even consider the virtual-world option, having long since decided that simulated experiences were best for entertainment. To determine which video to use, she chooses to see video clip summaries of 45 frames per second (she has learned through experience that 50% increases in display still allow her to get the sense of motion images – she envies her sister's ability to comprehend 75% increases) rather than to view the written summaries or hear the verbal summaries of each. Because she said she is looking for overview information at this time, the system presents 100 video summaries ranked according to statistical and knowledge-based retrieval analyses of her verbal problem statement. The fourth clip looks interesting and includes some spectacular views of the Utah desert area she plans to explore next summer. Her gesture freezes the summary window and begins the 30-minute presentation on windmills throughout history narrated by a prominent Japanese professor of materials science. As the video progresses, Deanna cuts and pastes single frames and short sequences into her notebook, in some cases including textual transcripts.

About 10 minutes into the video, she freezes the presentation and goes back to the summary window to scan through several more possible choices. After viewing one complete video and speeding through several more, she begins to focus on the trade-offs between the number of blades and production tolerances. Requesting blueprints for a two-blade optimal windmill for moderate wind conditions and for the traditional prairie design, she runs the simulations under different wind speeds to make sure that the two-blade design is superior. Fortunately, she noted that the narrator had commented on how critical blade balance was to the two-blade design and on the high costs of ceramic blades. She wonders what the cost–performance trade-offs will be, given the group's inexperience with the manufacturing processes and their severe cost constraints. She types this problem (she found long ago that she can type as fast as she can talk), attaches it to her notes, and copies it to the rest of the group to get their thoughts on whether they should aim for an optimal design that they may not be able to implement or a more practical design.

### Scenario two: Intelligent agents

Brian has 15 years of experience as a clinical psychologist in a state-run long-term care facility for the elderly and also has a thriving private practice. Because government services are increasingly contracted out to private enterprise, Brian has begun to consider opening a for-profit long-term facility. He has first hand experience with the needed services, and he has many colleagues who may be interested in joining his venture. He needs information about the administrative aspects of the concept, however, before he can begin serious discussions with others. Brian sits down at his workstation and begins to compose intelligent agents that he will send into the Global Web. Although he does not have the latest agent-construction set, he does have experience using and confidence in Knowboty Better (Version 5.8.1, trademark Megasmart Inc.).

Brian defines an agent to gather information on local and state regulations for medical facilities, specifying the finest grain of detail (he wants regulations on all aspects of buildings and services) but the narrowest set of sources (he wants the regulations only for a single state and a few specific counties). He defines another agent to explore financial sources for investment costs, profit data, and competition in the long-term care field, setting broad parameters for sources and overview information (he knows he will eventually refine this agent to seek more specific data once he has gained a sense of the financial aspects). He requires this agent to report back daily and to include public-domain simulation models that he can use for analyzing the data. He configures another agent to locate and organize coverage data for the various public and private health insurance options, specifying weekly reports. Another agent is defined to examine the availability of human resources in the region and typical credentials and salaries for physicians, nurses, attendants, social workers, and other health care workers. He suggests several professional jobline sources with which he is familiar and allows flexibility for the agent to consult others with high-similarity profile coefficients (including the newspaper want ads). Other specific agents are similarly constructed for topics such as the availability of buildings in the region, tax codes, and venture capital sources. A global agent is also constructed to gather medical and psychological case studies conducted at long-term care facilities. This agent's parameters are set to report back every other day and deposit cases in a database of psychological cases that Brian has constructed as part of his professional growth over the years (he views this as a sort of hedge, for even if he eventually decides not to develop a formal prospectus for the venture, he will have augmented his psychological database with some physiological cases that may help him in his work).

### Scenario three: Implants, ubiquitous computing, and human–machine symbiosis

Suzanne has a busy medical practice in a large metropolitan area. When she arrives at her office, she notes that the day wall displays today's appointments, most of which involve routine checkups or well-defined symptoms, but eight of them glow softly to indicate that some special preparations must be made. The first special case is a patient she has not seen in 2 years, a middle-aged man with little medical history who is coming because of persistent headaches and a low fever for the past 10 days. Suzanne selects one of the hundreds of implant modules displayed on the info wall and activates the radio link between the wall and her knowplant. Her knowplant (Real Intelligence Inc.) was recently upgraded to provide better visual/ kinesthetic fidelity and coordination, although she wishes she had invested the extra money to get the newly developed olfactory link.

In the milliseconds it takes for the module to come inmind (beyond online), she gasps at the visual/auditory burst, a sensation she has never quite gotten used to in her years of using her various implants. Although thinking about headache and fever will yield sensations and visual/auditory images of the latest causal probability diagrams with accompanying case studies, Suzanne verbalizes the words as well. The Symbiosis Society has long debated whether multiple channel inputs improve the focus or the vividness of memories, but she has always found it reassuring to verbalize while thinking. As specific cases race through her mind, she turns her attention to possible diagnostic tests. Various instruments and monitors in her examination room snap to attention as she considers the data collection strategies she may want to use during her examination later that day. The various instruments are alerted by Suzanne's implant through signals sent to their internal computers and subsequently are updated from the patient medical record by the info wall.

Suzanne recalls her mentor from medical school, who told stories about searching huge bibliographic files just to locate paper journal articles that were then obtained through interlibrary loan. What was the name of that system? It never ceased to amaze her that simple fact retrieval was more difficult with knowplants because their organizations were conceptual in nature (top down from concepts to cases) rather than organized by discrete tokens like those old retrieval systems. As the first patient of the day arrives, it occurs to Suzanne that her patients believe they are coming to her office but that in many ways they are coming into her mind and enveloped by her augmented expertise disguised as an office.

Each of these scenarios offers some appeal and some repulsion. Although cast in positive contexts, each scenario could just as easily have presented the same technological perspective in horrific settings. It seems certain that aspects of each of these scenarios will come to pass, with the order of presentation likely correlating with the passage of time. Certainly, most of the technical components of scenario one would be available today if the cost constraints and the dilemma of technology/database push–pull (if there were an installed base of hardware, the programming would come, and vice versa) could be ignored.

Scenario two represents an active area of research and speculation, and surely today's ability to send queries to multiple databases on a "canned" user profile basis will continue to become more sophisticated. A major problem here is "agent management": Controlling a group of agents itself requires time and effort, let alone making sense out of and integrating the fruits of their searches.

Scenario three is the least technically feasible, but research in monitoring and controlling electromagnetic and electrical activity in the brain continues to progress toward mapping and understanding how the brain works. Moreover, the trends toward installing computing power in many devices rather than a single workstation is strong, positive, and irreversible. In fact, we should concentrate on putting computers into books rather than writing books on computers. The main problem here, of course, is not the technology but the failure to distinguish between brain and mind. We can conceive of a brain that contains all the external representations of knowledge in the world, but not a mind that can survive without learning and interpretation.

More specifically, these scenarios do not obviate the importance of the information-seeking process. Information problems must be recognized, accepted, and defined. Although recognition and definition may be aided by external factors, acceptance is a strictly human factor. Moreover, recognition and definition must be driven by conscious attention and thought, and consciousness is the antithesis of machinery. Information problems must be articulated, and search systems selected.

These subprocesses require mapping mental concepts to words, icons, or other physically represented tokens. System selection requires knowledge about alternatives and evaluative judgments of coverage and value. Evaluation and selection are perhaps the most critical elements of human information-seeking activity and are most directly applied during the subprocesses of system selection, examination of results, and reflection. In all these scenarios, the information seeker makes judgments about the possible relevance of high-level representations such as video summaries or memory modules. Relevance judgments regarding specific primary information related to the problem also must take into account applicability, accuracy, and expected value. These decisions in turn determine what is extracted and eventually used in solving the information problem. In sum, the technology may evolve beyond anything we can now imagine, but information seekers will always be required to think, make inferences and decisions, and develop confidence in these processes.

## Conclusion

The aim of information seeking is to get relevant information into one's head and either use it in conjunction with known information to take some action or integrate it into the knowledge base. This is accomplished by coordinating information-seeking factors in systematic and heuristic ways. Our personal information infrastructures are central to this process. Domain knowledge helps us determine where to look and what to look for; information-seeking skills help us to formulate queries and browse; and system knowledge allows us to manipulate the many devices that provide access to the various representations available. Search systems not only deliver information, but they also provide structure and format that guides and influences search. A critical need is for human–computer interaction research to address how electronic systems can enhance and go beyond the delivery and structuring techniques available in manual environments. Domains of knowledge are organized to distinguish themselves from other domains. These organizations and protocols guide information seeking for those familiar with the domain, but those systems used by domain novices must illustrate and make explicit such features.

There can be no doubt that we are immersed in a set of complex relationships with the environment. The things we do choose to think about are influenced by the world around us. Likewise, as part of the environment, we influence the world – sometimes in devastating ways. People are incredibly adaptable to positive as well as adverse conditions and also adapt the world to their needs. In the case of information environments, we have adapted to systems, collections, and organizations that have been put together in either haphazard ways or for the sake of efficiencies of scale. A more balanced, ecological, and sustainable view of information seeking in electronic environments is to design systems that amplify human capabilities and propensities so that the resulting augmentations will be positive and natural rather than sophisticated workarounds that we pass on to future generations of information seekers.

Our personal information infrastructures are constantly developing and changing throughout our lives. Systems designed principally for the convenience of the designer or the institution rather than the end user impede productive and satisfying work and inhibit the continued development of personal information infrastructures. What we have argued for in this book is design based on taking advantage of natural human capabilities and propensities rather than systems that magically or transparently think for users. This is particularly important to information seekers because information seeking is primarily an intellectual rather than a physical activity. We may like the thought of machines that can find the information we need, and in fact, we can observe systems that retrieve well-defined facts that we may need. What we cannot imagine and what we will not admit are machines that think for us. Somewhere in between is where most of information seeking falls. Information seeking is thinking in that most of the time we are not quite sure what we need – we are not quite sure what the information problem is – and it is the seeking itself that illuminates, informs, and assists us in defining, growing, learning, and succeeding. Directly hardwiring one's brain to a world encyclopedia database may ultimately facilitate more rapid associations and more broad-based associations, but ultimately it is our personal struggles with the problems, concepts, and abstractions of information that define not only intellectual tasks but also what we are as human beings.

Two principles obtain from this point of view. First, we should design systems that amplify and enhance natural capabilities. Second, we should pay more attention to the information-seeking process and the interactions among the information-seeking factors rather than to technology itself. An ecological point of view that bases design on how the different components interact with and influence one another is what is needed. The information-seeking process has become much more integrated, fluid, and parallel because of electronic environments, but most of the tools and techniques that have been developed focus on the query formulation and examination subprocesses. These are clearly needed, but what is more critical is attention to the problems of acceptance, definition, extraction, and use and, in fact, integrating the entire information-seeking process into the larger tasks of learning, working, and planning.

# Notes

## Chapter 1

1. Shoshana Zuboff used the more action-oriented term *informated society* in her book *In the Age of the Smart Machine* (1988). Although this phrase is more appropriate to the highly interactive environments discussed in this book, we use the more popular term *information society*. Drucker (1968) used the term *knowledge society* and Bell (1973) described the knowledge-driven, technological society as *postindustrial*.
2. According to the 1990 U.S. Census, 46% of American children use computers in school or at home, and 37% of American adults use computers at work (*Communications of the ACM,* June 1991). The *Statistical Abstracts of the United States, 1993* reports that 99.4% of all high schools have computers (a mean of 45 per school) and 98.5% of elementary schools have computers (a mean of 19 per school). A Times Mirror Center survey (*Communications of the ACM,* July 1994) reports that one-third of all households in the United States contain a personal computer, that 23 million adults use a home computer every day, that 46% of the teenagers have a home computer, that 28% of the children use a home computer for educational purposes, and that 10% of the home computers have modems.
3. An examination of today's remote controls for home entertainment systems supports the wag's observation that the tools we use to control our tools are more complex than those we use to build them.

## Chapter 2

1. The term *system* is used to include information objects such as books or people, as well as electronic objects.
2. Shannon and Weaver (1949, p. 56) report 50% redundancy in ordinary English language; that is, about half of what we write is determined by the structure of the language itself rather than the content we wish to present.
3. Card, Moran, and Newell (1983) report cycle times for perceptual and cognitive cycles processors. The time to recognize distinct flashes of light ranges from 50 to 200 milliseconds (ms); Card, Moran, and Newell use 100 ms as an average. Times for various object recognition, counting, and selection tasks vary from 25 to 170 ms, so they use 70 ms as average. An estimate of 10 cycles per second is based on these data. Potter and Levy (1969) cite ranges from 50 to 300 ms for single pictures with low to high levels of visual noise, and their studies demonstrate that the accuracy of visual recognition improved as display times increased from 125 ms (16% accuracy) to 1000 ms (80% accuracy).
4. Human speech (both speaking and listening) averages 120 words per minute (wpm), or roughly 80 bits per second (bps) (Streeter, 1988). Human reading averages between 200 and 300 wpm, roughly 140 to 200 bps (Streeter, 1988, cites 200 to 300 wpm, and Hulme, 1984, cites 250 to 300 wpm). If we consider the 100 million rods and cones in the human eye as capable of accepting a bit in a "glance," visual input is approximately 100 million bits per glance. It is important to note that these values have not changed over the last 6000 years!
5. For example, much of our social intercourse depends on current events and "trivia" that we accumulate. More important, insights and research advances come as a result of humans' making

connections among seemingly unrelated ideas or events. The development of highly constrained filtering agents can have serious consequences for us individually as well as for civilization itself.

6. For example, the parallel architecture of the Connection machine has been applied to send a query concurrently to multiple databases in a wide area information server (WAIS) (Kahle & Medlar, 1991).

7. In practice, commonly occurring words (stop words) are not included, and word-stemming principles are often applied. See Belkin and Croft (1987) or Salton (1989) for an overview of information retrieval principles.

8. String search based on inverted files or on signature files (Faloutsos, 1985) is more properly called *full-text* or *word* search, because in true string search, each character or character group is scanned in linear fashion at the time of search. Scanning techniques are impractical in large databases because every character must be examined and compared; thus strategies such as indexes are applied in advance of search.

## Chapter 3

1. Fidel and Soergel (1983) identified scores of interacting variables in eight categories related to online bibliographic retrieval. Their analysis included intermediaries and end users as categories.

2. *Precision* is the ratio of relevant documents retrieved to the total number of documents retrieved, and *recall* is the ratio of relevant documents retrieved to the total number of relevant documents in the database.

3. Note that this assignment of terms depends on the information seeker's vocabulary, not the system's. The mapping from personal to system terminology takes place later during query formulation.

4. Saracevic and Kantor (1988b) classified questions into five categories: domain, clarity (semantic and syntactic), specificity (of both the task statement and the content of task), complexity (number of concepts), and presupposition (number of implied concepts not explicitly stated in the task statement). Marchionini and his colleagues (Wang, Liebscher, & Marchionini, 1988) used five criteria to classify questions in their studies of hypertext use: complexity (number of concepts), specificity (variability of appropriate answers), focus (determinability of the primary concept), path (length of the optimal route to find the answer in a specific database), and accessibility (difficulty of finding the optimal path).

5. These assignments of "aboutness" are never perfect, as information specialists who originally catalog books can attest, and the assignment of subject headings to databases of all sorts is a challenge that has long been constrained both physically (limitations on the number of subject headings allowed) and conceptually (unambiguously capturing the many terms related to a topic). Gomez, Lochbaum, and Landauer (1990) suggested assigning as many terms as possible to improve retrieval – something that is much easier in electronic environments.

6. Waltz (1990) reports $4 \times 10^{16}$ bytes as an estimate of human long-term memory capacity, but no one has officially reported running out of memory!

7. Display units include cathode ray tubes (CRTs) that depend on electrons systematically striking phosphorus-coated screens, liquid-crystal panels that require a separate light source and depend on the electronic realignment of organic liquid crystals, and electroluminescent displays that depend on thin phosphor layers that allow a thin, flat screen. See Helander (1987) for an overview of visual display technology and human factors.

8. There is a clear trend toward use of multiple I/O devices to enhance interactivity. Multiple I/O devices are the basis for telepresence (virtual reality), and it remains to be seen how multiple channels of information flow will affect information seeking.

9. Communication systems can be characterized as simplex (the source is always the source, and the destination cannot reply), half duplex (both the source and the destination can send and receive but

must take turns to do so), and full duplex (both the source and the destination can send and receive simultaneously).

10. It is interesting that most formal instruction is carefully sequenced but that discussions are likely to be less well structured. The benefits of the two instructional strategies in combination may help guide our thinking about the mix of linear and nonlinear presentations in electronic systems.

11. In chapter 4 we argue that information-seeking knowledge and skills represent a domain of knowledge.

12. Examples of high-performance computing leading to new discoveries in physics, meteorology, and other fields are common (e.g., see Billingsley, Brown, & Derohanes, 1992). Examples of retrieval systems leading to new knowledge include Swanson's (1991) use of medical literature retrieval systems to gain new medical knowledge (e.g., he discovered previously unknown relationships between migraine headaches and magnesium by using bibliographic searches of medical literature to locate common terms or citations in disparate literatures) and scholars' use of the morphological tools in Perseus to discover new philological insights (Marchionini & Crane, 1994).

13. Problem definition is the first step in Polya's (1957) classic treatment of problem solving through heuristic and deductive thinking. His suggestions for problem definition include an examination of what is known and what the problem conditions are, consideration of whether the problem can be solved, the introduction of suitable notation, the separation and writing down of parts of the conditions, and the drawing of figures.

14. For example, CONIT (Marcus, 1983) includes assistance in selecting a database as well as its primary mission of aiding the online search process; $I^3$ R (Croft & Thompson, 1987) includes user models and a variety of experts that help users conduct a search; and CODER (Fox, 1987) takes document structure into account in providing expert search assistance.

15. The main entries for a given document in most large U.S. academic libraries are determined according to an elaborate set of rules published as the Anglo-American Cataloging Rules. In most cases, the main entry for a document is the first author's last name, although many variations are possible.

16. Willett and his colleagues (Willett, 1991) proposed paragraph ranking as an access mechanism for full-text retrieval. Such approaches also offer good opportunities for aiding information extraction as well.

## Chapter 4

1. Davis uses the term *abduction,* "lead from," rather than *adduction,* "lead to."

2. Professional information specialists need additional specialized skills, as they are often removed from the problem, and they must also develop skills in helping clients articulate the problem.

3. There has also been considerable study of business databases in business settings that are designed to support well-defined fact retrieval tasks. This work has led to significant improvements in interfaces, especially query languages, and alternative interaction styles, such as query by example.

## Chapter 5

1. Combining sets in a pairwise fashion, or other than all at once, is considered by Harter (1986) as a distinct strategy called *pairwise facets.*

2. A series of technical reports on the project evaluation is available as Perseus working papers Nos. 8, 9, 11, 12, and 14, 15, 16, and 17 (Perseus Project, Harvard University). The current version of Perseus includes texts from more than 100 books and plays and 25,000 24-bit color images.

3. Perseus is somewhat unusual in that there are few explicit hypertext links but, rather, a series of indexes and tools enabling users to create their own links as needed. Thus, Perseus is much more like a library than a computer-based instruction system. This design philosophy is expressed by the system architects in Mylonas (1992) and Crane (1988).

**Chapter 6**

1. Skimming is not considered here because it is peculiar to text, whereas scanning is independent of the medium.
2. Norman (1988) discusses the importance of matching "knowledge in the head" and "knowledge in the world" for successful human–computer interaction.

**Chapter 8**

1. A 10-million volume collection (most large academic libraries have a few million volumes) of 150,000-word books (this book has about 90,000 words), at a generous 7 characters per word on average, yields about 8.5 terabytes.
2. This point should not be underestimated. It is one thing to collect and store huge volumes of data and quite another to process and use them. For example, without parallel processing, it would take 25 years to load and process the 115 terabytes of GOES data currently archived on 27,000 three-quarter-inch videotapes!
3. Some school libraries have addressed this problem by marking serial titles that are available in the local collection.
4. It is interesting to observe the steps of system evolution in this regard. We are progressing from having huge printed volumes of subject headings placed near OPACs, to putting the subject headings online as a separate file or function, to integrating them as a feature of the interface.

# References

Akscyn, R. (1991). *The Association for Computing Machinery hypertext compendium.* New York: ACM Press.

Allen, B. (1992). Cognitive differences in end user searching of a CD-ROM index. In *Proceedings of the fifteenth annual international ACM SIGIR Conference on Research and Development in Information Retrieval* (Copenhagen, June 21–24, 1992), pp. 298–307.

Allen, R. B. (1990). User models: Theory, method, and practice. *International Journal of Man–Machine Studies, 32,* 511–543.

Allen, T. J. (1977). *Managing the flow of technology: Technology transfer and the dissemination of technological information within the R&D organization.* Cambridge, MA: MIT Press.

Andriole, S. J. (Ed.). (1984). *Computer-based national information systems.* New York: Petrocelli Books.

Apple Computer Inc. (1992). *The virtual museum, release 1.0.* Cupertino, CA: Apple Computer Inc.

Apted, S. M. (1971). General purposive browsing. *Library Association Record, 73*(12), 228–230.

Arthur D. Little, Inc. (1967). *The 3 R's program: Report to division of library development New York State Library.* Cambridge, MA: Arthur D. Little, Inc.

Auster, E. & Choo, C. W. (1993). Environmental scanning by CEOs in two Canadian industries. *Journal of the American Society for Information Science, 44*(4), 194–203.

Auster, E., & Lawton, S. (1984). Search interview techniques and information gain as antecedents of user satisfaction with online bibliographic retrieval. *Journal of the American Society for Information Science, 35*(2), 90–103.

Barrett, E. (Ed.). (1988). *Text, conText, and hyperText: Writing with and for the computer.* Cambridge, MA: MIT Press.

Bates, M. (1979a). Idea tactics. *Journal of the American Society for Information Science, 30*(5), 280–289.

Bates, M. (1979b). Information search tactics. *Journal of the American Society for Information Science, 30*(4), 205–214.

Bates, M. (1986). Subject access in online catalogs: A design model. *Journal of the American Society for Information Science, 37*(6), 357–376.

Bates, M. (1989). The design of browsing and berrypicking techniques for the online search interface. *Online Review, 13*(5), 407–424.

Bederson, B. (1994). Pad++: Advances in multiscale interfaces. In *Proceedings of CHI '94, Conference Companion* (Boston, April 24–28, 1994), p. 315. New York: ACM Press.

Beheshti, J. (1992). Browsing through public library catalogs. *Information Technology and Libraries, 11*(3), 220–228.

Belew, R. (1986). *Adaptive information retrieval: Machine learning in associative networks.* Unpublished doctoral dissertation, University of Michigan.

Belge, M., Lokuge, I., & Rivers, D. (1993). Back to the future: A graphical layering system inspired by transparent paper. *INTERCHI '93 Adjunct Proceedings* (Amsterdam, April 24–29, 1993), pp. 129–130. New York: ACM Press.

Belkin, N. J. (1978). Information concepts for information science. *Journal of Documentation, 34*(10), 55–85.

Belkin, N. J. (1980). Anomalous states of knowledge as a basis for information retrieval. *Canadian Journal of Information Science, 5,* 133–143.

Belkin, N. J., & Croft, W. B. (1987). Retrieval techniques. In M. Williams (Ed.), *Annual review of information science and technology* (Vol. 22, pp. 109–145). White Plains, NY: Knowledge Industries.

Belkin, N. J., & Croft, W. B. (1992). Information filtering and information retrieval: Two sides of the same coin? *Communications of the ACM, 35*(12), 29–38.

Belkin, N. J., Marchetti, P. G., & Cool, C. (1993). BRAQUE: Design of an interface to support user interaction in information retrieval. *Information Processing & Management, 29*(3), 325–344.

Belkin, N. J., Oddy, R. N., & Brooks, H. M. (1982). ASK for information retrieval: Part 1. Background and theory. *Journal of Documentation, 38*(2), 61–71.

Bell, D. (1973). *The coming post-industrial society: A venture in social forecasting.* New York: Basic Books.

Bellardo, T. (1985). An investigation of online searcher traits and their relationship to search outcome. *Journal of the American Society for Information Science, 36,* 241–250.

Berk, E., & Devlin, J. (1991). *Hypertext/hypermedia handbook.* New York: McGraw-Hill.

Bernstein, M., Bolter, J. D., Joyce, M., & Mylonas, E. (1991). Architectures for volatile hypertext. In *Proceedings of Hypertext '91* (San Antonio, December 15–18, 1992), pp. 243–260.

Billingsley, K. R., Brown, H. U., & Derohanes, E. (Eds.). (1992). *Scientific excellence in supercomputing: The IBM 1990 contest prize papers* (Vols. 1 & 2). Athens, GA: Baldwin Press.

Bolt, R. A. (1984). *The human interface: Where people and computers meet.* Belmont, CA: Lifetime Learning Publications.

Bolter, J. D. (1991). *Writing space: The computer, hypertext, and the history of writing.* Hillsdale, NJ: Erlbaum.

Bookstein, A. (1985). Probability and fuzzy-set applications to information retrieval. In M. Williams (Ed.), *Annual review of information science and technology* (Vol. 20, pp.117–151). White Plains, NY: Knowledge Industries.

Borgman, C. L. (1986a). The user's mental model of an information retrieval system: An experiment on a prototype online catalog. *International Journal of Man–Machine Studies, 24*(1), 47–64.

Borgman, C. L. (1986b). Why are online catalogs hard to use? Lessons learned from information-retrieval studies. *Journal of the American Society for Information Science, 37*(6), 387–400.

Borgman, C. L. (1989). All users of information systems are not created equal: An exploration into individual differences. *Information Processing & Management, 25*(3), 237–252.

Borgman, C. L., Case, D., & Meadow, C. (1989). The design and evaluation of a front-end user interface for energy researchers. *Journal of the American Society for Information Science, 40*(2), 99–109.

Borgman, C. L., Gallagher, A. L., Krieger, D., & Bower, J. (1990). Children's use of an interactive catalog of science materials. In *Proceedings of the ASIS* (Toronto, November 4–8, 1990) pp. 55–68.

Botafogo, R. A., & Shneiderman, B. (1991). Identifying aggregates in hypertext structures. In *Proceedings of Hypertext '91* (San Antonio, December 15–18, 1991), pp. 63–74.

Bransford, J., Sherwood, R., Hasselbring, T., Kinzer, C., & Williams, S. (1990). Anchored instruction: Why we need it and how technology can help. In D. Nix & R. Spiro (Eds.), *Cognition, education, and multimedia: Exploring ideas in high technology,* pp. 115–141. Hillsdale, NJ: Erlbaum.

Brockmann, R. J. (1990). *Writing better computer user documentation from paper to hypertext: Version 2.0.* New York: Wiley.

Brown, J. S., Collins, A., & Duguid, P. (1989). Situated cognition and the culture of learning. *Educational Researcher, 18*(1), 32–41.

Buckland, M. (1991). *Information and information systems.* New York: Praeger.

Buckland, M., & Lynch, C. (1987). The linked systems protocol and the future of bibliographic networks and systems. *Information and Technology Libraries, 6*(2), 83–88.

Burke, F. (1981). The future course of archival theory in the United States. *American Archivist, 44,* 40–46.

Carbonell, J. (Ed.). (1992). *Machine learning: Paradigms and methods* (2nd ed.). Cambridge, MA: MIT Press.

Card, S., Moran, T., & Newell, A. (1983). *The psychology of human–computer interaction.* Hillsdale, NJ: Erlbaum.

Card, S., Robertson, G., & Mackinlay, J. (1991). The information visualizer, an information workspace. In *Proceedings of CHI '91* (New Orleans, April 28–May 2, 1991), pp. 181–188. New York: ACM.

Carmel, E., Crawford, S., & Chen, H. (1992). Browsing in hypertext: A cognitive study. *IEEE Transactions on Systems, Man, and Cybernetics, 22*(5), 865–884.

Carroll, J. M. (1990). *The Nurnberg funnel: Designing minimalist instruction for practical computer skill.* Cambridge, MA: MIT Press.

Carroll, J. M., & Aaronson, A. P. (1988). Learning by doing with simulated intelligent help. *Communications of the ACM, 31*(9), 1064–1079.

Chang, S-J., & Rice, R. E. (1993). Browsing: A multidimensional framework. In M. Williams (Ed.), *Annual review of information science and technology* (Vol. 28, pp. 231–276). White Plains, NY: Knowledge Industries.

Chase, W. G., & Simon, H. A. (1973). Perception in chess. *Cognitive Psychology, 4,* 55–81.

Chi, M., Glaser, R., & Farr, M. (1988). *The nature of expertise.* Hillsdale, NJ: Erlbaum.

Connelly, D., et al. (1990). Knowledge resource preferences of family physicians. *Journal of Family Practice, 30*(3), 353–359.

Cooper, W. (1971). A definition of relevance for information retrieval. *Information Storage and Retrieval, 7*(1), 19–37.

Corkill, C., & Mann, M. (1978). *Information needs in the humanities: Two postal surveys.* Sheffield: Centre for Research on User Studies, University of Sheffield. CRUS Occasional Paper 2, BLB & DD Report No. 5455.

Cove, J. F., & Walsh, B. C. (1988). Online text retrieval via browsing. *Information Processing & Management, 24*(10) 31–37.

Covell, D., Uman, G., & Manning, P. (1985). Information needs in office practice: Are they being met? *Annals of Internal Medicine, 103,* 596–599.

Crane, G. (1988). Redefining the book: Some preliminary problems. *Academic Computing, 2*(5), 6–11, 36–41.

Crane, G. (Ed.). (1992). Perseus 1.0: *Interactive sources and studies on ancient Greece.* New Haven, CT: Yale University Press.

Croft, W. B., & Thompson, R. H. (1987). I³R: A new approach to the design of document retrieval systems. *Journal of the American Society for Information Science, 38*(6), 389–404.

Croft, W. B., & Turtle, H. (1989). A retrieval model for incorporating hypertext links. In *Hypertext 89 Proceedings* (Pittsburgh, November 5–8, 1989), pp. 213–224. New York: ACM Press.

Cummings, A. M., Witte, M. L., Bowen, W. G., Lazarus, L. O., & Ekman, R. H. (1992). *University libraries and scholarly communication: A study prepared for the Andrew W. Mellon Foundation.* Washington, DC: Association of Research Libraries.

Cutting, D. R., Karger, D. R., Pedersen, J. O., & Tukey, J. W. (1992). Scatter/gather: A cluster-based approach to browsing large document collections. In *Proceedings of the fifteenth annual international ACM SIGIR Conference on Research and Development in Information Retrieval* (Copenhagen, June 21–24, 1992), pp. 318–329.

Daniels, P. (1986). Cognitive models in information retrieval – An evaluative review. *Journal of Documentation, 42*(4), 272–304.

Davis, E. (1990). *Representations of commonsense knowledge.* San Mateo, CA: Morgan Kaufmann.

Deerwester, S., Dumais, T., Furnas, G., Landauer, T., & Harshman, R. (1990). Indexing by latent semantic analysis. *Journal of the American Society for Information Science, 41*(6), 391–407.

Dervin, B. (1977). Useful theory for librarianship: Communication, not information. *Drexel Library Quarterly, 13*(3), 16–32.

Dervin, B., & Nilan, M. (1986). Information needs and uses. In M. Williams (Ed.), *Annual review of information science and technology* (Vol. 21, pp. 3–33). White Plains, New York: Knowledge Industries.

Dillon, M., Jul, E., Burge, M., & Hickey, C. (1993). Accessing information on the Internet: Toward providing library services for computer-mediated communication. *Internet Research, 3*(1), 54–69.

Dorr, B. J. (1992/93). The use of lexical semantics in linterlingual machine translation. *Machine Translation, 7,* 135–193.

Doszkocs, T., Reggia, J., & Lin, X. (1990). Connectionist models and information retrieval. In M. Williams (Ed.), *Annual review of information science and technology* (Vol. 25, pp. 208–260). White Plains, NY: Knowledge Industries.

Doyle, L. B. (1965). Is automatic classification a reasonable application of statistical analysis of text? *Journal of the Association of Computing Machinery, 12*(4), 473–489.

Drucker, P. (1968). *The age of discontinuity: Guidelines to our changing society.* New York: Harper & Row.

Dumais, S. (1988). Textual information retrieval. In M. Helander (Ed.), *Handbook of human–computer interaction,* pp. 673–700. Amsterdam: North-Holland.

Egan, D. E. (1988). Individual differences in human–computer interaction. In M. Helander (Ed.), *Handbook of human–computer interaction,* pp. 541–568. Amsterdam: North-Holland,.

Egan, D. E., Remde, J. R., Gomez, L. M., Landauer, T. K., Eberhardt, J., & Lochbaum, C. C. (1989). Formative design evaluation of Superbook. *ACM Transactions on Office Information Systems, 7*(1), 30–42.

Elliot, E., & Davenport, G. (1994). Video streamer. In *Proceedings of CHI '94 Conference Companion* (Boston, April 24–28, 1994), pp. 65–66.

Engelbart, D. (1963). A conceptual framework for augmentation of man's intellect. In P. Howerton & D. Weeks (Eds.), *Vistas in information handling* (Vol. 1, pp. 1–29). Washington, DC: Spartan Books.

Erickson, T., & Salomon, G. (1991). Designing a desktop information system: Observations and issues. In *Proceedings of CHI '91, Human Factors in Computing Systems* (New Orleans, April 27–May 2, 1991), pp. 49–54.

Ericsson, K. A., & Staszewski, J. J. (1989). Skilled memory and expertise: Mechanisms of exceptional performance. In D. Klahr & K. Kotovsky (Eds.), *Complex information processing: The impact of Herbert A. Simon,* pp. 235–267. Hillsdale, NJ: Erlbaum.

Estes, W. K. (1982). Learning, memory, and intelligence. In R. Sternberg (Ed.), *Handbook of human intelligence,* pp. 170–224. Cambridge: Cambridge University Press.

Evans, P. (1993). *The enabling and disabling effects of a hypermedia information environment on information seeking and use in an undergraduate course.* Unpublished doctoral dissertation, University of Maryland.

Faloutsos, C. (1985). Access methods for text. *Computing Surveys, 17*(1), 49–74.

Feigenbaum, E., & McCorduck, P. (1983). *The fifth generation: Artificial intelligence and Japan's computer challenge to the world.* Reading, MA: Addison-Wesley.

Fidel, R. (1984). Online searching styles: A case-study-based model of searching behavior. *Journal of the American Society for Information Science, 35*(4), 211–221.

Fidel, R. (1991). Searchers' selection of search keys: I. The selection routine. II. Controlled vocabulary or free-text searching. III. Searching styles. *Journal of the American Society for Information Science, 42*(7), 490–527.

Fidel, R., & Soergel, D. (1983). Factors affecting online bibliographic retrieval: A conceptual framework for research. *Journal of the American Society for Information Science, 34*(3), 163–180.

Fischer, G., & Girgensohn, A. (1990). End-user modifiability in design environments. In *Proceedings of CHI '90* (Seattle, April 1–5, 1990, pp. 183–191). New York: ACM Press.

Fischer, G., & Stevens, C. (1991). Information access in complex, poorly structures information spaces. In *proceedings of CHI* (New Orleans, April 28–May 2, 1992, pp. 63–70). New York: ACM Press.

Flavell, J. H. (1985). *Cognitive development* (2nd ed.). Englewood Cliffs, NJ: Prentice-Hall.

Florance, V. (1992). Medical knowledge for clinical problem solving: A structural analysis of clinical questions. *Bulletin of the Medical Library Association, 80,* 140–149.

Fogg, D. (1984). Lessons learned from "Living in a Database" graphical query interface. In *Proceedings of SIGMOD* (Boston, June 1984, pp. 100–106). New York: ACM Press.

Forester, T., & Morrison, P. (1990). *Computer ethics: Cautionary tales and ethical dilemmas in computing.* Cambridge, MA: MIT Press.

Fox, E. A. (1987). Development of the CODER system: A testbed for artificial intelligence methods in information retrieval. *Information Processing & Management, 23*(4), 341–366.

Fox, E. A. (1991). Standards and the emergence of digital multimedia systems. *Communications of the ACM, 34*(4), 26–29.

Frakes, W. B., & Baeza-Yates, R. (1992). *Information retrieval: Data structures & algorithms.* Englewood Cliffs, NJ: Prentice-Hall.

Frisse, M. E. (1988). Searching for information in a hypertext medical handbook. *Communications of the ACM, 31*(7), 880–886.

Frisse, M. E., & Cousins, S. B. (1989). Information retrieval from hypertext: Update on the dynamic medical handbook project. In *Proceedings of Hypertext '89* (Pittsburgh, November 5–8, 1989), pp. 199–212.

Fuchi, K., Kowalski, R., Furukawa, K., Ueda, K., Kahn, K., Chikayama, T., & Tick, E. (1993). Launching the new era. *Communications of the ACM, 36*(3), 49–101.

Furnas, G. W. (1986). Generalized fisheye views. In *Proceedings of CHI '86, Human Factors in Computer Systems Conference* (Boston, April 13–17, 1986), pp. 16–23.

Furuta, R., & Stotts, P. D. (1989). Programmable browsing semantics in Trellis. In *Proceedings of Hypertext '89* (Pittsburgh, November 5–8, 1989), pp. 27–42.

Garber, S. R., & Grunes, M. B. (1992). The art of search: A study of art directors. In *Proceedings of CHI '92, Human Factors in Computing Systems* (Monterey, CA, May 3–7, 1992), pp. 157–163.

Garfield, E. (1955). Citation indexes for science: A new dimension in documentation through association of ideas. *Science, 122,* 108–111.

Garner, R. (1987). *Metacognition and reading comprehension.* Norwood, NJ: Ablex.

Garner, R. (1990). When children and adults do not use learning strategies: Toward a theory of settings. *Review of Educational Research, 60*(4), 517–529.

Garner, R., Gillingham, M. G., & White, C. S. (1989). Effects of "seductive details" on macroprocessing and microprocessing in adults and children. *Cognition and Instruction, 6,* 41–57.

Gecsei, J., & Martin, D. (1989, September–October). Browsing access to visual information. *Optical Information Systems,* pp. 237–241.

Glaser, R. (1987). Thoughts on expertise. In C. Schooler & W. Schaie (Eds.), *Cognitive functioning and social structure over the life course.* Norwood, NJ: Ablex.

Glaser, R., & Chi, M. T. H. (1988). Overview. In M. Chi, R. Glaser, & M. Farr (Eds.), *The nature of expertise,* pp. xv–xxviii. Hillsdale, NJ: Erlbaum.

Gomez, L., Lochbaum, C., & Landauer, T. (1990). All the right words: Finding what you want as a function of richness of indexing vocabulary. *Journal of the American Society for Information Science, 41*(8), 547–559.

Gould, J. D., Alfaro, L., Barnes, V., Finn, R., Grischkowsky, N., & Minuto, A. (1987). Reading is slower from CRT displays than from paper: Attempts to isolate a single-variable explanation. *Human Factors, 29*(3), 269–299.

Greene, S. L., Gomez, L. M., & Devlin, S. J. (1986). A cognitive analysis of database query production. *Proceedings of the Human Factors Society* (Dayton, OH, September 29–October 3, 1986). pp. 9–13.

Greeno, J. (1989). Situations, mental models, and generative knowledge. In D. Klahr & K. Kotovsky (Eds.), *Complex information processing: The impact of Herbert A. Simon,* pp. 285–318. Hillsdale, NJ: Erlbaum.

Griffiths, J-M., & King, D. W. (1991). *A manual on the evaluation of information centers and services.* New York: American Institute of Aeronautics and Astronautics.

Grudin, J. (1991). CSCW Introduction. *Communications of the ACM, 34*(12), 30–34.

Grudin, J. (1993). Interface: An evolving concept. *Communications of the ACM, 36*(4), 110–119.

Guilford, J. P. (1967). *The nature of human intelligence.* New York: McGraw-Hill.

Hancock-Beaulieu, M. (1992). Query expansion: Advances in research in online catalogues. *Journal of Information Science, 18,* 99–103.

Hansen, W. J., & Haas, C. (1989). Reading and writing with computers: A framework for explaining differences in performance. *Communications of the ACM, 31*(9), 1080–1089.

Harmon, D. (1992). Relevance feedback revisited. In *Proceedings of the fifteenth annual international ACM SIGIR Conference on Research and Development in Information Retrieval* (Copenhagen, June 21–24, 1992), pp. 1–10.

Harter, S. P. (1986). *Online information retrieval: Concepts, principles, and techniques.* Orlando, FL: Academic Press.

Harter, S. P., & Rogers-Peters, A. (1985). Heuristics for online information retrieval: A typology and preliminary listing. *Online Review, 9*(5), 407–424.

Hawkins, D. T., & Wagers, R. (1982). Online bibliographic search strategy development. *Online, 6*(3), 12–19.

Hefley, W. E. (1990). Architectures for adaptable human–machine interfaces. In W. Karwowski & M. Rahimi (Eds.), *Ergonomics of hybrid automated systems II,* pp. 575–585. Amsterdam: Elsevier.

Heilprin, L. B. (1985). Paramorphism versus homomorphism in information science. In L. Heilprin (Ed.), *Toward foundations of information science,* pp. 115–136. White Plains, NY: Knowledge Industries.

Helander, M. G. (1987). Design of visual displays. In G. Salvendy (Ed.), *Handbook of human factors,* pp. 507–548. New York: Wiley.

Herner, S. (1970). Browsing. In *Encyclopedia of Library and Information Science.* (Vo.l 3, pp. 408–415). New York: Dekker.

Herot, C. F. (1980). Spatial management of data. *ACM Transactions on Database Systems, 5*(4), 493–514.

Hildreth, C. (1982). The concept and mechanics of browsing in an online library catalog. In *Proceedings of the third national online meeting* (New York City, March 30–April 1, 1982), pp. 181–193.

Hildreth, C. (1989). General introduction, OPAC research: Laying the groundwork for future OPAC design. In C. Hildreth (Ed.), *The online catalogue: Developments and directions,* pp. 1–24. London: Library Association.

Huang, M-S. (1992). *Stopping behavior of end-users in online searching.* Unpublished doctoral dissertation, University of Maryland.

Hulme, C. (1984). Reading: Extracting information from printed and electronically presented text. In A. Monk (Ed.), *Fundamentals of human–computer interaction,* pp. 35–47. London: Academic Press.

Humphrey, S. (1989). MedIndEx System: Medical indexing expert system. *Information Processing & Management, 25*(1), 73–88.

Huth, E. (1987). *Medical style and format: An international manual for authors, editors, and publishers.* Philadelphia: ISI Press.

Ingwersen, P. (1984). A cognitive view of three selected online search facilities. *Online Review, 8*(5), 465–492.

Jacob, R., Leggett, J., Myers, B., & Pausch, R. (1993). Interaction styles and input/output devices. *Behavior and Information Technology, 12*(2), 69–79.

Janosky, B., Smith, P., & Hildreth, C. (1986). Online library catalog systems: An analysis of user errors. *International Journal of Man–Machine Studies, 25,* 573–592.

Johnson-Laird, P. (1983). *Mental models.* Cambridge, MA: Harvard University Press.

Jonassen, D. (1989). *Hypertext/hypermedia.* Englewood Cliffs, NJ: Educational Technology Publications.

Kahin, B. (Ed.). (1992). *Building information infrastructure.* New York: McGraw-Hill Primus.

Kahle, B., & Medlar, A. (1991, September). An information system for corporate users: Wide Area Information Servers. *Online,* pp. 55–60.

Kahn, H., & Robertson, I. T. (1992). Training and experience as predictors of job satisfaction and work motivation when using computers: A correlational study. *Behaviour & Information Technology, 11*(1), 53–60.

Kahneman, D., Slovic, P., & Tversky, A. (Eds.) (1982). *Judgment under uncertainty: Heuristics and biases.* Cambridge: Cambridge University Press.

Katz, W. A. (1987). *Introduction to reference work* (5th ed.) . Vol. 1: *Basic information sources.* Vol. 2: *Reference services and reference processes.* New York: McGraw-Hill.

Kay, A. (1984). Computer software. *Scientific American, 251*(3), 53–59.

Koegel-Buford, J. (Ed.). (1994). *Multimedia systems.* Reading, MA: Addison-Wesley.

Korfhage, R. R. (1991). To see or not to see – Is that the query? In *Proceedings of the fourteenth annual international ACM SIGIR Conference on Research and Development in Information Retrieval* (Chicago, October 13–16, 1991), pp. 134–141.

Kuhlthau, C. (1988). Longitudinal case studies of the information search process of users in libraries. *Library and Information Science Research, 10,* 257–304.

Kuhlthau, C., Turock, B., George, M., & Belvin, R. (1990). Validating a model of the search process: A comparison of academic, public and school library users. *Library and Information Science Research, 12,* 5–31.

Kwasnik, B. H. (1989). *The influence of context on classificatory behavior.* Unpublished doctoral dissertation, Rutgers University.

Kwasnik, B. H. (1992). A descriptive study of the functional components of browsing. In *Proceedings of the IFIP TC2ᵍG2.7 Working Conference on Engineering for Human–Computer Interaction* (Ellivuori, Finland, August 10–14, 1992), pp. 191–202.

Lai, K. Y., Malone, T., & Yu, K-C. (1988). Object lens: A spreadsheet for cooperative work. *ACM Transactions on Office Information Systems, 34*(121), 65–73.

Lancaster, F. W. (1972). *Evaluation of on-line searching in MEDLARS (AIM-TWX) by biomedical practitioners.* Urbana: University of Illinois, Graduate School of Library Science (Occasional Paper No. 101).

Lancaster, F. W. (1978). *Toward paperless information systems.* New York: Academic Press.

Larson, J. A. (1986). A visual approach to browsing in a database environment. *IEEE Computer, 19*(6), 62–71.

Larson, R. (1983). *Users look at online catalogs. Part 2: Interacting with online catalogs final report.* ERIC Document No. 231–401. Syracuse, NY: ERIC Clearinghouse on Information Resources.

Larson, R. (1991). The decline of subject searching: Long-term trends and patterns of index use in an online catalog. *Journal of the American Society for Information Science, 42*(3), 197–215.

Larson, R. (1992). Evaluation of advanced retrieval techniques in an experimental online catalog. *Journal of the American Society for Information Science, 43*(1), 34–53.

Laurel, B. (1991). *Computers as theater.* Reading, MA: Addison-Wesley.

Laurini, R., & Thompson, D. (1992). *Fundamentals of spatial information systems*. London: Academic Press.

Lee, E. S., & Whalen, T. (1993). Computer image retrieval by features: Suspect identification. In *Proceedings of InterChi '93* (Amsterdam, April 24–29, 1993), pp. 494–499.

Lenat, D. B., Guha, R. V., Pittman, K., Pratt, D., & Shepherd, M. (1990). CYC: Toward programs with common sense. *Communications of the ACM, 33*(8), 30–49.

Lesgold, A., Rubinson, H., Feltovich, P., Glaser, R., Klopfer, D., & Wang, Y. (1988). Expertise in a complex skill: Diagnosing x-ray pictures. In M. Chi, R. Glaser, & M. Farr (Eds.), *The nature of expertise*, pp. 311–342. Hillsdale, NJ: Erlbaum.

Liebscher, P. (1992). *Information seeking in hypertext: Multiple access methods in a full-text hypertext database*. Unpublished doctoral dissertation, University of Maryland.

Liebscher, P., & Marchionini, G. (1988). Browse and analytical search strategies in a full-text CD-ROM encyclopedia. *School Library Media Quarterly, 7*, 223–233.

Lin, X. (1993). *Self-organizing semantic maps as graphical interfaces for information retrieval*. Unpublished doctoral dissertation, University of Maryland.

Lin, X., Liebscher, P., & Marchionini, G. (1991). Graphic representation of electronic search patterns. *Journal of the American Society for Information Science, 42*(7), 469–478.

Lindsay, P. H., & Norman, D. A. (1977). *Human information processing: An introduction to psychology* (2nd ed.). New York: Academic Press.

Luhn, H. P. (1957). A statistical approach to mechanized encoding and searching of literary information. *IBM Journal, 1*(4), 309–317.

Luhn, H. P. (1958). The automatic creation of literature abstracts. *IBM Journal, 2*(2), 159–165.

Lynch, C. A. (1991). The client–server model in information retrieval. In M. Dillon (Ed.), *Interfaces for information retrieval and online systems: The state of the art*, pp. 301–318. New York: Greenwood Press.

Mackinlay, J., Robertson, G., & Card, S. (1991). The perspective wall: Detail and context smoothly integrated. In *Proceedings of CHI '91, Human Factors in Computing Systems* (New Orleans, April 27–May 2, 1991), pp. 173–179.

Malone, T., Grant, K., & Turbak, F. (1986). The information lens: An intelligent system for information sharing in organizations. In *Proceedings of CHI '86* (Boston, April 13–17, 1986), pp. 1–8.

Mantei, M. (1982). *Disorientation behavior in person-computer interaction*. Unpublished doctoral dissertation, University of Southern California.

Marchionini, G. (1987). An invitation to browse: Designing full-text systems for casual users. *Canadian Journal for Information Science. 12*(3/4), 69–79.

Marchionini, G. (1989a). Information seeking in electronic encyclopedias. *Machine-Mediated Learning, 3*(3), 211–226.

Marchionini, G. (1989b). Information-seeking strategies of novices using a full-text electronic encyclopedia. *Journal of the American Society for Information Science, 29*(3), 165–176.

Marchionini, G. (1989c). Making the transition from print to electronic encyclopedias: Adaptation of mental models. *International Journal of Man–Machine Studies, 30*, 591–618.

Marchionini, G. (1990). Evaluating hypermedia-based learning. In D. Jonassen & H. Mandl (Eds.), *Designing hypermedia for learning*, pp. 355–373. Berlin: Springer-Verlag.

Marchionini, G. (1992). Interfaces for end-user information seeking. *Journal of the American Society for Information Science, 43*(2), 156–163.

Marchionini, G., Ashley, M., & Kortzendorfer, L. (1993). ACCESS at the Library of Congress. In B. Shneiderman (Ed.), *The sparks of innovation in human–computer interaction*, pp. 251–258. Norwood, NJ: Ablex.

Marchionini, G., & Barlow, D. (1994). *A comparison of Boolean-based retrieval to the WAIS system for retrieval of aeronautical information: Final report to NASA STI program*. NASA CR-4569. Washington: NASA.

Marchionini, G., Barlow, D., & Hill, L. (1994). Extending retrieval strategies to networked environments: Old ways, new ways, and a critical look at WAIS. *Journal of the American Society for Information Science, 45*(8), 561–4.

Marchionini, G., & Crane, G. (1994). Evaluating hypermedia and learning: Methods and results from the Perseus Project. *ACM Transactions on Information Systems, 12*(1), 5–34.

Marchionini, G., Dwiggins, S., Katz, A., & Lin, X. (1993). Information seeking in full-text end-user-oriented search systems: The roles of domain and search expertise. *Library and Information Science Research, 15*(1), 35–69.

Marchionini, G., & Liebscher, P. (1991). Performance in electronic encyclopedias: Implications for adaptive systems. *Proceedings of the fifty-fourth annual meeting of the ASIS* (Washington, DC, April 27–31, 1991), pp. 39–48.

Marchionini, G., Lin, X., & Dwiggins, S. (1990). Effects of search and subject expertise on information seeking in a hypertext environment. *Proceedings of ASIS* (Toronto, November 4–8, 1990), pp. 129–142.

Marchionini, G., Neuman, D., & Morrell, K. (1994). Directed and undirected tasks in hypermedia: Is variety the spice of learning? In *Proceedings of ED-Media 94: World Conference on Educational Multimedia and Hypermedia* (Vancouver, June 25–30, 1994), pp. 373–378.

Marchionini, G., Norman, K., & Boerner, S. (1992). *Final Project Report: Computer interface design for intermediate results for Grateful Med.* Report to the National Library of Medicine. Bethesda, MD: NLM.

Marchionini, G., & Shneiderman, B. (1988). Finding facts vs. browsing knowledge in hypertext systems. *IEEE Computer, 21*(1), 70–80.

Marcus, R. (1983). An experimental comparison of the effectiveness of computers and humans as search intermediaries. *Journal of the American Society for Information Science, 34*(6), 381–404.

Markey, K. (1984). *Subject searching in library catalogs: Before and after the introduction of online catalogs.* Dublin, OH: OCLC.

Markey, K., & Cochrane, P. (1981). *Online training and practice manual for ERIC data base searchers* (2nd ed.). Syracuse, New York: ERIC Clearinghouse on Information Resources.

Matthews, J. (1982). *A study of six online public access catalogs: A review of findings. Final report.* ERIC Document No. 231 389. Syracuse, New York: ERIC Clearinghouse on Information Resources.

McClure, C., Bishop, A., Doty, P., Rosenbaum, H. (1991). *The national research and education network: Research and policy perspectives.* Norwood, NJ: Ablex.

McKnight, C., Dillon, A., & Richardson, J. (1991). *Hypertext in context.* Cambridge: Cambridge University Press.

Meadow, C. T. (1988). OAKDEC, A program for studying the effects on users of a procedural expert system for database searching. *Information Processing and Management, 24*(4), 449–457.

Meadow, C. T. (1992). *Text information retrieval systems.* San Diego: Academic Press.

Meadow, C. T., Cherry, B., Borgman, C., & Case, D. O. (1989). Online access to knowledge: System design. *Journal of the American Society for Information Science, 40*(2), 86–98.

Meadow, C.T., & Cochrane, P. (1981). *Basics of online searching.* New York: Wiley.

Mesthene, E. G. (1968). How technology will shape the future. *Science, 161,* 135–143.

Milstead, J. L. (1992). Methodologies for subject analysis in bibliographic databases. *Information Processing & Management, 28*(3), 407–431.

Minsky, M. (1975). A framework for representing knowledge. In P. Winston (Ed.), *The psychology of computer vision,* pp. 211–277. New York: McGraw-Hill.

Mylonas, E. (1992). An interface to classical Greek civilization. *Journal of the American Society for Information Science, 43*(2), 192–201.

Nagy, G., Seth, S., & Viswanathan, M. (1992). A prototype document image analysis system for technical journals. *IEEE Computer, 25*(7), 10–22.

Nardi, B. A. (1993). *A small matter of programming: Perspectives on end user computing.* Cambridge, MA: MIT Press.

Nelson, T. H. (1987). All for one and one for all. *Hypertext 87 Proceedings* (Chapel Hill, NC, November 13–15, 1987), pp. v–vii.

Neuman, D. (1993). Designing databases as tools for higher-level learning: Insights from instructional systems design. *Educational Technology Research and Development, 41*(4), 25–46.

Newell, A., & Simon, H. (1972). *Human problem solving.* Englewood Cliffs, NJ: Prentice-Hall.

Nielsen, J. (1989a). The matters that really matter for hypertext usability. In *Proceedings of Hypertext '89* (Pittsburgh, November 5–8, 1989), pp. 239–248.

Nielsen, J. (1989b). Usability engineering at a discount. In G. Salvendy & M. J. Smith (Eds.), *Designing and using human–computer interfaces and knowledge based systems,* pp. 394–401. Amsterdam: Elsevier.

Nielsen, J. (1990a). *Hypertext and hypermedia.* Boston: Academic Press.

Nielsen, J. (1990b) The visual presentation of information: Miniatures versus icons as a visual cache for videotex browsing. *Behaviour & Information Technology, 9*(6), 441–450.

NISO Committee G. (1989). *Z39.50, American national standard for information sciences – Common command language for online interactive information retrieval.* New Brunswick, NJ: NISO.

Nonogaki, H., & Ueda, H. (1991). FRIEND21 Project: A construction of 21st century human interface. In *Reaching through technology: CHI '91 Proceedings,* pp. 407–414.

Norman, D. (1983). Some observations on mental models. In D. Gentner & A. Stevens (Eds.), *Mental models,* pp. 7–14. Hillsdale, NJ: Erlbaum.

Norman, D. (1988). *The psychology of everyday things.* New York: Basic Books.

O'Connor, J. (1964). Mechanized indexing methods and their testing. *Journal of the Association for Computing Machinery, 11*(4), 437–449.

Paisley, W. (1990). An oasis where many trails cross: The improbable cocitation networks of a multidiscipline. *Journal of the American Society for Information Science, 41*(6), 459–468.

Payne, D. G., & Lang, V. A. (1991). Visual monitoring with spatially versus temporally distributed displays. *Human Factors, 33*(4), 443–458.

Peck, V. A., & John, B. E. (1992). Browser-Soar: A computational model of a highly interactive task. *Proceedings of CHI '92, Human Factors in Computing Systems* (Monterey, CA, May 3–7, 1992), pp. 165–172.

Pejtersen, A. M. (1989). A library system for information retrieval based on a cognitive task analysis and supported by an icon-based interface. In *Proceedings of SIGIR '89 twelfth annual international ACM SIGIR Conference, Research and Development in Information Retrieval* (Cambridge, MA, June 25–28, 1989) pp. 40–47.

Penniman, W. D. (1975). *Rhythms of dialogue in human–computer conversation.* Unpublished doctoral dissertation, Ohio State University.

Perlin, K. (1991). A multiscale approach to interactive display organization. In *Coordination theory and collaboration technology workshop.* Washington, DC: National Science Foundation.

Plaisant, C. (1993). A guide to volunteer opportunities in archaeology: Case study on the use of a hypertext system in a museum exhibit. In B. Shneiderman (Ed.), *Sparks of innovation in human–computer interaction,* pp. 223–229. Norwood, NJ: Ablex.

Polya, G. (1957). *How to solve it.* Princeton, NJ: Princeton University Press.

Potter, M. C., & Levy, E. I. (1969). Recognition memory for a rapid sequence of pictures. *Journal of Experimental Psychology, 81*(1), 10–15.

Prescott, S., & Griffith, B. (1970). *A descriptive study of information needs and practices of clinical psychologists.* Washington, DC: American Psychological Association.

Quillian, M. R. (1968). Semantic memory. In M. Minsky (Ed.), *Semantic information processing,* pp. 227–270. Cambridge, MA: MIT Press.

Rasmussen, E. (1992). Clustering algorithms. In W. Frakes & R. Baeza-Yates (Eds.), *Information retrieval: Data structures and algorithms,* pp. 419–442. Englewood Cliffs, NJ: Prentice-Hall.

Raymond, D. R. (1992). Flexible text display with Lector. *IEEE Computer, 25*(8), 49–60.

Rayner, K. (1978). Eye movements in reading and information processing. *Psychological Bulletin, 85*(3), 618–660.

Reinhardt, A. (1993). Smarter e-mail is coming. *Byte, 18*(3), 90–108.

Rice, R. E., & Borgman, C. L. (1983). The use of computer-monitored data in information science and communication research. *Journal of the American Society for Information Science, 34*(4), 247–257.

Robertson, G., Mackinlay, J., & Card, S. (1991). Cone trees: Animated 3D visualizations of hierarchical information. In *Proceedings of CHI '91, Human Factors in Computing Systems* (New Orleans, April 27–May 2, 1991), pp. 189–194.

Rohmert, W. (1987). Physiological and psychological work load measurement and analysis. In G. Salvendy (Ed.), *Handbook of human factors,* pp. 402–428. New York: Wiley.

Rorvig, M. E. (1993). A method for automatically abstracting visual documents. *Journal of the American Society for Information Science, 44*(1), 40–56.

Salton, G. (1989). *Automatic text processing: The transformation, analysis, and retrieval of information by computer.* Reading, MA: Addison-Wesley.

Salton, G., & Buckley, C. (1990). Improving retrieval performance by relevance feedback. *Journal of the American Society for Information Science. 41*(4), 288–297.

Salton, G., Fox, E. A., & Voorhees, E. (1983). Advanced feedback methods for information retrieval. *Journal of the American Society for Information Science, 36*(3), 200–210.

Salton, G., & McGill, M. (1983). *Introduction to modern information retrieval.* New York: McGraw-Hill.

Samuelson, P. (1992). Updating the copyright look and feel lawsuits. *Communications of the ACM, 35*(9), 25–31.

Samuelson, P., & Glushko, R. J. (1991). Intellectual property rights for digital library and hypertext publishing systems: An analysis of Xanadu. *Proceedings of Hypertext '91* (San Antonio, December 15–18, 1991), pp. 39–50.

Saracevic, T. (1976). Relevance: A review of the literature and a framework for thinking on the notion in information science. In M. Voigt & M. Harris (Eds.), *Advances in Librarianship* (Vol 6), pp. 81–138. New York: Academic Press.

Saracevic, T., Kantor, P., Chamis, A. Y., & Trivison, D. (1988). A study of information-seeking and retrieving. I. Background and methodology. *Journal of the American Society for Information Science, 39*(3), 161–176.

Saracevic, T., & Kantor, P. (1988a). A study of information seeking and retrieving. II. Users, questions and effectiveness. *Journal of the American Society for Information Science, 39*(3), 177–196.

Saracevic, T., & Kantor, P. (1988b). A study of information seeking and retrieving. III. Searchers, searches, and overlap. *Journal of the American Society for Information Science, 39*(3), 197–216.

Schank, R., & Abelson, R. (1977). *Scripts, plans, goals and understanding.* Hillsdale, NJ: Erlbaum.

Schneider, W., & Shiffrin, R. (1977). Controlled and automated human information processing. I: Detection, search, and attention. *Psychological Review, 84,* 1–66.

Sears, A. (1992). *Layout appropriateness: A metric for user interface evaluation.* Technical Report CAR-TR-603/CS-TR-2823, College Park: University of Maryland.

Sewell, W., & Teitelbaum, S. (1986). Observations of end-user online searching behavior over eleven years. *Journal of the American Society for Information Science, 37*(4), 234–245.

Shannon, C., & Weaver, W. (1949). *The mathematical theory of communication.* Urbana: University of Illinois Press.

Shiffrin, R., & Schneider, W. (1977). Controlled and automatic human information processing. II:

Perceptual learning, automatic attending, and a general theory. *Psychological Review, 84,* 127–190.

Shneiderman, B. (1983). Direct manipulation: A step beyond programming languages. *IEEE Computer, 16*(8), 57–69.

Shneiderman, B. (1990). Tree visualization (TV) with tree-maps (TM): A 2-d space-filling approach. *ACM Transactions on Graphics, 11*(1), 92–99.

Shneiderman, B. (1992). *Designing the user interface: Strategies for effective human–computer interaction* (2nd ed.). Reading, MA: Addison-Wesley.

Shneiderman, B. (1993). Protecting rights in user interface designs. In B. Shneiderman (Ed.), *The sparks of innovation in human-computer interaction,* pp. 351–354. Norwood, NJ: Ablex.

Shneiderman, B., & Kearsley, G. (1989). *Hypertext hands-on! An introduction to a new way of accessing and organizing information.* Reading, MA: Addison-Wesley.

Simon, H. A. (1979). *Models of thought.* New Haven, CT: Yale University Press.

Smeaton, A. (1992). Europe, ESPRIT II, and information retrieval. *Journal of the American Society for Information Science, 43*(1), 89–91.

Soergel, D. (1985). *Organizing information: Principles of data base and retrieval systems.* Orlando, FL: Academic Press.

Spiro, R., Feltovich, P., Coulson, R., & Anderson, D. (1989). Multiple analogies for complex concepts: Antidotes for analogy-induced misconception in advanced knowledge-acquisition. In S. Vosniadou & A. Ortony (Eds.), *Similarity and analogical reasoning,* pp. 498–531. Cambridge: Cambridge University Press.

Sternberg, R. J. (Ed.). (1982). *Handbook of human intelligence.* Cambridge: Cambridge University Press.

Sternberg, R. J. (1985). *Beyond IQ: A triarchic theory of human intelligence.* Cambridge: Cambridge University Press.

Stielow, F., & Tibbo, H. (1988). The negative search, online reference and the humanities: A critical essay in library literature. *RQ, 27,* 358–365.

Story, G. A., O'Gorman, L., Fox, D., Schaper, L. L., & Jagadish, H. V. (1992). The RightPages Image–based electronic library for alerting and browsing. *IEEE Computer, 25*(9), 17–26.

Stotts, P. D. & Furuta, R. (1989). Petri-net-based hypertext: Document structure with browsing semantics. *ACM Transactions on Information Systems, 7*(1), 3–29.

Streeter, L. (1988). Applying speech synthesis to user interfaces. In M. Helander (Ed.), *Handbook of human–computer interaction,* pp. 321–343. Amsterdam: North-Holland.

Stueben, S., & Vockell, E. L. (1993). Reformatting text for learners with disabilities. *Educational Technology, 41*(6), 46–50.

Suchman, L. A. (1987). *Plans and situated actions: The problem of human–machine communication.* Cambridge: Cambridge University Press.

Sumner, W. (1990). Processes – The new technology. *ASIS Bulletin 16*(5), 14.

Swanson, D. (1991). Complementary structures in disjoint science literatures. *Proceedings of the fourteenth annual international ACM/SIGIR Conference on Research and Development in Information Retrieval,* pp. 280–289.

Tasman, P. (1957). Literary data processing. *IBM Journal, 1*(3), 249–256.

Taviss, I. (1972). *Our tool-making society: Its politics, values, and life styles.* Englewood Cliffs, NJ: Prentice-Hall.

Taylor, R. (1962, October). The process of asking questions. *American Documentation, 391*–397.

Teich, A. H. (Ed.). (1990). *Technology and the future* (5th. ed.). New York: St. Martin's Press.

Tenopir, C. (1984). Full-text databases. In M. Williams (Ed.), *Annual review of information science and technology,* pp. 215–246. White Plains, NY: Knowledge Industries.

Tenopir, C. (1985). Full-text database retrieval performance. *Online Review, 9*(2), 149–164.

Tenopir, C., & Ro, J. S. (1990). *Full-text databases.* New York: Greenwood Press.

Thompson, R. H., & Croft, W. B. (1989). Support for browsing in an intelligent text retrieval system. *International Journal of Man–Machine Studies, 30,* 639–668.

Tibbo, H. (1989). *Abstracts, online searching, and the humanities: An analysis of the structure and content of abstracts of historical discourse.* Unpublished doctoral dissertation, University of Maryland.

Torkzadeh, G., & Angulo, I. E. (1992). The concept and correlates of computer anxiety. *Behaviour and Information Technology, 11*(2), 99–108.

Travers, M. (1989). A visual representation for knowledge structures. *Proceedings of Hypertext '89* (Pittsburgh, November 5–8, 1989), pp. 147–158.

Tufte, E. R. (1990). *Envisioning information.* Cheshire, CT: Graphics Press.

Tukey, J. A. (1977). *Exploratory data analysis.* Reading, MA: Addison-Wesley.

Turkle, S. (1984). *The second self: Computers and the human spirit.* New York: Simon & Schuster.

Tversky, A., & Kahneman, D. (1974). Judgment under uncertainty: Heuristics and biases. *Science, 185,* 1124–1131.

U.S. Department of Energy. (1992). *Human genome: 1991–92 program report.* Springfield, VA: National Technical Information Service.

U.S. Office of Science and Technology Policy. (1991). *Grand challenges: High performance computing and communications. The FY 1992 U.S. research and development program.* Washington, DC: National Science Foundation.

Vicente, K. J., Hayes, B. C., & Williges, R. C. (1987). Assaying and isolating individual differences in searching a hierarchical file system. *Human Factors, 29*(3), 349–359.

Vigil, P. J. (1983). The psychology of online searching. *Journal of the American Society for Information Science, 34*(4), 281–287.

Wagers, R. (1989, May). Can easy searching be good searching? A model for easy searching. *Online,* 78–85.

Walker, S. (1987). Okapi: Evaluating and enhancing an experimental online catalog. *Library Trends, 35,* 631–645.

Walker, W. H., & Kintsch, W. (1985). Automatic and strategic aspects of knowledge retrieval. *Cognitive Science, 9,* 261–283.

Waltz, D. (1990). The prospects for building truly intelligent machines. In A. Teich (Ed.), *Technology and the future,* pp. 366–388. New York: St. Martin's Press.

Wang, X. (1990). *An algorithm for knowledge-based selection of databases.* Unpublished doctoral dissertation, University of Maryland.

Wang, X., Liebscher, P., & Marchionini, G. (1988). *Improving information seeking performance in hypertext: Roles of display format and search strategy.* Technical Report CAR-TR-353, Center for Automation Research, University of Maryland.

Waterworth, J. A., & Chignell, M. H. (1991). A model for information exploration. *Hypermedia, 3*(1), 35–58.

White, M. (1985, fall). Evaluation of the reference interview. *RQ,* 76–84.

Wiberley, S., & Daugherty, R. (1988). Users' persistence in scanning lists of references. *College and Research Libraries, 49*(2), 149–156.

Wickens, C. D. (1987). Information processing, decision-making, and cognition. In G. Salvendy (Ed.), *Handbook of human factors,* pp. 72–107. New York: Wiley.

Wiederhold, G., Wegner, P., & Ceri, S. (1992). Toward megaprogramming. *Communications of the ACM, 35*(11), 89–99.

Willett, P. (1991). The ranking of paragraphs as an access mechanism for full-text documents. In P. Gillman (Ed.), *Text retrieval: Information first,* pp. 34–45. London: Taylor Graham.

Williams, M. D. (1984). What makes RABBIT run? *International Journal of Man–Machine Studies, 21,* 333–352.

Williamson, C., & Shneiderman, B. (1992). The dynamic HomeFinder: Evaluating dynamic queries in a real-estate information exploration system. In *Proceedings of the fifteenth annual International ACM SIGIR Conference on Research and Development in Information Retrieval* (Copenhagen, June 21–24, 1992), pp. 338–346.

Wilson, P. (1973). Situational relevance. *Information Storage and Retrieval, 9,* 457–471.

Young, D., & Shneiderman, B. (1993). A graphical filter/flow representation of Boolean queries: A prototype implementation and evaluation. *Journal of the American Society for Information Science, 44*(6), 327–339.

Zloof, M. M. (1977). Query-by-example: A database language. *IBM Systems Journal, 16*(4), 324–343.

Zoellick, W. (1987). Selecting an approach to document retrieval. In S. Ropiequet, J. Einberger, & W. Zoellick (Eds.), *CD-ROM* Vol 2. *Optical publishing,* pp. 63–82. Redmond, WA: Microsoft Press.

Zuboff, S. (1988). *In the age of the smart machine.* New York: Basic Books.

# Index